# Languages in Migratory Settings

Research on migration has often focused on push and pull factors; and on the mobilities which drive migration. What has often received less attention, and what this book recognises, is the importance of the creative activities which occur when strangers meet and settle for long periods of time in new places. Contributions consider case studies in Italy, Kyrgyzstan, France, Portugal and Australia, as well as taking a careful look at the city of Glasgow during the Commonwealth games of 2014. They explore the making and use of literature (for adults and children) of art installations; translation processes in immigration law; education materials; and intercultural understanding. The research reveals the extent to which migration takes a place, and takes different forms, as life is made anew out of intercultural encounters which have a geographical specificity. This shift in focus allows a different lens to be placed on languages, intercultural communication and the activities of migration, and enables the settings themselves to come under scrutiny. This book was originally published as a special issue of *Language and Intercultural Communication.*

**Alison Phipps** is Professor of Languages and Intercultural Studies at the University of Glasgow, UK; and co-convener of the Glasgow Refugee, Asylum and Migration Network.

**Rebecca Kay** is Professor of Russian Gender Studies at the University of Glasgow, UK; and co-convener of the Glasgow Refugee, Asylum and Migration Network.

# Languages in Migratory Settings

Place, politics, and aesthetics

*Edited by*
**Alison Phipps and Rebecca Kay**

LONDON AND NEW YORK

First published 2016
by Routledge

2 Park Square, Milton Park, Abingdon, Oxon OX14 4RN
711 Third Avenue, New York, NY 10017, USA

*Routledge is an imprint of the Taylor & Francis Group, an informa business*

First issued in paperback 2017

*British Library Cataloguing in Publication Data*
A catalogue record for this book is available from the British Library

ISBN 13: 978-1-138-91197-0 (hbk)
ISBN 13: 978-1-138-08469-8 (pbk)

Typeset in Times New Roman
by RefineCatch Limited, Bungay, Suffolk

**Publisher's Note**
The publisher accepts responsibility for any inconsistencies that may have
arisen during the conversion of this book from journal articles to book chapters,
namely the possible inclusion of journal terminology.

**Disclaimer**
Every effort has been made to contact copyright holders for their permission to
reprint material in this book. The publishers would be grateful to hear from any
copyright holder who is not here acknowledged and will undertake to rectify
any errors or omissions in future editions of this book.

# Contents

# Citation Information

The chapters in this book were originally published in *Language and Intercultural Communication*, volume 14, issue 3 (August 2014). When citing this material, please use the original page numbering for each article, as follows:

**Chapter 1: Introduction**
*Editorial: Languages in migratory settings: place, politics and aesthetics*
Alison Phipps and Rebecca Kay
*Language and Intercultural Communication*, volume 14, issue 3 (August 2014)
pp. 273–286

**Chapter 2**
*Divorce and dialogue: intertextuality in Amara Lakhous'* Divorzio all'islamica a viale Marconi
Mariangela Palladino
*Language and Intercultural Communication*, volume 14, issue 3 (August 2014)
pp. 287–303

**Chapter 3**
*Visualizing intercultural literacy: engaging critically with diversity and migration in the classroom through an image-based approach*
Evelyn Arizpe, Caroline Bagelman, Alison M. Devlin, Maureen Farrell and Julie E. McAdam
*Language and Intercultural Communication*, volume 14, issue 3 (August 2014)
pp. 304–321

**Chapter 4**
*The social and symbolic aspects of languages in the narratives of young (prospective) migrants*
Giovanna Fassetta
*Language and Intercultural Communication*, volume 14, issue 3 (August 2014)
pp. 322–338

**Chapter 5**
*Learning across borders – Chinese migrant literature and intercultural Chinese language education*
Yongyang Wang
*Language and Intercultural Communication*, volume 14, issue 3 (August 2014)
pp. 339–351

For any permission-related enquiries please visit:
http://www.tandfonline.com/page/help/permissions

# Notes on Contributors

**Evelyn Arizpe** is Senior Lecturer in the School of Education at the University of Glasgow, UK. Her research interests include children's literature and literacies, particularly in relation to picturebooks, Young Adult literature, reader-response, Latin America, migration and intercultural communities.

**Caroline Bagelman** is currently a Post-Graduate Research Student in the School of Education at the University of Glasgow, UK. Her research is entitled 'Picturing Transformative Texts: an exploration of food politics through picturebooks'.

**Alison M. Devlin** is a Research Associate in DALLAS Evaluation in the School of Education at the University of Glasgow, UK.

**Maureen Farrell** is Senior Lecturer in the School of Education at the University of Glasgow, UK. Her research interests focus on children's literature, particularly Scottish children's literature; picture books; and children's literature and religious education.

**Giovanna Fassetta** is a Research Associate in the School of Education at the University of Strathclyde, Glasgow, UK.

**Moya Flynn** is a Senior Lecturer in Central and East European Studies at the University of Glasgow, UK. Her research interests include social support and migration in Scotland; and lesbian, gay and bisexual migration.

**Robert Gibb** is a Lecturer in Sociology at the University of Glasgow, UK. His research interests include asylum, refugees and migration, with a particular focus on Bulgaria, Denmark and France. He is also interested in contemporary social theory.

**Anthony Good** is Professor Emeritus in Social Anthropology at the University of Edinburgh, UK. His principal overseas field research was in Tamil Nadu, South India, though he also has considerable experience of Sri Lanka as a physical chemistry lecturer and later a human rights researcher.

**Rebecca Kay** is Professor of Russian Gender Studies at the University of Glasgow, UK; and co-convener of the Glasgow Refugee, Asylum and Migration Network.

**Natalya Kosmarskaya** is a Senior Researcher at the Department of Central Asia and the Caucasus–Institute of Oriental Studies–Russian Academy of Sciences, Moscow. She has published extensively on post-Soviet migration to Russia; Russian-speakers' position in the newly independent states (especially those of Central Asia); the trajectories of ethnic/social identity change in the post-Soviet context; and diaspora formation in the NIS.

# NOTES ON CONTRIBUTORS

**Elsa Lechner** is a Senior Researcher in the Centre for Social Studies at the University of Coimbra, Portugal.

**Julie E. McAdam** is currently a Post-Graduate Research Student in the School of Education at the University of Glasgow, UK. Her research is entitled 'Supporting Educators to realise the potential of children's literature in developing 21st century citizens'.

**Mariangela Palladino** is a Lecturer in English at Keele University, UK. Her research interests lie at the intersection of Postcolonial literatures and cultures, migration and diaspora, as well as in narratology and narrative ethics. She is currently working on a monograph, *The Forms of Ethics*, which focuses on the ethical import of narrative in Toni Morrison's fiction.

**Alison Phipps** is Professor of Languages and Intercultural Studies at the University of Glasgow, UK; and co-convener of the Glasgow Refugee, Asylum and Migration Network.

**Olga Solovova** is an Associate Researcher at the Centre for Social Studies at the University of Coimbra, Portugal.

**Yongyang Wang** is based in the Graduate School of Education at the University of Melbourne, Australia.

# Languages in migratory settings: place, politics and aesthetics

## Introduction

In their grounding-breaking collection of essays, *Migratory Settings*, Aydemir and Rotas make a subtle conceptual and discursive shift in order to unsettle prevailing assumptions about migration. The juxtaposition of an adjective of movements with a plural noun suggesting fixture highlights a paradox inviting 'a shift in perspective from migration as movement from place to place to migration as installing movement within place' (Aydemir & Rotas, 2008, p. 7). It is a tension with which each of the papers in this special issue of *Language and Intercultural Communication* wrestles in different ways, approaching the subject of migration from different disciplinary perspectives and using diverse methodologies and analysis. It is also a tension inherent in languages and intercultural communication as a field of research and practice. Transcriptions and thick descriptions capture and fix, installing – to echo Aydemir and Rotas – what is an aural and oral flow in interview narratives, as text. One medium is rendered as another, a medium which is human sound becomes a medium of human technology – that of writing, or of vision. The senses are translated and dissonance occurs, marking an awareness that something has shifted, something has changed, something is not as it was.

## GRAMNet and context setting

We shall return to this and other paradoxes during the course of our discussion of the themes, which this collection of papers raises. First, we wish to provide some context to this special issue. As editors we also act as founding co-conveners of Glasgow Refugee, Asylum and Migration Network (http://www.gla.ac.uk/gramnet), in Scotland, UK. This is a research and knowledge exchange network, supported by the University of Glasgow, which was set up in 2010 to 'think with the City' of Glasgow. Whilst drawing inspiration from Glasgow as a migratory setting with a long and diverse history and both exciting and challenging contemporary interconnections, the network has never been parochial in focus or scope. Instead, and like this special issue, it considers different migratory settings and how researchers approach these migratory settings, teasing out similarities and differences. Consequently in developing this special issue, calling for contributions and editing submissions, we encouraged a focus on place-specific projects where researchers were able to engage critically and with different methodological foci, which have engaged with migration, refugees and asylum seekers.

In doing so, and in the context of our work with GRAMNet, we were mindful of and motivated by contemporary concerns relating to Glasgow and Scotland as specific and fascinating migratory settings. The special issue and its themes connected to Scotland as a country facing a Referendum on Independence and self determination, to be held on 18 September 2014 – and to the importance of 2014 for Glasgow as a place for a present thickening of languages and intercultural experience as it prepares to play host to the

Commonwealth Games. At the time of writing this editorial, the preparations for this sporting occasion include the setting up of the first Pan-African Orchestra – the Ha Orchestra (http://www.haorcestra.com) made up of musicians from diverse countries of Africa – including Ghana, Morocco, Zimbabwe, – and musicians from European countries, especially those with a Celtic connection, who are creating a new soundscape through a fusion of musical traditions and movements. There are festivals of Mutlicultural Homecoming which focus on the Scottish diasporas, established and new migrant communities and which are seeing new dances being created out of the traditions of dance which are meeting at this moment.

Responses to migration have also historically been accompanied by both hospitality and hostility. A look at Glasgow's history finds particular animus towards the Irish in the late 1920s and early 1930s, which sowed the seeds for later concerns relating to sectarianism between catholics and protestants, and between two rival football teams: Celtic and Rangers. In response to what has been a more recent rise in xenophobia in the UK, mirroring new waves of xenophobia and racism in Europe more widely, the Scottish Refugee Council organised its Refugee Week Festival 2014 under the title of 'Welcome'. The festival included a 'Welcome Van' and a 'Welcome Tent' as deliberate responses to the 'Go Home Vans' used recently by the UK Government to create a hostile environment for migrants, and to reflect as a temporary material presence, the tented cities of the refugee camps of the world. In the social media campaigns which accompany this effort of migratory aesthetics a thread of resistance and graffiti art has emerged as virtual and viral direct action, somewhat inspired by the graffiti artist 'Banksy' (http://banksy.co.uk/) where the political campaigns to assert monocultural identities and to demonise languages other than English, and intercultural initiatives are literally written over with counter messaging. The hashtag #IWelcome Refugees is an example of this kind of more recent technological and lingusitic aeasthetic and political placing of migratory experience. This said, the writing over of offending signs with counter slogans is not a new feature of migratory settings and contested spaces. In the eleventh century on Orkney Mainland, the neolithic tomb Maes How was visited by Vikings who overnighted within its walls and left their runes equivalent to 'Siegrid was here'.

As Scotland debates the possibilities of secession and prepares for the Referendum on Independence, the implications of and for migratory experience are palpable. Whatever the outcome of this historical vote, the present debate is creating a space for imagining futures, for testing possibilities, for changing aesthetics and for reflecting on the intercultural relations and languages which have shaped Scotland to date.

**Editorial overview of themes in the papers**

We have sketched out this context as editors, as our work with these papers through this latest season of change in Scotland has been illuminated by the breadth of the authors' focus on migratory politics, law, aesthetics and intercultuality from contexts outside of our own. Though several of the authors in this special issue are drawn from Glasgow Refugee Asylum and Migration Network they have not primarily researched these aspects of the Scottish context, but their contributions come from work in Italian, Kyrgyz, French, UK, Portuguese and Australian contexts. The work also focuses on different aesthetic and linguistic aspects of migrancy, interculturality and of the place of languages in these settings. Arzipe et al., for example, take 'visual literacies' as their main focus; Wang – chinese literature and curriculum; Lechner and Solovova – clinical silences; Gibb and Good – the law and its translation; Fassetta – children's narratives; Flynn and Kosmarskaya – imaginings of the city and languages of belonging; Palladino – film and divorce. Consequently this special issue, through its diverse contributory strands, reflects shifts in the discourse of migration studies from a direct concern with geography, politics or the now outdated framings of sending and receiving countries, to a focus on aesthetic and symbolic aspects of communication, in languages, and in the multimodal forms of intersemiotic translations. In short, by encouraging submissions to this special issue of *Language and Intercultural Communication* which drew on research projects relating to language, translation, interpretation, mediation, visual and intercultural literacy, in a range of discipline specific and interdisciplinary contexts, a dialogue has emerged, between methods, theory and approaches to the study of language and languages in the broad field of area and cultural studies.

In the call for contributions, as editors, we asked for work which reflected on the following themes:

- Language and intercultural dimensions of transnationalism as these relate to both migrants/asylum seekers/refugees and local populations.
- Legal and social policy on migration, asylum and refugees relating to languages and policy on integration.
- Narratives of migration, asylum and refugees in art, literature, film, drama, etc.
- Critical perspectives on intercultural language education – schooling, higher, adult and community education.
- Translation and interpreting especially as they relate to law, health, education and the arts.
- Language and social psychological consequences of migration and asylum.
- Intercultural and language dimensions of faith groups and faith practices.
- Intercultural and linguistic perspectives on human security as it relates to migration.

## Aesthetic resonance

What has been striking in editing the papers for this special issue has been the extent to which the aesthetic resonance has come to the fore both in individual papers and as a connecting theme. *Language and Intercultural Communication* tends, as a journal, to lean towards Applied Linguistics and Foreign Language/English Language Education fields with critical theorising of empirical work, and its empiricism often follows the conventions laid out in the scientific trainings of applied linguistics and education. It tends, therefore, towards the social scientific, though the rigour of its theorising is of note. From early papers in the journal on Gadamer, contributions from critical scholars such as Henry Giroux, Adrian Holliday, Manuela Guilherme and Shanta Nair Venugopal together with interviews with key thinkers such as Stella Ting Toomey, Noam Chomsky and Boa Ventura de Sousa Santos have created a scholarly context of theoretical and methodological openness, conceptual development and reception. Nonetheless, this does mean that the symbolic and subjective dimensions of language and intercultural communication have often been overlooked, as methodological and theoretical approaches have not heard or seen these aspects. Kramsch (2006, 2009) has more recently pioneered arguments for an inclusion of both aesthetic and affective dimensions to study in this field:

To survive linguistically and emotionally the contradictions of everyday life, multilingual subjects draw on the formal semiotic and aesthetic resources afforded by various symbolic systems to reframe these contradictions and create alternative worlds of their own. (Kramsch, 2009, p. 29)

By stressing the way multilinguals – in the formal classroom or in informal, everyday settings – attend to the subtle cues and codes of the social world, Kramsch highlights the adaptation to and modification of language practices. Be it through switching codes, i.e. registers, languages, accents or listening for patterns in discourse which align subjects politically, geographically, socially and culturally, this practice is one which sits well with the study of aesthetic dimensions to language and also to migration. In the study of migration such dimensions come to the fore as the displacements involved mean taken for granted and normative dimensions to speech and action have to be made anew, in a different context, and smooth aesthetics are complicated by new interactions and the creation of new forms. This emerges very clearly in the contributions from Fasetta and from Arizpe et al., both of which explore children's renegotiations of and creative engagements with new contexts of communication. These new or overwritten forms become important in their own right, indexing happenings in migratory settings, and this is as true for the runes on Maes How left by vikings as evidence of their temporary settlement as it is for layers of multilingual grattifi in Kreuzberg, Berlin, which outwardly manifest the dynamics of migration as it makes its mark and settles into the physical environment.

Reception is an important dimension to work on migration and intercultural language studies. Reception may be hostile or it may be challenging. Reception can take time and it is, in terms of acceptance or rejection, a one-way process. Scholarly reception is no exception and as editors we are aware that in offering aesthetic dimensions to debates with languages and intercultural communication, through work on migration, we are seeking to enable the reception of new ideas, methods, concepts into the field and we will be testing what are relatively new boundaries and may be at risk of making claims for newness which do not stand the test of time. Migratory aesthetics offer the prospect here, through reception, for a linguistic and intercultural aesthetics to emerge as a mode of reflection and also suggest the need for methodologies and theoretical perspectives drawn from the humanities as well as from the social sciences, for understanding and analysing what is happening in different settings. As the contributions by Gibb and Good and by Lechner and Solovova clearly demonstrate, a lack of attention to the aesthetic and affective aspects of intercultural communications can in fact render multilingual interventions at best meaningless and at worst harmful, especially in contexts of coercive power such as the courtroom or the clinical setting.

**North and South**

The aesthetic thematics are not the only elements which this collection of papers highlight. Of note is an aspect which recurs in several papers – that of North and South. These cardinal points of the compass orient the analysis and act as symbols where the North tends towards privilege and the South is 'othered' and relegated to a subordinate positioning. These geographical markers organise the placement of migrants, and empirical work also reflects this, notably in Flynn and Kosmarskaya, as the cardinals are used by residents of the city to describe the migratory aesthetics of the city-scape and the city's history. This has consequences for domestic Kyrgyz migration politics. Similarly in Fassetta's analysis, with an international focus, the northern and southern slopes of the Mediterranean become symbols of the international border, policed by FRONTEX and the European Union. The North represents arrival, security, hope and even economic prospects of care for family back home. The South represents that being left behind. Both have their ambivalences, and both 'stand in for' gritty discussions of the reality of poverty in the empirical material here. Poverty is not often discussed directly in *Language and Intercultural Communication*. Discussion does take place, however, relating to the dominance of academic discourses formed by the histories and thought of the 'West' (Graeber, 2007) and in recent contributions, notably from Shanta Nair Venugopal (2012) this has been challenged by occidental critiques from the 'East'. Thus, the cardinals which have emerged as key to discussions of languages and intercultural communication in the contributions to this volume are also present, albeit along different axes, in *Language and Intercultural Communication's* scholarly debates. It should also be noted that Boa Ventura de Sousa Santos has discussed the critical potential of Nord-Sul (north south) perspectives offered by the Centro de Estudos Sociais, Coimbra University (Santos, 2002). In Lechner and Solovova's contribution the inequalities of North and South, which are often discussed in scholarship as those of West gazing on East, come through in the complex inadequacies of comunication in clinical settings of mental health, with migrants from the global south. Roberts and Sarangi and Corbett and Lu have both discussed these complexities in their work. Roberts and Sarangi (1999) have questioned whether clinical workplaces really constitute settings for intercultural communication given some of the formulaic ways in which interaction is undertaken, and Lu and Corbett (2012) have raised the question of empathy and time asking how intercultural consultations of 7–10 minutes might perform empathy and to what extent this is possible. What Lechner and Solovova bring to this particular discussion is a strand of theorising, which also echoes that of migratory aesthetics. Citing Michael Agier's work in refugee camps in sub-Saharan Africa (2011), Lechner and Solovova show how metaphorical borders are created between north and south through administrative discourses, and how identity, e.g. refugee, foreigner, gives way to markers of *place*. This, Lechner and Solovova argue, following Agier 'corresponds to a political status of extra-territoriality and dependency that determines the terms and contents of possible communication with non-refugees.' Borders cease to be points of contact and exchange and become part of metaphorical and symbolic 'daily-life' politics to be survived.

## Inter-

The final thematic aspect we wish to highlight here, following on from that of migratory aesthetics and the symbolic use of cardinals, is that of the prefix 'inter-'. This is present, of course, in *Language and Intercultural Communication* – 'intercultural' – and we will not add to discussions about this term and its definitions here. Rather the 'inter-' prefixes which interest us here are those of 'intersemiotics', 'intertextuality' and 'intersectionality'. The papers deal with these interstices, which adds to a liminal layering in the papers, a sense of their setting in places which are thick with border crossings of many physical and metaphorical kinds, a space where the English language has to stretch and add to its root words in order to, somewhat clumsily, render in a single word what are complex processes of experience and being. The papers in this special issue reflect the intersemiotics of language with film, literature, clinical interview, law and administrative justice, visual image, film. In each case language itself is intersected as text and/or as verbal utterance. This creates a rich setting and also creates a requirement for much deeper analysis than is within the scope of this paper.

Similarly with the intersectional elements here which, from the starting point of migrancy, race and ethnicity, bring in a range of elements. These cover childhood, (Arizpe et al.; Fassetta); marital status and divorce (Palladino), disability and mental health (Lechner and Solovova); learner status (Arizpe et al; Wang); legal immigrant status (Good and Gibb); rural/urban background (Flynn and Kosmarkya). And throughout these,

languages emerge as a key intersectional dimension, little discussed as such, but of equal standing and requiring equal scholarly attention, as the original insectional trinity of race, gender and class. What the contributions show, in some cases starkly, is that markers in language and of languages create aesthetic settings, especially in aural perspective, which heighten the likelihood at one and the same time of xenophobic discrimination and inequality rooted in fear of what is not understood, and of cosmopolitan celebratory aesthetics such as those found in tourism to many so-called 'world cities' or 'arrival cities' (Goldin, Cameron, & Balarajan, 2011; Saunders, 2010). Which language you speak and how your language is judged acts in ways which bear comparison with the discrimation of markers of race, gender and class. It makes a difference which language you speak and how you speak, where and with whom. Code switching analysis discusses these elements at length within Applied Linguistics, but not readily as an element requiring political and critical analysis (exceptions include Block, 2012; Duchêne & Heller, 2007; Heller & Duchêne, 2011). The move to wrap language and languages into scholarly terms such as 'discourse' or 'code' has also had the effect of masking the intersectional aspects of language. These markers are held in place by particular political economies (O'Regan, 2014) which adapt themselves to different contexts and connect to discussions of English as a global/world/international language often referred to as English as a lingua franca (ELF). The limitations of this latter element have been discussed rigorously by Jenks (2013), in *Language and Intercultural Communication* and by O'Regan (2014). Both criticise ELF for its theoretical incoherence and lack of contextual nuance, and have provoked considerable discussion (Baker, Jenkins & Baird 2014; Widdowson, 2014).

The special issue therefore offers the intersectional dimension of languages, in intercultural communication and across the arts, humanities and social sciences, as a field for analysis and of political economy. As editors we argue that the 'Inter-' prefix, with its considerable liminal valence also underscores our first point relating to migratory aesthetics. Liminal zones (Turner, 1987; van Gennep, 1909) are also zones of contact and of notable creativity and even carnivalesque performance. Following Bakhtin it is clear that heteroglossia have carnivalesque potential, troubling, thickening the aesthetics, performing difference and acting as sites of language-making. They can also be spaces in which extreme measures are taken to strip out the aesthetic diversity and insert template-like formats for interviews as noted above. These templates seek to offer sameness as fairness to ensure all are equal before the law (Gibb and Good) and before the clinician (Lechner and Solovova).

Migratory settings, with their interstices, aesthetics and geographical orientations, offer significant challenges in terms of methodology for intercultural communicative research. The normative frameworks of social scientific methods begin to falter when faced with phenomena – aesthetics, aural resonance, intertextuality, symbolic representation of north and south – which fall more comfortably into the broad domains of the arts and humanities. Theoretically, too, the terrain is tricky and the operational approaches which focus on process and acquisition meet suggestion, interpretation, and abstract concepts such as beauty, ugliness, sound, kindness, strangeness, hospitality and carnival. The search for solutions to social problems – of language and intercultural communication – is queered by critical suggestion that these may not exist and their pursuit may be highly problematic (Ahmed, 2000). Adapting to new situations and making new forms of life are part of the arts of intercultural practice.

In what follows we wish to analyse this problematic in a case study from Glasgow which incorporates the dimensions we have highlighted in this special issue. Rather than beginning with a set of research questions, with a research design and then presenting data and our analysis of it, we begin instead in an aesthetic setting where arts and residents have been working interculturally and doing new things with language.

## Future memory at Red Road

One of the pressing dangers of language and intercultural communication is its presentism. The focus on empirical data within applied linguistics and in linguistics, together with the privileging of the 'transcript' and 'audio recording' as pre-eminent and rarely questioned forms of data collection, creates something of a fetish of these forms. Training in the field of language and intercultural communication means setting data in the certain scientific conventions which dominate its presentation. The data, which have migrated from the field to the research setting, and have thus undergone a considerable transformation from their original state, become coded, enumerated, analysed and thematised. Of itself, this method has proved helpful in privileging systematic study of language in social settings, including migratory settings, more or less within the present. A give away for this is the reliance on audio recording. Disciplines concerned with the historical record before the twentieth century barely have recourse to comparative, aural, historical sources, for instance, and it is therefore relatively easy for claims to be made regarding the present which are rather more claims about the kinds of methods available for data collection than any definitive statement about how people really live with languages and in intercultural interaction through history. It is, however, only one convention which may be used in what is an interdisciplinary field.

The study of migration takes many forms and different disciplinary fields come to the languages and forms of intercultural communication which manifest within their purview, with different methods and theoretical frameworks. The project we discuss below found its initial form in a collaboration between an ancient historian, Elena Isayev, and a landscape artist, Catrin Webster, in an AHRC-funded project called 'Future Memory in Place' which aimed to consider how archaeological and ancient historical artefacts and records showed through their aesthetics and symbols, the kinds of activities which had form in migratory settings. By taking, for instance, a *tessera hospitalis* – friendship token, Elena Isayev was able to demonstrate the complexity of journeys between families, trading partners and loved ones around the ancient Mediterranean, over long periods of time. No aural transcripts are present in her work as none existed, but the comparative records of the archaeological finds, in different settings, point to the use of these tokens in journeys made and traces left of those journeys. They also tell of the affective dimensions which took form in the *tessera* and in a gift economy. Together with Catrin Webster a project seeking to recreate this aesthetic form in the twenty-first century Welsh context with schoolchildren allowed for an encounter with objects across historical timeframes and also for new forms to be made which would 'set' a new work in situ. Linkages between visual arts and musical 'soundscapes', bringing in a collaboration with composer and conductor Marion Wood furthered the interaesthetic scope of the project and culminated in public performances of '1000 colours blue'(http://projects.beyondtext.ac.uk/deplacingfu-turememory-fo/index.php). As such participants were involved in making memories anew, out of the forms made by others in the past, focused on the dynamics of migration in the present, but equally conscious of the dynamics and forms of migration in the past.

## Singing goodbye to the Red Road flats

The imaginative and artistic methods used in the project became the inspiration for a further iteration of 'Future Memory'.

The migratory setting for this new iteration of the project was the social housing scheme: 'Red Road' in Glasgow. It was an example of the kinds of large-scale, high-rise housing schemes which were built in the 1960s in order to re-house those who had been evicted as part of the slum clearance programmes of the post-war period. These modernist forms dominate the cityscapes of many large cities, icons of the positivist faith in modernist architecture. Plans to demolish the Red Road flats have led to the gradual rehousing of former residents. They have also inspired a number of literary and artistic projects seeking to capture the hopes and fears, friendships and divisions, joy and sadness of life in the flats (Irvine, 2011). Many of these projects were brought together through a partnership of Glasgow Housing Association and Glasgow Life (http://www.redroadflats. org.uk/) including the work of photographer Iseult Timmermans of Street Level Photoworks, who coordinated the work of the Red Road community studio for many years. Through the community studio and other community art projects Iseult has worked collaboratively with residents and the particular architecture of the flats since the late 1990s. In the project 'Future Memory at Red Road' Iseult worked alongside the original Future Memory in Place team, as well as archaeologist Michael Given and Rebecca Kay, to co-create a particular aesthetic which would neither overly celebrate nor overly grieve these ambiguous homes and landmarks but would weave the need for a migratory aesthetics into what were originally housing for indigenous Glaswegians and became housing equally strongly associated with asylum seekers. The images below, for example, show how the history of the residents was brought to life along the garage doors leading to the foot of one particular block (Figures 1 and 2).

Through a series of archaeological and artistic workshops led by Elena Isayev, Michael Given, Catrin Webster and Marion Wood, children at the local primary school collected objects, created stories and reconceived these as swathes of colour. Strips of fabric were painted with colours which moved in and out of shades and tones, blended

Figure 1. Photographic portraits of former residents, from the archive created by Iseult Timmermans were displayed on the now derelict garage doors. (Image by Alison Phipps).

Figure 2.  Resident's portraits were foregrounded against the remaining blocks of flats where many had lived. (Image by Alison Phipps).

and bled into one another and merged to create a new colour. These along with stories, anecdotes and life histories of former residents were then translated into sound by a scratch community choir bringing together residents of all ages and backgrounds. Working with Marion Wood they were taught to sing tonally, using a methodology inspired by Mongolian throat singing and the sounds of nature, and allowing each member of the choir to find their own note by which to sing goodbye to Red Road. On the day of the performance the coloured fabric strips adorned the fences surrounding the deserted and derelict flats and were mirrored and magnified by brightly dyed bedsheets, created by Catrin Webster hanging from the now empty windows in a colourful echo of the everyday needs for washing and also of prayer flags from Tibet (Figure 3). Recordings of songs sung in the flats in many different languages were collected by the team and these as well as excerpts from life history interviews and day-to-day noises such as crying babies and kitchen sounds played out from speakers installed in the shell of the building, which became the largest musical instrument in Europe, resembling a giant ghetto blaster. This broadcast soundscape combined with the bedsheet flags of colour was visible and audible from afar and had an unforeseen aesthetic impact, acting as a call to the event which brought former residents and interested passersby from across the district. A middle-aged man driving up in his van explained that his attention had been originally caught by hearing a rendition of 'You are my sunshine' echoing from the building and catching sight of the fluttering colours at the windows. 'A used tae sing that song tae ma weans', he explained 'It brought a tear tae ma eye tae hear it, and I hud tae come and see whit was goin on (Figure 3)'. By crossing from the intimacy of what had been sung in domestic settings and moving it into the air of the city, a public sound expression of an intercultural domestic memory was created, if only for a moment. Judith Butler writes of moments of social change occurring when the domestic makes a home for itself on the streets:

The body is constituted through perspectives it cannot inhabit; someone else sees our face in a way that none of us can. We are in this way, even as located, always elsewhere, constituted in a sociality that exceeds us. This establishes our exposure and our precarity, the ways in which we depend on political and social institutions to persist. (Butler, 2011)

Standing in the rain at the foot of the flats was reminiscent of the many pieta in art history, witnessing to a dying and human suffering and hearing in the breeze despite the darkness and heaviness of the place, the sounds of singing which tells of past life and future memory. It was also a migratory aesthetics, made through migratory experiences layering themselves through history but merging into new forms, strongly constituted by place and by the northern geography of the City of Glasgow giving up ghostly voices to remind of the ambiguities which work themselves inside homes and lives. For those standing alone in the rain it allowed for the witnessing of an intercultural sociality which exceeded any one person's experience and offered a challenge to language and intercultural researchers as to how to allow in the aesthetic dimensions of research as they escape from and exceed those edges which form the inter-space of intercultural studies (Figure 4).

For those within the crowded out community centre to which the choir and their audience retreated from the rain, these aesthetics merged and emerged into new exchanges and shifting identities and interactions. A young boy whose family had come to Red Road as asylum seekers and were still housed in one of the remaining part-inhabited blocks grew visibly in stature and confidence as he sang alongside his two Glaswegian pals. Their gaudy foam rubber crowns perched precariously on their heads they raced off after the performance to visit his home together for the first time and to reenact the 'flinging of pieces' from a top floor window that they had just been singing about.[1] Meanwhile back at the community centre, staff and regular visitors made up

Figure 3. Brightly coloured bedsheets hung from the empty windows of the derelict block were visible from afar. (Image by Alison Phipps).

Figure 4. The empty and derelict block was the setting for an event which brought memories to life through sound, image and colour.

primarily of long-term residents of the flats, commented on the concert as the first time that many of the newer residents, those whose journeys across continents had brought them to Glasgow in the 2000s, had set foot in the building. Mutual wariness and even hostility faded into mutual curiosities and cautious interactions through a shared sensory and embodied experience of song, laughter and the (re)making of future memories.

## Aesthetic unsettling

Our description and reflection on the case of the Red Road flats in Glasgow give an example of how the arts hold together aesthetic, affective, situational and liminal layers which coexist in migratory settings. Beginning with the description and analysis of artistic practice allows themes to come to the fore in similar ways as Palladino demonstrates with the filming of novels; or Lechner and Solovova through attention to the resonance of silence; or Arizpe et al. in the sketches emerging from visual picture books used in the migratory setting of the classroom.

The road to the Red Road project involved much messy serendipity, collaborative patience and artistic tenacity as well as participatory ways of working. It required a shift in thinking and a letting go of disciplinary certainties regarding method and data for those of us more used to particular ways of academic working. It demonstrated, perhaps, that there is a case to be made for not going into the data but for taking the data into new aesthetic domains, migrating the data not into platforms but into artistic forms, which pay attention to aesthetic qualities as part of communicating an element which is missed when codifications remain resolutely positivist.

One way of doing this is to improvise with different presentations of language data in the context of language and intercultural communication. We might therefore use the relatively new work of providing poetic transcriptions of data alongside traditional forms. If we take Fassetta's work with Ghanaian migrant children we could re-render their words in poetic form following Anna Jones work with poetic forms of data (2010), attending to a language aesthetic in this context which perhaps heightens some of the poignancy of the words collected:

> Eleven-year-old Jackson
> thought he knew
> what the problem was:
> 'You don't understand
> because you are white'
> Marty had
> a different explanation:
> 'No.
> White
> has nothing
> to do with it'
> 'She doesn't understand
> our
> language'.
> I
> was forgotten,
> two boys
> pondering an insight.
> 'True'
> I did not understand
> *their* language.

What is clear from working in aesthetic dimensions to language and intercultural communication is that new questions present themselves which go beyond some of the standard concerns of the field. The questions of misunderstanding, for instance, are reframed into a context of interpretation and hermeneutics for the aesthetic asks for comment rather than offering an answer. It also brings affect centre stage demanding a judgement, not on the correctness or clarity of an argument made but on the new insight which has joined the intercultural setting, which has migrated from one imagination, taken form, settled and moved in on another imagination. It may also provoke what MacDonald and O'Regan (2012) have termed a 'discourse of responsibility' as aesthetics produce strong sensibilities of care and protection, as well as of repulsion and destruction, which shed light on some of the perennial questions of tolerance and empathy which have beset intercultural studies.

Where migration is involved, as Sarah Nuttall (2007) has shown, questions of beauty and ugliness become politicised in particular ways. This is clear in some of the papers in this volume, which attend to judgments on the aesthetic quality of migratory forms and settings. What is not understood or seen as familiar is quickly judged to be ugly, or is celebrated as exotic and orientalised. It may change and move into a range of social economies: broadcast, smuggled, exchanged, displayed, hidden. These activities, to bring our reflections full circle, are part of the process of installing movement within place. Attention to aesthetics, the making of new forms or the appearance and description in language, judgement and description of new aesthetic forms points to what Karin Barber

(2007) has termed 'the art of making things stick.' By concentrating attention on aesthetic processes in migratory settings it becomes possible to shift the perspective from movement and encounter in intercultural language relations to the acts of 'installing movement within place.' (Aydemir & Rotas, 2008, p. 7). Such a focus detaches intercultural research, of necessity, from models of intercultural communication and towards the work of thick description, phenomenology and improvisation. It allows it to follow an immanent ethics, as described by MacDonald and O'Regan (2012) which is not focused on a final correct transcendental 'solution' to questions of intercultural interaction but is instead free 'to engage critically and transformatively with regard to the exorbitant cultural acts of the other' (p. 12). Aesthetic acts are in their own way 'exorbitant' and as such provide both a site and a method for such critical and transformative work in migratory settings.

## Note

1. The 'Jeeley Piece song', based on a poem by Adam McNaughton, 1967 recalls the common practice of mothers handing their children a slice of bread and jam (a jeely piece) out of the windows of their tenement flats and how this was disrupted by the move to high-rise accommodation following the slum clearances of the 1950s and 1960s. Its chorus became a key refrain throughout the workshops and events of the Future memory at Red Road project. http://www.roblightbody.com/scotland/scotlandjeely.htm

## References

Agier, M. (2011). *Le couloir des exilés. Être étranger dans un monde commun* [Corridors of exile: A worldwide web of camps by Michel Agier]. (E. Rosencratz, Trans.). Bellecombe-en-Bauge: éditions du Croquant.

Ahmed, S. (2000). *Strange encounters: Embodied others in post-coloniality.* London: Routledge.

Aydemir, A., & Rota, A. (2008). *Migratory settings.* Amsterdam: Rodopi.

Baker, W., Jenkins, J. & Baird, R. (2014). ELF researchers take issue with 'English as a lingua franca: an immanent critique. *Applied Linguistics.* Retrieved from http://applij.oxfordjournals. org/content/early/2014/07/02/applin.amu026.short?rss=1

Barber, K. (2007). Improvisation and the art of making things stick. In E. Hallam & T. Ingold (Eds.), *Creativity and cultural improvisation* (pp. 25–45). Oxford: Berg.

Block, D. (2012). Class and second language acquisition research. *Language Teaching Research, 16*, 2.

Butler, J. (2011). Bodies in alliance and the politics of the street. *Transversal, 10.* Retrieved from http://www.eipcp.net/transversal/1011/butler/en

Duchêne, A., & Heller, M. (2007). *Discourses of endangerment: Interest and ideology in the defence of language.* New York, NY: Continuum.

Goldin, I., Cameron, G., & Balarajan, M. (2011). *Exceptional people: How migration shaped our world and will define our future.* Princeton, NJ: Princeton University Press.

Graeber, D. (2007). *Possibilities: Essays on hierarchy, rebellion and desire.* Oakland: AK Press.

Heller, M., & Duchêne, A. (2011). *Language in late capitalism: Pride and profit.* London: Routledge.

Irvine, A. (2011). *This road is red.* Edinburgh: Luath Press.

Jenks, C. (2013). Are you an ELF? The relevance of ELF as an equitable social category in online intercultural communication. *Language and Intercultural Communication, 13*(1), 95–108.

Jones, A. (2010). Not some shrink-wrapped beautiful package: Using poetry to explore academic life. *Teaching in Higher Education, 15*(5), 591.

Kramsch, C. (2006). From communicative competence to symbolic competence. *Modern Language Journal, 9*, 249–252. doi:10.1111/j.1540-4781.2006.00395_3.x

Kramsch, C. (2009). *The multilingual subject.* Oxford: Oxford University Press.

Lu, P.-Y., & Corbett, J. (2012). *English in medical education.* Bristol: Multilingual Matters.

MacDonald, M. N., & O'Regan, J. P. (2012). The ethics of intercultural communication. *Educational Philosophy & Theory, 45*(10), 1005–1017. doi:10.1111/j.1469-5812.2011.00833.x

Nair Venugopal, S. (2012). *The gaze of the west and framings of the east*. New York, NY: Palgrave Macmillan.

Nuttall, S. (2007). *Beautiful/ugly: African and diaspora aesthetics*. Durham, NC: Duke University Press.

O'Regan, J. P. (2014). English as a lingua franca: An immanent critique. *Applied Linguistics*. Retrieved from http://applij.oxfordjournals.org/content/early/2014/01/27/applin.amt045.full.pdf +html?sid=299a887e-125a-4dc3-9f57-aad5e0a7f98a

Santos, B. d. S. (2002). Between prospero and caliban: Colonialism, postcolonialism, and inter-identity. *Luso-Brazilian Review, 39*(2), 9–44.

Sarangi, S., & Roberts, C. (1999). *Talk, work and institutional order: Discourse in medical, mediation and mangagement settings*. Berlin: Mouton de Gruyter.

Saunders, D. (2010). *Arrival city: How the largest migration in history is reshaping our world*. London: Heinemann.

Turner, V. (1987). *The anthropology of performance*. New York, NY: PAJ.

van Gennep, A. (1909). *The rites of passage*. London: Routledge and Kegan Paul.

Widdowson, H. G. (2014). Contradiction and conviction. A reaction to O'Regan. *Applied Linguistics*. Retrieved from http://applij.oxfordjournals.org/content/early/2014/07/02/applin. amu026.short?rss=1

Alison Phipps and Rebecca Kay
*University of Glasgow, Glasgow, UK*

# Divorce and dialogue: intertextuality in Amara Lakhous'
## *Divorzio all'islamica a viale Marconi*

Mariangela Palladino

*Department of English, Keele University, UK*

This study addresses the underdeveloped dialogue in contemporary intercultural relations between Italy and its 'others' to examine the ways in which Amara Lakhous' novel *Divorzio all'islamica a viale Marconi* (2010) [Divorce Islamic style in viale Marconi] articulates a postcolonial response to Pietro Germi's 1961 film *Divorzio all'italiana* [Divorce Italian style] by initiating an intercultural dialogue among preexistent and emerging cultures. Foregrounding intertextuality and 'writing back' in a postcolonial context as intercultural communication modes, this paper explores the intertextual relations between the novel and the film; it examines the use of irony and multivocal narrative in Lakhous' novel as strategies of intercultural mediation. Moreover, it interrogates the works' social, cultural, historical and linguistic movements to analyse the narrativizations of familiarity and estrangement. *Divorzio all'islamica a viale Marconi* enables a dialogue between local cultures and 'guest' cultures by tracing (obliterated) common histories, shared experiences and similar social and cultural predicaments across the northern and southern shores of the Mediterranean, remapping geographical and cultural terrains.

Questo saggio, che intende perlustrare le trame del dialogo, tuttora marginale negli studi interculturali contemporanei, tra l'Italia ed i suoi 'altri', propone un'analisi del romanzo di Amara Lakhous *Divorzio all'islamica a viale Marconi* (2010), inteso come risposta postcoloniale al film di Pietro Germi *Divorzio all'italiana* (1961) e come opera che instrada un dialogo tra culture preesistenti ed emergenti. Considerando l'intertestualità e la'riscrittura' nel contesto postcoloniale come modalità di comunicazione interculturale, l'articolo esamina le relazioni intertestuali tra il romanzo ed il film, prestando particolare attenzione all'uso dell'ironia e della narrativa multi-vocale quali peculiari strategie di mediazione interculturale. Il saggio si sofferma inoltre sugli aspetti sociali, culturali, storici e linguistici del romanzo al fine di evidenziare la narrativizzazione dei concetti di familiarità ed estraniamento. *Divorzio all'islamica a viale Marconi* incoraggia un dialogo tra culture locali e culture'altre', tracciando (ormai dimenticate) storie comuni, esperienze, condizioni sociali e culturali condivise tra le due sponde del Mediterraneo e, quindi, *ri-mappando* nuovi territori geografici e culturali.

## Introduction

Amara Lakhous claims that 'one must make a huge effort to communicate. [...] it is necessary to understand others' point of view, we must put ourselves in their shoes'[1]; he advocates for the necessity to find 'punti in comune', common grounds by recreating a shared imaginary (Brogi, 2011, p. 7). An Algerian-born author who writes in Italian, Lakhous is concerned with communication, especially in the intercultural context of contemporary Italy. His work brings to the surface a common, Mediterranean 'identitarian context' (Esposito, 2011, p. 7) which seeks to enable social relations between migrants and hosts and foster intercultural communication. In a country like Italy where media is mostly controlled by Berlusconi and his 'empire', and where postcolonial debates are only just emerging – unlike the Francophone and Anglophone contexts –'Lakhous' works forge a space of necessary awareness and dialogue' (Esposito, 2011, p. 2).

Intercultural communication is primarily concerned with creating and enabling spaces for dialogue. In the era of globalization and social networking, communication has paradoxically become more complex. The global war on terror, conservative politics and concerns over dwindling natural resources in the face of climate change significantly increase social and cultural tensions. As the past three decades have seen an intensification of migratory routes towards Europe, there is an urgent need for both 'a new conceptual framework to understand the dynamics of global flows [...as well as] a new perspective on the relationship between the stranger and the resident' (Papastergiadis, 2006, pp. 429–432). Debates about intercultural communication are becoming more prominent; Liu claims that intercultural communication enables us to attain knowledge of other peoples and cultures, and it enhances our knowledge about our own culture. 'The result is invariably greater intercultural understanding' (Liu, Volcic, & Gallois, 2011, p. 23).

However, intercultural communication theory is not unproblematic and without aporias. As O'Regan and MacDonald point out, there is a risk of incurring intercultural relativism and inertia. Responsibility 'to the Other' and 'responsibility to openness in opposition to closure' is their answer to this issue:

> the point is to determine not whether different truths are good or bad, but whether putting a particular discourse or set of discourses into practice might lead to a silencing of open alternatives and therefore also a turning away from the Other. (O'Regan & MacDonald, 2007, p. 275)

Paying due acknowledgement to the scholarship on intercultural communication theory, this paper approaches the subject from a postcolonial literary perspective. As Condon (1986) puts it: '[l]iterature and film can enhance intercultural communication [...] by expressing the significance of certain relationships, values, communication styles' (p. 155). Further, a postcolonial literary perspective offers critical strategies which are alert to the (inter)textual interplay of cultures, languages and narrative modes, thus providing a space of interaction between worlds.

This study addresses the underdeveloped dialogue in contemporary intercultural relations between Italy and its 'others' to examine the ways in which Amara Lakhous' novel *Divorzio all'islamica a viale Marconi* (2010) [Divorce Islamic style in viale Marconi] articulates a postcolonial response to Pietro Germi's (1961) film *Divorzio all'italiana* [Divorce Italian style]. It is argued that this is achieved by initiating an intercultural dialogue among preexistent and emerging cultures. Foregrounding inter-textuality and 'writing back' in a postcolonial context as intercultural communication modes, this paper explores the intertextual relations between the novel and the film; it examines the use of irony and multivocal narrative in Lakhous' novel as strategies of intercultural mediation. Moreover, it interrogates the works' social, cultural, historical and linguistic movements to analyse the narrativizations of familiarity and estrangement.

*Divorzio all'islamica a viale Marconi* enables a dialogue between local cultures and 'guest' cultures by tracing (obliterated) common histories, shared experiences and similar social and cultural predicaments across the northern and southern shores of the Mediterranean, remapping geographical and cultural terrains.

## Italy's early days of postcolonial literature

Describing the social and cultural map of contemporary Italy, Amara Lakhous (2011) says that:

> there are all types: young Africans and Asians selling counterfeit goods on the sidewalks, Arab children walking with father and veiled mother, Gypsy women in long skirts begging. In other words, I'm in the Italy of the future, as the sociologists say. (p. 41)

Multicultural Italy is already a reality. Interestingly, Allievi points out that there are some limitations to Italy being a multicultural country. Indeed, while demographics point in this direction, Italy is usually perceived and understood as a 'monocultural and mono-religious' (Catholic) country (Allievi, 2010, p. 85). The ever-increasing number of migrants has contributed to the proliferation of nationalist sentiments – systematically fuelled by institutional discourses – hence, the relationships between preexistent and emerging cultures remain problematic, tense and surrounded by anxieties. 'This nation-alistic mythology'[2], as Bourchard calls it, is complemented by restrictive border (both geographical and juridical) politics which police and regulate the inside/outside boundaries, and those between 'the native and the foreign, the self and the other' (Bouchard, 2010, p. 106).

Italy's struggle to acknowledge the redefinition of its national subjectivities and to deal with its migrant population is rooted in its postcolonial unconscious, as Ponzanesi (2004, p. 26) puts it. Indeed, whilst other European countries have dealt with the legacy of colonialism and the recent global migratory flows, Italy has only just started confronting its colonial past and the consequences of global migration (Coppola, 2011, p. 121). 'The colonial adventure is removed from the Italian imaginary and from historical memory; it is not studied in school, and until recently has rarely been the object of research and reassessment' (Curti, 2007, pp. 60–62). Italy's colonial chapter is erased by a cultural amnesia; its colonial expansion to Africa was archived until very recently, as 'mainstream culture selectively recollected the past while cultivating the idea of Italians as "*brava gente*," or good people, and of their colonialism as "*straccione*," that is to say, done on the cheap and somehow benign' (Bouchard, 2010, p. 109). Bouchard's view on the allegedly 'benign' Italian colonial enterprise, hence not really significant, echoes other critics (Allievi, 2010; Coppola, 2011; Curti, 2007; Parati, 2005; Ponzanesi, 2004).

The country's failure to acknowledge its colonial memory, its histories of racism and cultural plurality, its chapters of mass emigration, prevent it from understanding migrants' sociocultural and legal situation (Allievi, 2010, p. 97). Indeed, Curti (2007) reminds us that Italy, with its history of emigration unconsciously mirrors itself in today's migrants and ignores or forgets that some of them come from its ex-colonies (p. 62). In order to reconceptualize and understand contemporary migration, it is crucial to retrieve the legacy of Italian colonialism and Italian emigration, to be reminded that 'the face of the other is also the face that was one's uncle or one's father, that the affective and cultural dispositions necessary to overcome separations and divisions can be mobilized' (Bouchard, 2010, p. 110).

Whilst Italy slowly and belatedly recalls its colonial experiences, contemporary postcolonial writers are enabling the recovery of the country's colonized, colonialist and migrant pasts, as well as challenging the dominant nationalistic agenda sustained by social, legal and political institutions. Postcolonial Italian literature facilitates the rehabilitation of texts from Italy's colonial and migrant past, as the country 'morphs from an emigrant to an immigrant country' (Bouchard, 2010, pp. 105–106). Furthermore, Parati (2005) argues that due to its history of internal migrations and social and cultural divisions (north and south), Italian culture offers an ideal space to reopen the discussion on the relationship between outside and inside (p. 25). In a context of hostile conservatism, Italian postcolonial authors initiate a necessary dialogue among cultures and shake the grounds of Italy's indifferent attitude to its increasingly culturally diverse population. This body of counter-discourses consolidates the literary postcolonial in Italian language; indeed, there is an 'urge [for] incorporating more linguistic contexts other than the Anglophone and the francophone into postcolonial discourse' (Brancato, 2008, p. 1); a position which echoes Moore-Gilbert's (2000) [1997] call for a postcolonial in 'non-Anglophone worlds' (p. 187).

In the past two decades, the Italian literary scene has witnessed a proliferation of postcolonial, 'migrant', 'hyphenated', 'in-between' authors. There are ongoing debates on the labelling of this specific literary strand; however, as Curti (2007) observes, there are limits to the term 'migrant' (p. 66); '"migrancy" is now ubiquitous as a theoretical term. It specifically refers to migration not as an act, but as a condition of human life' (Smith, 2004, p. 257). Thus, the creation of a discursive category on this basis is far more complex. Alternative terms have been suggested; for instance, Portelli (2006) considers the label 'migrant literature' inadequate and suggests 'multicultural Italian literature' instead (p. 475). Although the debate about 'labeling' goes beyond the purpose of this study, I want to briefly challenge and depart from one of the proposed terms: 'Afro-Italian' literature (Brancato, 2007; Ponzanesi, 2003; Portelli, 2004). Reproducing problematic power relations – extensively explored in the black American context – the 'Afro' included in this hyphenated labelling literally reduces (and suppresses) the African presence in the definition; indeed the term 'Afro-American' has been replaced with the more inclusive, non-hyphenated African American. Postcolonialism in the Italian context – whilst being a belated experience – has the opportunity to avoid the shortcomings of previous critical discourses; thus, it seems irresponsible to replicate previous faux pas of discoursive categories.[3]

## Migrancy, intertextuality and intercultural dialogue

Lakhous' work posits itself amidst this social and cultural scene, in an effort to 'speak back' to dominant mis-representations and engage in an intercultural and intertextual dialogue. In Parati's (2005) words, this is a literary 'writing back' 'both to the alarmist press releases concerning mass invasions[4] from poorer countries and to the opposite excess embodied in the construction of immigrants as pitiful entities in constant need of assistance' (p. 31). Although Lakhous consciously seeks – in his own words – to 'extricate [him]self from this postcolonial discourse' (Esposito, 2011, p. 3) by writing in Italian rather than in French (his colonial language),[5] his work participates in the production of counter-discursive strategies, endemic to the postcolonial process (Tiffin, 1995, p. 98). Lakhous' writing represents an anti-systemic act which challenges coercive social and cultural practices and initiates liberation. As Edward Said (1994) reminds us, liberation as an intellectual mission has shifted from settled, sedentaries and established cultural dynamics and is enabled by 'unhoused, decentred, and exilic energies, energies whose incarnation today is the migrant' (p. 403). Echoing Said's stance, Andrew Smith (2004) explores the relationship between migrancy, postcolonial literature and liberatory narratives:

> [i]t is often the migrant writer who is taken to be the figure of this new liberation, prizing the lid from locked histories and self-centred stories. [...] By becoming mobile and by making narratives out of this mobility, people escape the control of states and national borders *and* the limited, linear ways of understanding themselves which states promotes in their citizens. (p. 245)

Interestingly, intercultural communication is realized by those who move across borders and cultures (Piller, 2011, p. 174); thus, without romanticizing migrancy, its link with agency in the intercultural dialogue seems evident. In the context of contemporary Italy, Italophone literature by African writers facilitates intercultural communication (Brancato, 2007, p. 657). Lakhous' *Divorzio all'islamica a viale Marconi*, recasting past histories and reaching back and forwards among cultures and places, contributes to the postcolonial process of re-drawing and re-charting contemporary Italy's identitarian cartographies.

One of the devices for the postcolonial author to write back is 'intertextuality' (Weir, 2006, p. 1). Coined by Julia Kristeva in her essay 'The Bounded Text' (1960), *intertextualité* is a series of relationships between texts, as well as between readers and texts. For Kristeva (as cited in Guberman, 1996), a literary text 'borrows always from the discourses of the press, from oral discourses, from political discourses, and from other texts that preceded it, that provide vehicles in turn for those cultural and political texts of history' (p. 53). Textual and intertextual encounters generate radical and – to recall Edward Said – liberating energies that allow redefinition of subjectivities. Texts and discourses interrelate and interpose, opening up any intrinsic ideologies and recombine in unpredictable and politically liberating fashions. 'As a theory of textuality and sub-jectivity, Kristevan intertextuality addresses such liberative concerns of the postcolonial critique and its continual attempt to level any essentializing discourse insisting upon the arbitrary boundaries between Self and Other' (Weir, 2006, p. 10).

Intertextuality in Lakhous' novel functions as re-writing or writing back to re-appropriate and reclaim histories that have been erased by the canon. Further, it maps out a novel literary territory in which intercultural encounters are made possible; as López-Varela Azcárate (2011) observes, the intertextual phenomenon is strictly bound up not only with negotiation of authority but also with issues of mediation of values and cultural forms (p. 10). Mediation is a key concept in intercultural communication (Baraldi, 2003; Deardorff, 2009; Fox, 1997; Ting-Toomey &Chung, 2012), especially with reference to contemporary Italy where migrancy is experienced, both by 'hosts' and 'guests', with anxiety, fear, misunderstanding and prejudice. Intertextuality is not mainly a 'matter of multilingual punning and allusion-mongering broadly within the same culture [...] but [it has] the function of a more deeply permeating intermingling of two radically different cultures' (Trivedi, 2007, p. 132).

*Divorzio all'islamica a viale Marconi* is a re-writing of Germi's film *Divorzio all' italiana*, a comedy milestone in Italian cinema, and in itself an intertextual, satirical response to a precedent text, Giovanni Arpino's novel *Un delitto d'onore* (1960). A parallel between Lakhous' and Germi's titles begs for consideration: whilst *Divorzio all'italiana* suggests homogeneity – a divorce Italian style – Lakhous' work immediately signifies difference and heterogeneity both by associating an Islamic element to the

Italian context, and by localizing it to viale Marconi in Rome, one street in one city. Germi's film – a parodic remediation – narrativizes and problematizes the indissolubility of marriage in 1960 Italy, while Lakhous recounts how divorce is easily obtained in Islamic law. Starring Marcello Mastroianni, *Divorzio all'italiana* tells the story of a Sicilian baron, Ferdinando Cefalù, called Fefè, and his machinations to rid himself of an unwanted wife. Taking advantage of article 587 of the Italian Penal Code (only abolished in 1981) – whereby the killing of a wife, daughter or sister caught in flagrante in an adulterous relationship, was punished with 3–7 years imprisonment – Fefè plans to find a lover for his wife Rosalia and then to murder her. In *Divorzio all'islamica a viale Marconi*, Safia, an Egyptian migrant living in Rome, is in conflict with her husband over his overzealous approach to Islamism and his marital demands. Safia often challenges him and, in the course of their marriage, she is repudiated by her husband three times. As Islam prescribes, the third repudiation renders the divorce definitive; thus, whilst Safia's husband, Said, tries to win her back, she turns the repudiation into a liberation and releases herself from social and cultural oppressions. A re-vision of the film, Lakhous' novel transfers it to the female realm, indeed whilst in the case of Safia it is a woman who is empowered by the divorce, in the film divorce only serves the interests of male desire (Spackman, 2011, p. 11).

Postcolonial Italian texts provide a comparative perspective and enable a dialogic process to take place between the culture of origin and the 'host' culture. By engaging with a diverse set of cultural references such as food, weather, landscape, customs, clothing and by drawing on shared cultural practices, postcolonial narratives in Italian literature enable readers to familiarize themselves 'with cultures often remote to them, but they are also offered a view from the outside of their own culture and society, so that they can look at it from a different – and critical – angle' (Brancato, 2007, p. 656). Ironically, it is through divorce that Lakhous' novel articulates a dialogue among cultures to annul divisions and to bridge gaps in communication. Narrativizing 'Islamic style' divorce in contemporary Italy by re-visiting a 1960 canonical text, Amara Lakhous' postcolonial counter-discourse opens up multiple spaces of intercultural communication. Bringing to the fore the arbitrary boundaries between self and other, between Italian and foreigner, the novel draws 'punti in comune', common grounds, to begin an intercultural dialogue.

## The intertextual as intercultural

*Divorzio all'islamica a viale Marconi* adopts and adapts the style of 1960 'commedia all'italiana' a genre which very subtly derides serious matters. In an interview, Lakhous explores the significance of self-irony in contemporary postcolonial Italy: 'when a world that suffocates us is so irrational [...] there is no way to face it rationally. But we have irony and the possibility of sacralizing. [...] if you use irony, you shake things up, move things around' (Esposito, 2011, pp. 9–10). Lakhous' use of irony responds to rigid and nationalist identitarian discourses produced by institutions; in his words: 'when people say Italians are those who speak Italian [...] this discourse of identity being tied to some sort of grid, of linguistic entrapment, of nationalism, is troubling. With irony one can create doubt' (Esposito, 2011, p. 9). Orton (2001) points out the values and effectiveness of re-appropriation when deploying irony in relation to institutional and dominant discourses. Irony is a powerful, centuries-old form of social critique to challenge discourses of power by exposing their inherent contradictions and absurdities (p. 383). Irony is inscribed in the predicaments of Christian, one of the protagonists in *Divorzio all'islamica a viale Marconi*; he is a Sicilian who studied Arabic at the University of

Palermo and in 2005 is asked by the SISMI (Servizio per le Informazioni e la Sicurezza Militare) to work on a mission as part of George W. Bush's War on Terror. Christian – renamed Issa for the purpose of this operation – has to impersonate a Muslim Tunisian migrant and gain access to an alleged terrorist cell in the Roman neighbourhood of viale Marconi, known as 'Little Cairo', home to an immigrant community, mainly from northern Africa.

Set in the alarmist climate that followed the 2005 London and Madrid bombings, the novel follows Christian/Issa on his mission to uncover the allegedly imminent Rome bombing being plotted in Viale Marconi. Parati (2005) recalls Étienne Balibar's concept of the 'imaginary singularity of national formations', that is to say that institutions '"produce" homogeneous national communities (and identities). [...] A construction of homogeneous *italianità* is necessary in order to create dichotomies such as "us" and "them", "Italians" and "foreigners", *comunitari* and *extracomunitari*' (pp. 24–25). In Lakhous' oeuvre, the use of irony challenges the dominant view of a monolithic and homogenous Italian identity. Christian/Issa plays the Fanonian dictum black skin/white masks in reverse. In *Black Skin White Masks* (1952) Fanon explores racial drama, colonial desire and the 'masquerade of Western Man'(Bhabha, 2008, p. xxxii). In Issa's case, black skin/white masks is inverted as the 'white', Western man plays the 'black' man; the drama of identity has been staged till – as Bhabha puts it in the foreword to the 1986 edition –the 'black mask *slips* to reveal the white skin' (p. xxxiv). Thus, the blending of Christian into Issa is a reminder that one can be the other,[6] that otherness is inscribed in the self: '"Black skin, white masks" is not a neat division; it is a doubling, dissembling image of being in at least two places' (p. xxviii). Aptly referring to 'terror' and the anxieties surrounding otherness in our contemporaneity, de Sousa Santos observes that '[t]error shows us what Benjamin had already demonstrated, that the other is inside us and is not a foreigner, so we need to develop new strategies of trust and reciprocity in this context' (Phipps, 2007, p. 99). Lakhous' character, Christian 'exits' his Italian identity to inhabit that of a migrant, Issa; he shares a flat in Little Cairo with other migrants and works as kitchen porter in one of the neighbourhood's pizzerias. As Lakhous points out this is 'una grandissima opportunità', a very big opportunity, as certitudes produce fundamentalism (Brogi, 2011, p. 8).

Christian/Issa's narrative is parallel to that of an Egyptian woman, Safia, who comments on her culture of origin and shares her experiences as a Muslim migrant in contemporary Italy. Obliged to wear the veil by her husband, Said – a devout Muslim and a pizza chef in Rome who renamed himself Felice – Safia is an acute observer caught in between Islamic religious practices, and contemporary Italy's discriminatory patterns. In this context, Safia develops a series of empowerment strategies to defy both her husband's patriarchal power and the discriminatory gaze she is often subjected to in a reluctantly multicultural Rome. She becomes a clandestine hairdresser and happily embraces the name Sofia, both for her resemblance to Italian 1960 cinema star Sofia Loren, and because often people fail to grasp her name correctly (Lakhous, 2010, p. 25). This re-naming, for Safia – whilst seemingly suggesting an acceptance of hegemonic norms – represents in fact an act of empowerment as she uses this to her advantage. The ambiguity imbricated in the naming and the slippage of one into the other is reflected in the novel's narrative strategies, in which both Christian/Issa and Safia/Sofia – the two narrators – articulate a dialogue between the centre and the margin, between Muslim northern Africa and catholic Italy.

It is through the 'Islamic style' divorce that the stories of Safia/Sofia and Christian/ Issa meet. In a series of accidental encounters along the streets of 'Little Cairo', the two characters/narrators exchange glances; interest, fascination and attraction grow between them. Safia/Sofia fantasizes about Christian/Issa and significantly renames him 'il Marcello Arabo', the Arabian Marcello. A reference to Italian actor Marcello Mastroianni (and also a further intertextual reference to Germi's film), Safia/Sofia's re-naming multiplies Christian/Issa's identities in an intricate sequence of ironic performative acts: a Sicilian (Italian) plays a Tunisian who in turns embodies a male, Italian icon. This series of ironic identitarian slippages is imbricated in an entanglement of roots and routes between the northern and southern shores of the Mediterranean. Moreover, at the end of the novel we discover that – ironically – Christian/Issa's mission to uncover a bomb plot was just a test concocted by the SISMI to train him; hence the notion of performance and *mise-en-scène* reaches yet another narrative level. As Spackman (2011) has it: 'the revelation that the migrant reality in which Christian/Issa posed and passed was itself one big pose erodes the ground upon which any reliable distinction might be made'(p. 13) between the self and the *other* self assumed as part of a *mise-en-scène*.

In Germi's film Mastroianni 'plays' the role of a stereotyped and stigmatized southerner and participates in the generalization and proliferation of stereotypes. Mastroianni's enacting of southern-ness is made apparent by an exaggerated facial tic, 'greasily pomaded hair, and a use of the *passato remoto* [preterit] that stands out from his otherwise standard spoken Italian' (Spackman, 2011, p. 11). Germi's film is not only echoed in the novel's themes and plot, but also in its language – a preeminent aspect in the novel. Indeed, Christian is a Sicilian and his narrative combines both Sicilian dialect and standard Italian:'insomma, irriconoscibile sono' (Lakhous, 2010, p. 11), here words in Italian are arranged in a Sicilian sentence structure where the verb is placed in a non-normative position. Also, Christian speaks Arabic with a Tunisian accent, 'like a native'; his linguistic predicaments bespeak his family's history of emigration to Tunisia. A Sicilian Italian, Christian admits that 'in Rome I really am a stranger'[7] (Lakhous, 2010, p. 12). Thus, the ironic passing for a Tunisian Muslim only adds to the multiple migrations embedded in his cultural, geographical and linguistic identities.

Christian/Issa's linguistic predicaments articulate a 'double-voiced' narrative; its 'heteroglossic' characteristic reveals a non-heterogeneous, 'in-between' nature. His multiple identities as Sicilian–Tunisian–Italian and now Egyptian represent for Spackman (2011), a sort of metaphorical transposition of Italy's future: Christian/Issa 'becomes the site of the proliferation and crossing of languages and identities that is generalized as an Italian future in which it is no longer possible to say who is a migrant and who is not' (p. 13). Lakhous' text plays with performing 'otherness' through a multiplication of voices and identities that are fluidly cast upon his characters. Moreover, in *Divorzio all'islamica a viale Marconi* both narrators make extensive use of different languages: Italian, Sicilian, French, English, Moroccan, Egyptian and Standard Arabic (Lakhous, 2010, pp. 37, 53, 74, 87, 143, 170). Christian/Issa's hybridized language occurs with the juxtaposition of multiple idioms:

> non guardare in faccia a nessuno [Italian] e avere il tradimento rint 'e vvene, [Neapolitan] come dicono i napoletani. Però 'un sugnu fisso [Sicilian]. [...] Mi sottopose al suo quiz preferito, quello delle cinque 'w': where, when, why, who and what [English]. (Lakhous, 2010, p. 31)

This multilingual intermingling of proverbial and idiomatic expressions (condensed into a single sentence) – whilst inserting locality in a cross-cultural and global context – signifies Italy's diverse linguistic cartography; furthermore, it also challenges notions of homogeneity of Italian identity, so forcefully advocated by dominant, institutional and official discourses.

Amara Lakhous' novel draws attention to otherness in sameness: the multivocal narratives, the double-naming of characters, along with the linguistic shifts in the text alert to the intercultural embedded in Italy's own social, linguistic and identitarian tissues. Otherness is thus within, rather than in the foreign, beyond the borders; it is to be found in the allegedly homogenous Italianness, within Italy's very social, cultural and identitarian threads. For Parati (2005), destabilizing definitions of Italianness:

> generate[s] questions and answers that interpret the present multicultural profile of Italy, grounded in continuity with a Mediterranean, already multicultural, past. [...] Literature [...] tells stories that run counter to any homogenizing project and allows the individuation of experiences that are excluded from public political discourse. (p. 51)

Lakhous' *Divorzio all'islamica a viale Marconi* demonstrates this by articulating a series of intercultural and inter-identitarian encounters between 'hosts' and 'guests', challenging dominant discourses of homogeneity and enmeshing the inside and the outside.

## 'Southern' women: internal and external otherness

Fokkema (2004) observes that:

> there is more cross-cultural intertextuality now than ever before. [...] the creative assimilation of texts and ideas from another culture in new work – indicates an ultimate form of cultural integration, an explicit sign of transcending cultural barriers. (p. 8)

Safia/Sofia's accounts of her past are imbued with intercultural 'lessons'[8] in which Italian and Egyptian customs and cultures entwine. Taking the reader back to her life in Egypt as a child and young woman, she speaks about the importance of virginity for Islam 'an obsession, a sacred thing'[9] (Lakhous, 2010, p. 41). Similarly, Germi's film represents the significance of virginity in post World War II Sicilian moral codes. When Fefè's cousin, Angela, is suspected to have a lover (her father finds her diary in which she recounts a romantic and platonic encounter), a midwife is called to validate her purity. Addressed as 'svergognata', shameless, Angela is taken to her bed while the household women enact what looks like a ritual. A bowl of water and white cloths are taken into the room as a stern, old woman, comes in closing the door behind her. Dressed in black, this old, androgynous looking woman is a product of patriarchy, a menacing middle figure who enacts violence on the female body as a social ritual.

This powerful sequence is uncannily echoed in Lakhous' narrative. Safia/Sofia recalls 'a toothless old woman, she seemed the incarnation of the fables' evil witch' (p. 123), who practiced circumcision on young girls in her neighbourhood. This frightening figure was a 'specialist in this practice'; Safia/Sofia describes her as 'di una durezza incredibile'[10] (Lakhous, 2010, p. 123), incredibly harsh. The word 'durezza' also signifies toughness, cruelty, and austerity – Angela's midwife is compellingly recalled in this passage. Safia/Sofia remembers the psychological and physical violence inflicted on her sisters and the traumas left by this practice. Whilst being spared from this violence, she has been haunted by the image of the old, toothless woman, and afflicted by a sense of guilt for having been 'lucky' to escape circumcision.

Lakhous' narrative, through Safia/Sofia's perspective, explores the theme of violence against women as a widespread practice across east and west, south and north. An Italian radio programme catches Safia/Sofia's attention as it reveals statistics about the number of women victims of physical or sexual violence in Italy, 6.5 million (Lakhous, 2010, p. 122). This figure leaves her 'senza parole', speechless; Safia/Sofia admittedly thought that:

> women were victims of violence in places stricken by war like Afghanistan or Iraq, in countries where there is racial hatred like in some African or Muslim states, and where ignorance and poverty are widespread. But not in Italy! I mean, Italy is a European country, a Western country, part of the G8, and so on, am I not right?[11] (Lakhous, 2010, p. 123)

Safia/Sofia's rhetorical and ironic reflections challenge stereotypes about Muslims perpetrating violence against women as well as dominant and received views of Italy as an advanced, Western, democratic country. The reference to Europe and the G8 signifies Italy's intimate association with the powerful and rich global north; further, the unambiguous allusion to its status as a Western country, powerfully articulates the binary relations between war/violence/poverty/Africa and peace/democracy/Italy/Europe. Angela's and Safia/Sofia's past experiences and memories of violence function as backdrop to the theme of violence against women in both the West and the 'rest'.

Lakhous' text draws undeniable connections and intercultural paths between contemporary Italy and its 'others' which Safia/Sofia sarcastically groups as 'Afghanistan or Iraq', 'African or Muslim states', places with war and poverty. Whilst hinting at the vague and homogenous labelling of 'others', this reference alerts us to Italy's oblivious attitude to its internal issues. Safia/Sofia's surprise at the content of this radio programme is a metaphorical transposition of Italians' disbelief at how their cultural and social heritage is entwined with its 'others'; how it uncannily resonates with places elsewhere, beyond the Mediterranean. As a founding member of this democratic entity called Europe, Italy perceives itself as far removed from the worlds beyond the safe (southern) frontiers of Fortress Europe. With reference to intercultural theory, López-Varela Azcárate (2011) observes that with the intertextual 'the written text can become a contextualization cue in itself; an artefact for crosscultural negotiations' (p. 13); this is indeed the case in *Divorzio all'islamica a viale Marconi* where the use of intertextuality functions as (inter) cultural mediation.

Safia/Sofia has long and articulate debates about wearing the veil, about the general predicaments of Muslim women being marginalized in their home and rendered invisible, even in public, by their veil. Recalling her first discriminatory experiences and people's 'obsessive' gaze, for Safia/Sofia her 'veil was like a traffic light where people must stop. That compulsive stop was an ideal moment for people to unload tensions, fears, preoccupations, anxieties, and so on. People needed to unburden themselves'[12] (Lakhous, 2010, p. 62). In this passage she critically examines the social dynamics (and halts!) around the veil in contemporary Italy, where the scarfed woman becomes an embodiment of otherness, a visible alien to be scapegoated.[13]

These images powerfully echo Germi's film. As Fefè introduces viewers to the social and geographical reality of his village in Sicily, he tells of the 'invisible women of Agramonte [who] hid their beauty behind chaste shutters'; and of the 'natural reservation of *our* southern women'[14] (Germi, 1961).[15] In this discourse, Sicily is placed in the profound 'backward' south of an Italy striving to breakthrough as an advanced, and emancipated Western country whose stories of mass emigration, post-war depression and colonial enterprise were duly obliterated by the positivist dream of 'development'. This image is in sharp contrast with Safia/Sofia's ironic reference to Italy as a G8 country; as a matter of fact, Italy, in Safia/Sofia's words, 'is not too dissimilar to Arab and to third world countries'[16] (Lakhous, 2010, p. 82).

The reference to the subject of women in the 'south' is revisited towards the end of the film by a socialist politician from northern Italy (this can be inferred by his accent) in a speech to Agramonte's villagers: 'in your beautiful south it is time to tackle the problem of women's emancipation and to resolve it' (Germi, 1961). This quotation articulates a romanticized, paternalistic vision of the south: the politician fully celebrates Sicily's beauty alongside its women's 'problems' (omitting the fact that in the north of Italy too such 'problems' existed). This rather colonial approach towards Sicily is another reminder of Italy's multiple internal divisions and divisive nature: the country's south holds all the connotations of subalternity. Within this context, Agramonte's women occupy a similar peripheral space to Muslim migrant women, closed behind screens.

This association is rendered even more powerfully in the film by a solicitor's defence speech in court; addressing the judge, he presents the circumstances of his client, Mariannina Terranova, accused of murdering her unfaithful husband: 'a poor southern creature in the black shawl, that symbolizes *our*[17] women's modesty, her hands clasped in her lap, the lap which God condemns to the blissful torments of maternity' (Germi, 1961). This quotation is packed with patriarchal and orientalist references; whilst the word 'creature' faintly alludes to an animalistic semantic, 'poor' insists on her inferiority and vulnerability. The perfect portrait of a subaltern, the woman in question is shrouded in a black shawl, her visibility obliterated. The possessive adjective 'our' (echoing 'our women' in Fefè's account) signifies ownership; subjugated to patriarchy and to God's will, the Sicilian woman portrayed in this passage embodies a double subaltern in 1960 Italy: female and southerner. Having killed her husband because he 'dishonoured' her, Mariannina's case makes it to national news: 'southern honour found its heroine' (Germi, 1961). The rhetoric of this news headline articulates the dichotomic relationship between the richer, more advanced north and the poorer backward south of Italy. Despite being a national broadsheet, the paper speaks of a 'south' as a distinct entity with its distinct social and cultural heritage, its 'honour'.[18]

These examples from the film are paradigmatic instances of 'otherness' within 'sameness', of Italy's non-homogenous cultural and national identity. When Fefè manages to achieve his goal and kill his wife, his case too is recorded in the news with a similar orientalist rhetoric: 'tragedy of honour in Catania' (Germi, 1961). Parati points to a significant shift in the dominant rhetoric brought about in the 1980s and 1990s, whereby headlines like 'Calabrian kills his wife' or 'Sicilian involved in a brawl' were replaced by 'Albanian involved in the business of prostitution' or 'Moroccans arrested for selling drugs' (Parati, 2005, p. 36). The discourse of discrimination has consistently articulated 'difference', what changes is the 'other'. Italy's 'other' today, the migrant, the Muslim, the Moroccan, etc. is not solely a product of conservative political and legal discourses, but rather a heritage of the country's longstanding internal otherness. As Parati (2005) has it: '[p]ast and present narratives on internal and external otherness propose Italy as a crossroads where difference and the recognition of sameness meet and invade cultural and linguistic territories' (p. 37).

## Shared histories as intercultural dialogue

Said/Felice in Lakhous' novel, just like Fefè, concocts and organizes an arrangement for his wife to be with another man. In order to restore his marriage – undone by three repudiations – Said/Felice once again observes Islamic law. For Islam, after three repudiations the divorce is definite; the husband can reclaim his wife only by marrying her again. This can occur after she is married to another Muslim man and then divorced (Lakhous, 2010, p. 84). Thus Said/Felice asks Christian/Issa, his co-worker in the pizzeria, to marry his wife. Once again it is through the ironic use of tropes such as divorce, repudiation and division that texts, languages and cultures enter in dialogue. The machinations surrounding divorce – both Islamic and Italian style – are only a superficial intercultural connection. Indeed, the social rituals surrounding both divorces and Lakhous' intertextual references to Germi's film unveil common pasts and uncover shared histories between the southern and northern shores of the Mediterranean.

Digging into his wife's past, Fefè identifies a former lover, Carmelo Patanè, artist and painter. The revival of Carmelo Patanè in Rosalia's life – retrieved from her letters stored in an old trunk in the loft – is a metaphor for his 'resurrection' in the memory of Agramonte's community. Indeed, 'thought dead in the desert in Africa' (Germi, 1961), Carmelo's name figured among those of other fallen soldiers on a monument to commemorate victims of the Second World War in the village's 'piazza'. His name was subsequently removed when he reappeared in the village. Germi's film fleetingly refers to Patanè's predicaments in the El Alamein desert in Egypt in 1942 during a battle between Axis forces, Panzerearmee Afrika and the Allies. This short and peripheral sequence, whilst alluding to the marginality of Italy's colonial enterprise in the country's consciousness, 'resurrects' more than just Carmelo Patanè from the oblivion of the past. Germi's film brings Africa, in this specific case Egypt, at the heart of Italian social history, and reveals Italy's multiple others (quite literally) its skeletons in the closet. The intricate threads of intertextual and intercultural connections woven by Lakhous' text bring Safia/Sofia's world closer to Fefè's, as Egypt's and Italy's customs and histories entwine. Amara Lakhous' novel retrieves Italy's colonial past (only marginally narrativized in Germi's film) and draws attention to the undeniable social and historical proximity to Africa:

> [a]s a border area on the fringes of Europe and as a Mediterranean region whose still-recent history is marked by poverty and migration, Italy is often seen, both from a northern and southern perspective, as culturally and even racially closer to Africa than other European countries. (Brancato, 2007, p. 656)

As part of his mission, Christian/Issa shares a flat in Viale Marconi with other migrants. In a dialogue with one of his flatmates, the Moroccan Mohamed, they talk about the brutality of bureaucracy and Mohamed's anxieties about receiving his 'permesso di soggiorno', leave to remain. Mohammed explores the significance of the word 'Marocchino', Moroccan, in the Italian language: 'it does not refer to somebody who comes from Morocco. It is an offence, that's all, like nigger, faggot, bastard'[19] (Lakhous, 2010, p. 74). The 1990s saw the development of a significant migratory route – primarily from Morocco – to Italy. This might account for today's derogatory use of the term 'Marocchino',[20] a homogenizing label for all migrants and 'others', as Mohamed observes.

However, the origin of the term dates further back in Italian social history. Drawing on Miriam Mafai's work, Parati reminds us of the economic miracle that occurred in Italy in the late 1950s and early 1960s. The country's financial resurrection was also possible thanks to 'southern Italians [who] migrated to the urban Italian north [...] Often called *Marocchini* (Moroccans) at the time, some southern Italians chose to migrate within national boundaries because they were unable to obtain the necessary documentation to expatriate' (Parati, 2005, p. 144). This passage clearly spells out the dynamics of Italy's internal migration and its long history of discriminatory rhetoric, both linguistic and legal. The alleged homogeneity of Italy's identity and history is shattered by these stories of othering discourses within the peninsula itself. As Brancato (2007) notices, this continues to be the case in Italy today, where 'the marginal space to which African immigrants are relegated often coincides with the marginality of underprivileged locals, especially southern Italians' (p. 656).

Mohamed speaks of Italians' 'odio', hatred for Moroccans, rooted in the Second World War, when some Moroccan soldiers, fighting for the Allies, raped Italian women (Lakhous, 2010, p. 74). Thus, 'Marocchino' denotes foreign, alien, savage, violent, an exotic and uncivilized other. A parallel between Italy's past internal migrations and contemporary immigration seems apparent (Parati, 2005, p. 145): today's 'Marocchini' are – literally – Italy's past 'others'. A powerful reminder of the country's migrant history, this passage articulates correspondences between two sets of migrants (from southern Italy yesterday, and from abroad today) who share similar predicaments: issues in acquiring legal residency and civic legitimacy, discriminatory naming, stereotyping, etc.

After speaking to Mohamed, Christian/Issa reflects on these historical events involving Moroccans in Italy during the war – 'a taboo in the collective Italian imaginary, despite De Sica's famous film *La Ciociara*' (Lakhous, 2010, p. 74). While yet another intertextual reference (to *La Ciociara*) shakes the grounds of the Italian collective imaginary, Lakhous' text brings up another obliterated page of Italy's postcolonial unconscious. Through the use of a Sicilian proverb – 'the wolf with a bad conscience thinks the same as it acts'[21](Lakhous, 2010, p. 74)– he observes that Italian soldiers too are guilty of rape in Ethiopia and in Somalia. The proverb, which compellingly alludes to Italy's 'bad conscience', functions as a mediating (Sicilian) voice between Italy's and Morocco's histories of brutalities; both practicing violence against women, both pointing the finger at each other, both affected by historical amnesia. Dwelling in the 'centre' and the 'margin', Christian/Issa's double and multifaceted perspective revisits past and present anxieties and prejudices about colonialism and migrations; it offers intercultural mediation through intertextuality and vernacular, proverbial references. In fact, for Weir (2006) intertextuality enables a text to 'remain connected – even if arbitrarily – to the larger historical and social contexts in which it comes into production and/or interacts with its readership' (p. 6). In *Divorzio all'islamica a viale Marconi*, the use of intertextual references to shared memories and shared experiences, whilst opening up 'archived' pages of Italian history, offers numerous examples of intercultural routes/roots among peoples, cultures, languages, between Italy and its 'others'.

## Conclusion

In The Location of Culture, Bhabha (1994) rhetorically asks:

> [h]ow do strategies of representation or empowerment come to be formulated in the competing claims of communities, where despite shared histories of deprivation and discrimination, the exchange of values, meanings and priorities may not always be collaborative and dialogical, but may be profoundly antagonistic, conflictual and even incommensurate? (p. 2)

Homi Bhabha's preoccupation with the 'exchange of values' among groups divided by fears, prejudice and ignorance (about each other) pertains more than ever to our globalized humanity. In contemporary Italy, where new policies are implemented to defend the territory from 'illegal' migrants and Islamic terrorists, the different social and ethnic groups are struggling to enter into dialogue. The urgency to foster intercultural exchanges is key; '[i]ntercultural knowledge reduces anxiety and uncertainty, making the communication process more smooth and successful' (Liu et al., 2011, p. 25).

As Achille Mbembe (2011) observes, '[w]e are thus compelled [...] to pursue the question of all possible conditions of an authentic human encounter. Yet this encounter cannot begin with acute amnesia, [...] this encounter must begin through reciprocal disorientation' (p. 117). In order to pursue an intercultural 'encounter' it is imperative to rehabilitate the colonial past and to engage with it; thus, the 'reciprocal disorientation' advocated by Mbembe entails a renegotiation of subjectivities. This is what O'Regan and MacDonald (2007) defined, in Derridian terms, 'an infinite responsibility to the Other' which allows for 'the discursive terrain [to remain] open'(p. 275). The slippage of self into other, the use of irony, the intertextual references and the recuperation of past histories in Amara Lakhous' *Divorzio all'islamica a viale Marconi* 'disorientate' the reader and complicate homogeneous notions of national identity, national history and language.

Despite a delayed reception and production of postcolonial texts, postcolonial Italian literature represents an invaluable tool of mediation and dialogue among cultures, people and languages; '[t]he object of postcolonial critique is best described in terms of the *interlacing of histories and the concatenation of distinct worlds*' (Mbembe, 2011, p. 86). Amara Lakhous' *Divorzio all'islamica a viale Marconi* 'interlaces' contemporary Italy with its pasts, and 'concatenates' Italy with other worlds beyond its southern frontiers. Lakhous' work offers innovative narratives and verbal strategies of intercultural enunciation which both problematize normative discourses on migration and propose alternative ethics of communication among cultures.

## Acknowledgment

This article was written in Glasgow, an inspiring city, to which I am eternally thankful. I am grateful to Alex McCabe for sharing with me months of reading and writing (and gluten-free cooking). Thanks also to the editors of this special issue, Alison Phipps and Rebecca Kay. Finally, I owe Zoë Wicomb, Stefano Versace, Maria Vaccarella and John Miller a special debt of gratitude for reading drafts and providing feedback.

## Notes

1. '[b]isogna fare un grande sforzo per comunicare. Penso che sia necessario capire il punto di vista degli altri, dobbiamo metterci nei loro panni'. All translations from Italian in Amara Lakhous' text are my own.
2. Nationalist discourses are promoted in Italy through 'the revival of a mythology of Italian national identity based on imaginary notions of shared civic values, a territory linked to a common culture, and, at times, even a genealogical descent' and through the mobilization of 'latent Fascist fantasies of racial purity' (Bouchard, 2010, p. 106).
3. The term 'Afro-Italian' metaphorically reproduces current geo-political relationships between Africa and Italy: the hyphen keeps Africa away from Italian borders, it stands in between to curb interactions between the two shores, like European border control agency FRON-TEX does.
4. Moderate, left wing Italian broadsheet *La Repubblica* reports that the second most common surname in Milan is a Chinese one, as they put it: 'l'orientale Hu' [the oriental Hu]; however – the article reassures – no 'invasion' of Italy's demographic records is actually taking place (15 April 2012). Whilst acknowledging a change in the country's ethnic and social profile, *Repubblica* reproduces in plainly orientalist language the alarmist rhetoric surrounding migration.

5. In this context it is worth thinking about the significance of the 'colonial language'; is it just the language of the former colonial power in the country of origin (in Lakhous' case, French)? Is it not also the dominant language in the receiving country in which the migrant is usually treated as a subaltern?

6. *Divorzio all'islamica a viale Marconi* not only narrativizes the lives of 'foreign' migrants in Italy, it also forcefully reminds readers about the many Italians migrating abroad. Safia/Sofia's Italian friend, Giulia, announces that she is moving with her partner to Australia because in Italy 'non c'è futuro' [there is no future]; 'Gli italiani lasciano l'Italia pr cercare fortuna altrove! Ma noi immigrati veniamo qui per lo stesso ed identico motivo' [Italians leave Italy to find better chances elsewhere. But we immigrants come here for the very same reason!] (Lakhous, 2010, p. 152) This is another instance of shared experiences where differences between Italians and migrants are obliterated.

7. 'a Roma sono davvero uno straniero' (Lakhous, 2010, p. 12).

8. Lakhous' mapping of intercultural routes and dialogues does not fail to explore even the smallest details where 'North' and 'South' unsurprisingly meet. As Safia/Sofia seeks to escape her husband's attempts to conceive another child, she adopts 'il trucco femminile del mal di testa' [women's trick of the headache] (Lakhous, 2010, p. 130). This artifice, also employed by Rosalia, now fallen for her old time sweetheart, to deter her husband Fefè, allows both characters to escape marital obligations; moreover, it functions as an empowerment strategy to gain agency in the relationship. Within Lakhous' text, this trope narrows divisive gaps between the northern and southern shores of the Mediterranean, and identifies common social and behavioural patterns, shared experiences and secrets in the female world.

9. 'Un'ossessione, una cosa sacra' (Lakhous, 2010, p. 41).

10. '[u]na vecchietta senza denti, sembrava l'incarnazione della strega cattiva delle fiabe' 'una specialista in materia' (Lakhous, 2010, p. 123).

11. [l]e donne fossero vittime di violenza nei luoghi di guerra come in Afghanistan o in Iraq, nei paesi dove c'è odio razziale come in alcuni stati africani e musulmani, e dove sono diffuse la povertà e l'ignoranza. Ma non in Italia! Insomma, l'Italia è pur sempre un paese europeo, occidentale, che fa parte del G8, eccetera eccetera, o sbaglio? (Lakhous, 2010, p. 123)

12. 'Il mio velo era come un semaforo davanti al quale la gente deve fermarsi. Quella sosta obbligatoria era il momento ideale per scaricare tensioni, paure, inquietudini, ansia eccetera eccetera. Le persone avevano bisogno di sfogarsi' (Lakhous, 2010, p. 62).

13. Mbembe (2011) observes that the 'repeated controversies over the Islamic headscarf or the *burkha* are saturated with the kind of orientalist imagery that Said denounced' (p. 94).

14. My emphasis.

15. All citations from the film refer to the English subtitles.

16. 'L'Italia non è molto dissimile dai paesi arabi e del terzo mondo' (Lakhous, 2010, p. 82).

17. My emphasis.

18. The notion of honour, 'l'onore', begs for further discussion. Can the subaltern have 'honour'? The terms seem to appear in a chiasmic relationship.

19. 'non si riferisce a uno che viene dal Marocco. È un'offesa e basta, come negro, frocio, bastardo' (Lakhous, 2010, p. 74).

20. Growing up in the south of Italy, I have been used to hear the word 'Marocchino' as an accepted and widely used term to signify a black person – regardless of their national, ethnic background – usually a street vendor to be encountered along the beach under the scorching sun of the summer season. This term is employed still today, and often without any recognition or even realization of its homogenizing and discriminatory nature.

21. 'U lupu r'a mala cuscienza comu opera piensa' (Lakhous, 2010, p. 74).

## References

Allievi, S. (2010). Immigration and cultural pluralism in Italy: Multiculturalism as a missing model. *Italian Culture, 28*(2), 85–103. doi:10.1179/016146210X12790095563020

Baraldi, C. (2003). *Comunicazione interculturale e diversità* [Intercultural communication and diversity]. Rome: Carocci.

Bhabha, H. (1994). *The location of culture*. London: Routledge.

Bhabha, H. (2008). Foreword to the 1986 edition. In F. Fanon (Ed.), *Black skin white masks* (pp. xxi–xxxvii). London: Pluto Press.

Bouchard, N. (2010). Reading the discourse of multicultural Italy: Promises and challenges of transnational Italy in an era of global migration. *Italian Culture, 28*(2), 104–120. doi:10.1179/016146210X12790095563066

Brancato, S. (2007). From routes to roots afrosporic voices in Italy. *Callaloo, 30*, 653–661. doi:10.1353/cal.2007.0181

Brancato, S. (2008). Afro-European literature(s): A new discursive category? *Research in African Literatures, 39*(3), 1–13. doi:10.2979/RAL.2008.39.3.1

Brogi, D. (2011). Le catene dell'identità. Conversazione con Amara Lakhous [The chains of identity. Conversation with Amara Lakhous]. *Between, 1*(1), 1–10.

Condon, J. (1986). Exploring intercultural communication through literature and film. *World Englishes, 5*, 153–161. doi:10.1111/j.1467-971X.1986.tb00722.x

Coppola, M. (2011). 'Rented spaces': Italian postcolonial literature. *Social Identities, 17*(1), 121–135. doi:10.1080/13504630.2011.531909

Curti, L. (2007). Female literature of migration in Italy. *Feminist Review, 87*(1), 60–75. doi:10.1057/palgrave.fr.9400361

Deardorff, D. K. (2009). *The Sage handbook of intercultural competence*. London: Sage.

Esposito, C. (2011). Literature is language: An interview with Amara Lakhous. *Journal of Postcolonial Writing, 48*(4), 1–13. doi:10.1080/17449855.2011.55916

Fokkema, D. (2004). The rise of cross-cultural intertextuality. *Canadian Review of Comparative Literature, 11*, 5–10.

Fox, C. (1997). The authenticity of intercultural communication. *International Journal of Intercultural Relations, 21*(1), 85–103. doi:10.1016/S0147-1767(96)00012-0

Fra i Cognomi più diffusi a Milano il cinese Hu scalza 'sciur' Brambilla [Among the most popular surnames in Milan, Chinese Hu has replaced '*signor*' Brambilla]. (2012, April 15). *Repubblica*. Retrieved from http://repubblica.it

Germi, P. (1961). *Divorce Italian style* [DVD]. Italy: Lux Film.

Guberman, R. M. (Ed.). (1996). *Julia Kristeva: Interviews*. New York, NY: Columbia University Press.

Lakhous, A. (2010). *Divorzio all'islamica a viale Marconi* [Divorce islamic style in Viale Marconi]. Roma: Edizioni e/o.

Lakhous, A. (2011). Issa. *World Literature Today, 4*, 40–44.

Liu, S., Volcic, Z., & Gallois, C. (2011). *Introducing intercultural communication: Global cultures and contexts*. London: Sage.

López-Varela Azcárate, A. (2011). Intertextuality and intermediality as cross-cultural communication tools: A critical inquiry. Cultura. *International Journal of Philosophy of Culture and Axiology, 8*(2), 7–22.

Mbembe, A. (2011). Provincializing France?. (J. Roitman, Trans.). *Public Culture, 23*(1), 85–119. doi:10.1215/08992363-2010-017

Moore-Gilbert, B. (2000) [1997]. *Postcolonial theory*. London and New York, NY: Verso.

O'Regan, J. P., & MacDonald, M. N. (2007). Cultural relativism and the discourse of intercultural communication: Aporias of praxis in the intercultural public sphere. *Language and Intercultural Communication, 7*, 267–278. doi:10.2167/laic287.0

Orton, M. (2001). The economy of otherness: Modifying and commodifying identity. In S. Matteo (Ed.), *ItaliAfrica: Bridging continents and cultures* (pp. 376–392). New York, NY: Forum Italicum, Stony Brook.

Papastergiadis, N. (2006). The invasion complex: The abject other and spaces of violence. *Geografiska Annaler, Series B: Human Geography, 88*(4), 429–442. doi:10.1111/j.0435-3684.2006.00231.x

Parati, G. (2005). *Migration Italy: The art of talking back in a destination culture*. Toronto: University of Toronto Press.

Phipps, A. (2007). Other worlds are possible: An interview with Boaventura de Sousa Santos. *Language and Intercultural Communication, 7*(1), 91–101. doi:10.2167/laic262.0

Piller, I. (2011). *Intercultural communication: A critical introduction*. Edinburgh: Edinburgh University Press.

Ponzanesi, S. (2003). Il Multiculturalismo Italiano. L'identità frammentata dell'Italia. [Italian multiculturalism. Italy's fragmented identity] *Ibridazioni, 10*. Retrieved from www.sagarana.net/rivista/numero10/ibridazioni2.html

Ponzanesi, S. (2004). Il Postcolonialismo Italiano. Figlie Dell'impero e Letteratura Meticcia [Italian postcolonialism. Empire's daughters and *mestizo* literature]. *Quaderni del'900. Istituti Editoriali e Poligrafici Internazionali, IV*(2), 25–34.

Portelli, A. (2004). Le origini della letteratura afroitaliana e l'esempio afroamericano [The origins of afroitalian literature and the Africanamerican example]. *El Ghibli, 3B.* Retrieved from http://www.el-ghibli.provincia.bologna.it/

Portelli, A. (2006). Fingertips stained with ink. Notes on new 'migrant writing' in Italy. *Interventions: International Journal of Postcolonial Studies, 8*(3), 472–483. doi:10.1080/13698010600956113

Said, E. (1994). *Culture and imperialism.* London: Random House Vintage.

Smith, A. (2004). Migrancy, hybridity, and postcolonial literary studies. In N. Lazarus (Ed.), *The Cambridge companion to postcolonial literary studies* (pp. 241–261). Cambridge and New York, NY: Cambridge University Press.

Spackman, B. (2011). Italiani DOC? Passing and posing from Giovanni Finati to Amara Lakhous. *California Italian Studies Journal, 2*(1). ismrg_cisj_8973. Retrieved from http://escholarship.org/uc/item/9tp6d268

Tiffin, H. (1995). Post-colonial Literatures and Counter-discourse. In B. Ashcroft, G. Griffiths, & H. Tiffin (Eds.), *The post-colonial studies reader* (pp. 95–98). London: Routledge.

Ting-Toomey, S., & Chung, L. (2012). *Understanding intercultural communication.* New York, NY and Oxford: Oxford University Press.

Trivedi, H. (2007). Colonial influence, postcolonial intertextuality: Western literature and Indian literature. *Forum for Modern Language Studies, 43*(2), 121–133. doi:10.1093/fmls/cqm006

Weir, Z. (2006). How soon is now? Reading and the postcolonial present. *Postcolonial Text, 2*(4), 1–18.

# Visualizing intercultural literacy: engaging critically with diversity and migration in the classroom through an image-based approach

Evelyn Arizpe, Caroline Bagelman, Alison M. Devlin, Maureen Farrell and Julie E. McAdam

*School of Education, University of Glasgow, Glasgow, UK*

Accessible forms of language, learning and literacy, as well as strategies that support intercultural communication are needed for the diverse population of refugee, asylum seeker and migrant children within schools. The research project *Journeys from Images to Words* explored the potential of visual texts to address these issues. Working in Glasgow primary schools within critical pedagogical frameworks that invite sharing of personal narratives and of cultural knowledge, the researchers examined and evaluated an image-based approach, both for reading and responding to a selection of children's texts and for obtaining an insight into the home literacy practices of diverse communities. In this article, a 'generative theme', as used by Paulo Freire is used to examine how students engaged with reading visual texts, shared their responses and extended their intercultural understanding. The results from this project provide evidence for the inclusion of visual texts and methodologies within critical pedagogies in order to develop intercultural literacy in the classroom.

Para apoyar a la población diversa de niños refugiados, solicitantes de asilo y migrantes en el colegio, son necesarias tanto formas accessibles de lenguaje, aprendizaje y prácticas letradas, como también estrategias de comunicación intercultural. El proyecto de investigación, *Travesías desde las imágenes hacia las palabras* se dirige a este tema al explorar el potencial de textos visuales. Las investigadoras trabajaron en colegios de primaria en Glasgow a partir de marcos pedagógicos que invitaron a compartir narrativas personales y conocimientos culturales. Examinaron y evaluaron estrategias visuales, tanto para la lectura de una selección de textos para niños, como para obtener una mejor percepción de las prácticas de lectura de comunidades diversas. En este artículo, el 'tema generador', según Paulo Freire, se usa para examinar cómo los alumnos se acercaron a los textos visuales, compartieron sus respuestas y extendieron su con entendimiento intercultural. Los resultados de este proyecto aportan evidencia para incluir textos y metodologías visuales dentro de pedagogías críticas con el objetivo de desarrollar prácticas letradas interculturales en el aula.

**Boy A**: The rabbits came to invade, they needed more, they didn't have these things in their own country.
**Teacher**: *What could the animals do to understand each other better?*
**Girl A**: They can't understand the way they talk.
**Girl B**: They could write it down…

**Girl A**: They probably couldn't cos they're animals [referring to the native ones]
**Girl B**: The rabbits could write…
**Girl A**: The others can't read because language is difficult.
**Girl B**: …because the rabbits are more like humans.
**Boy B**: They could use sign language…

**Teacher**: Any other ways?
**Boy A**: They could give them gifts, a book.
**Boy C**: They could draw.

From a group of 10-year-old children (P7, Northside School) discussing *The Rabbits* (Marsden & Tan, 2000) with their teacher.

We live in a visual world, but despite children and adolescents spending increasingly long periods outside of school engaging with visual images on different types of screens, in ways that may seem to undermine traditional forms of reading and writing, it is only recently that multimodal texts and the multimodal literacies that accompany them are being explored within educational contexts (Bearne, 2004). Reading literature can provide powerful, life-changing experiences (Rosenblatt, 1938), so when the power of images, whether graphic or mental, is combined aesthetically with words, the transaction (Rosenblatt, 1978) between the reader and the text can have a transforming influence as the imaginary impact is exponentially multiplied.

We also live in a mobilized world, characterized by different forms of migration which demand more accessible forms of language learning and literacy as well as strategies to support intercultural communication amongst the diverse population of refugee, asylum seeker and migrant children within schools. This demand calls for further research into contemporary literacy practices, including how twenty-first century students are making meaning from the visual texts that surround them. Linked to this is a continuing need for a better understanding of the home literacy practices of diverse communities (Kenner, Mahara, & Gregory, 2010), as changing global and local practices influence the ways that reading is done.

While schools have recognized the importance of working with multimodal, 'multicultural' texts this is often done in ways that replicate traditional approaches to text. This results in missed opportunities for engagement that can lead to more critical understandings of the phenomenon of interculturalism to be found in both image and text (Short, 2009). Integrating visual methodologies with critical pedagogies may provide a way forward and, importantly, in a more ethical manner (Phipps, 2013). This article investigates the theoretical structures behind this integration through the example of an enquiry that involved students from diverse backgrounds, including asylum seekers and refugees, reading and creatively responding to picture books and non-visual texts on the topic of migration and journeys.

There are many definitions of the term 'intercultural' but we found the one proposed by Short (2009) best reflects our aims for this approach:

Interculturalism is an attitude of mind, an orientation that pervades thinking and permeates the curriculum. It is based on a broad understanding of culture as ways of living and being in the world that are designs for acting, believing, and valuing. (p. 2)

If we marry the term to 'literacy' and follow Crouch's (2008) definition of 'visual literacy', we end up with the idea that 'intercultural literacy' is 'an active process involving competencies (i.e. knowledge of/or awareness of other languages) that can lead from an awareness of self-identity/culture to a more empathetic analytical, critical reading of intercultural situations' (p. 195). We argue that this process should permeate school curricula and open spaces allowing both migrant and host children to connect and express themselves through creative possibilities. This would involve the development of the capacity for understanding, empathy, welcome and the acknowledgement of others' resilience (Arizpe, Colomer, & Martínez-Roldán, 2014).

Freire's (2008) understanding of the 'generative theme' is considered as a potential educational tool to examine the shared reading of visual texts within a diverse community. The pedagogical power of a good generative theme is its ability to engage students in educational material that reflects their lived experience. When combined with arresting visual or mental imagery, a theme opens up more easily to those who have not lived through that particular experience and encourages empathy and understanding for those who have. The dynamic and multimodal nature of contemporary children's literature allows readers to engage with complex topics at a variety of different aesthetic, cognitive and affective levels (Arizpe, Farrell, & McAdam, 2013). By linking the themes to ideas of culture and identity and bringing aspects of home cultures and literacies into the classroom and the discussions, students in this project made links between their own lives and those of others. By sharing their responses to the texts, they created a shared set of 'interpretive practices' that supported their language proficiency, sharpened meaning-making from texts, deepened their enjoyment of reading and encouraged intercultural awareness.

This article begins with a discussion of the role of the visual in literacy research, followed by a consideration of the impact of migration in the Scottish educational context. We describe the project *Journeys from Images to Words*[1] and use the idea of the 'generative theme' to examine the collected data. We discuss results in the light of critical, culturally responsive pedagogy and show how they provide evidence for the potential of integrating visual methodologies with critical pedagogies in order to develop intercultural literacy in a diverse classroom.

## Visual texts and visual methods

Qualitative visual research methods have proved effective when working with children who for a variety of reasons struggle to express themselves through words (Fransecky, 1969; Young & Barrett, 2001). They prove particularly effective when examining readers' responses to picture books, first, as a way for researchers to obtain insights into meaning-making from images and second, as a form of expression that sidesteps language barriers, and allows learners from diverse backgrounds to respond in creative ways that develop their visual literacy. Enquiry tools can also be pedagogical strategies, which engage and support children in their learning (Banks, 2001) and in their emotional response to visual texts (Perkins, 1994).

Research on children's responses to picture books (Kiefer, 1995; Pantaleo, 2008; Sipe, 2008) confirms that reading these visual texts can support the development of critical skills to examine 'a variety of texts and representational forms that incorporate a range of linguistic, discursive and semiotic systems' (Anstey, 2002, p. 449). Boal, pioneer of 'Theatre of the Oppressed', has also considered the importance of visual methods for transformative learning. He suggests that a crucial way of processing knowledge derived from these visual methods is to participate in the creative process:

We must develop our capacity not only to hear, but also to see. The creation of images produced by ourselves rather than by nature or a machine, serves to show that the world can be re-created. The creation of Images of the world as we want it to be, is the best way to penetrate the future. (Boal, 2006, p. 46)

The methods involved in reader-response research include open-ended questions and encourage speculation and alternative meanings. Dialogue and group discussion are usually at the centre of the activities, as are creative responses in the form of drawing or other art forms (Brice-Heath & Wolf, 2004). The objectives are based on enhancing the enjoyment of the reading experience and promoting analytical and critical thinking, however, few of these methods explicitly address intercultural literacy among their objectives. The project described here built on research which revealed the potential of picture books as an accessible entry point for those who are learning English or struggling with literacy skills (Arizpe, 2009; Arizpe & Styles, 2003; McGonigal & Arizpe, 2007). In particular, it extended the use of visual strategies for reading and responding to picture books employed in the *Visual Journeys*[2] enquiry, where intercultural learning did play a key role.

## Understanding migration in Scotland

The movement of people through ever-increasing flows of migration means not only a change of landscape for new arrivals, but also a change in the landscape of the host city itself in light of the intermingling of varied languages, religions and cultural practices in one space. Neither the new arrival nor the host are static entities (each is impacted by the other in a plethora of ways), and neither new arrivals nor hosts make up a homogenous group, making it necessary to respond to this social complexity in critical, creative and alinear ways. This has been an aim and challenge of our work and identifying a framework for understanding migration practices is an important step in this process.

Essentialized notions of a national coherent culture, which reflects shared beliefs and practices, have posed migration (resulting in a combination of many beliefs and practices in one space) as a threat (Vertovec, 2011). Vertovec suggests, however, that there is no nation prior to migration, and that cultural cohesion of uniform groups is an imagined notion in any context (historically or geographically). The multiplicity of beliefs and practices that exists in reality, making homogeneity of a host or a new arrival group impossible, means that migration represents a historical and social continuity, and not disruption or disjuncture. However, the massive displacement of populations in recent decades has intensified and issues around the crossing of borders (both literal and virtual) have become a central concern of most states.[3]

In recent years net migration to Scotland has reached its highest level as previous patterns and reasons for migration have changed, with immigrants entering Scotland from A8 and Commonwealth countries because of economic incentives. Between 2000 and 2010, Glasgow city was designated as a dispersal centre for children and young people from asylum seeker and refugee families. This has resulted in two trends in Scottish education, first the profile of children attending Scottish schools is now diverse with over 147 languages being recorded as home languages of children in Scottish schools (Scottish Government, 2009, pp. 14, 18), and second the school populations become more unstable as immigrants disperse around the UK. Terminology has also changed and the preferred term for referring to immigrant students in the UK is 'new arrivals'. In urban Local Authorities such as Glasgow, approximately 15% of young people use English as an additional language. The population changes make extensive demands on schools and specialist staff and HMIe (2009, pp. iv–v) comment that 'the same weaknesses exist in supporting the achievements of new arrivals with English as an additional language as have been present for at least the past ten years'.

Interculturality sees people as constructing complex identities based on their position within new contexts, reconstructing themselves and reconstructing culture as a fluid and, in a sense, hybrid entity (Botelho & Rudman, 2009). In this article, we use 'intercultural' rather than 'multicultural' because the latter has been too often based on a political discourse that celebrates isolated differences but does not seek integration, and does not recognize the potential of the migration process for the creation of *new* interrelated cultures. Similar concerns have led different scholars either to reject the concept of multiculturalism altogether or to highlight critical multicultural perspectives (Banks & Banks, 2001) on the education of immigrants and learners from different communities.

## Moving policy and practice towards intercultural literacy

In response to new challenges associated with migration, the United Kingdom Literacy Association (Reedy & UKLA, 2011) has called educators to move forward with a shared vision of literacy that promotes pedagogies and curricula that are locally and globally relevant to children. New arrival children bring higher demands to the educational system of the host country but, as Suárez-Orozco and Suárez-Orozco (2001) stress, they also bring many positive contributions and already possess a variety of resources. An 'engaging' curriculum should be provided as children acquire literacy and language skills and 'information must be provided multimodally in order to scaffold the children's available linguistic and cultural resources' (Suárez-Orozco & Suárez-Orozco, 2001, p. 588).

Current dialogue and debate on interculturalism, literacy and diversity in Scotland is often centred on the new *Curriculum for Excellence* which seeks to develop 'successful learners, confident individuals, responsible citizens and effective contributors' (Scottish Executive, 2004). This curriculum places the needs of the learner at its centre and these competencies are an aspiration for *all* children and young people in Scotland. The *Literacy Across Learning Principles and Practice* document outlines the need for all practitioners who work with children to engage in the process of supporting critical users of literacy with a range of texts in multiple contexts (Scottish Government, n.d.). Inclusion policy such as *Count Us In: Meeting the Needs of Children and Young People Newly Arrived in Scotland* (HMIe, 2009) places great value on sharing visions and values between home and school.

One potential resource which has been underexploited in this process is children's literature. Through these texts, children are presented with the possibility of reading/ viewing familiar and unfamiliar representations of self and others. The transaction between the reader and the literary (or visual) text has parallels with the 'transaction' that occurs during intercultural encounters as Gonçalves (2012) argues, based on the work of Iser (1978) and Rosenblatt (1978): 'Investigating the act of reading as a dialogical process revealed a significant affinity with intercultural processes which accounts for an understanding of the literary text as an intercultural catalyst and of reading as third place' (p. 12). The project described here is based on the strong belief that children's literature can help explore the intercultural worlds we inhabit.

Texts can pose options and alternatives (Gough, 1998) and present the idea of living in complex, culturally diverse worlds (Gopalakrishnan & Ulanoff, 2003). However, Short

(2009) warns that there is a danger in using 'multicultural' books and other resources without a clear and reflective approach on the teaching aims:

> Teaching for intercultural understanding involves far more than lessons on human relations and sensitivity training or adding a book or unit about a country into the existing curriculum. These approaches typically lead to superficial appreciations of cultural differences that reinforce stereotypes, instead of creating new understanding about cultural perspectives and global issues. (p. 2)

The curriculum framework she proposes instead is based on intercultural understanding as an 'orientation' which links to Freire's idea of 'reading the word and the world' and includes raising issues of power, oppression and social justice. The framework provides inviting spaces for students to 'wrestle' with these complex ideas/images and to begin to link visual features such as colours and symbols to particular meanings. In addition, it is only by realizing the Freirian ideal of the teacher as a dialogical facilitator (Freire, 1972), that shared explorations of the text can lead to new understandings of self (Cullingford, 1998), culture (Gopalakrishnan, 2011) and the grand narratives of politics and history that have shaped that culture. Critical reading allows encounters with 'otherness' as readers begin to imagine alternative and possible worlds (Kornfeld & Prothro, 2005) and form new understandings of others (Ee Loh, 2009). Sleeter and Grant (2002) would argue that this ability to see beyond the self is the beginning of practicing democracy and becoming active citizens in the world.

## 'Journeys from images to words' and back again

> I enjoyed this whole project [...] It's something that's you're learning and having fun at the same time [...] I've learned a very lot because when you're looking at the stories, we didn't really know much about asylum seekers, you know, other people that are in need, but now we've looked at the story you can see how bad it is and it doesn't show you how bad it is on the news but looking at the story, it tells you straight away it's bad because the world shouldn't be like this. It should be better and everybody should be at peace so they should. (Patrick)

> I loved reading the books... It made me think about my family and our journey from Pakistan. It made me write my own journey story so that other people can know more about what can happen to families around the world. (Munir)
>
> From a focus group with four boys to evaluate the project

*Journeys from Images to Words* aimed to develop and evaluate models of effective practice for the changing educational context in Glasgow, working in close partnership with teachers. The strategies emerging from the *Visual Journeys* project were extended to the reading of texts with both words and pictures and to texts with words only, within a whole class environment. These methods were designed to encourage students to use visual strategies to approach texts with a greater number of words and to read more critically. Using both fiction and non-fiction on the topics of migration and journeys, provided an additional stimulus for the sharing of experiences and intercultural understanding. Through a mixture of focus groups with the children, interviews with teachers and inviting parents/carers to comment on a visual display of the children's work at a scheduled event, it was hoped that responses would result in a more cohesive community both inside and outside the school. A final author event with author Morris

Gleitzman provided a real and current context for channelling some of the impulse for social action resulting from the engagements with the fiction texts.

### Research context and design

Two primary schools in Glasgow that had a large proportion of new arrivals in their catchment areas were involved in the enquiry. One of the schools (Southside Primary) is located in an area where there is a large but relatively well-established Asian community, as well as newly arrived families of Pakistani and Indian heritage, and more recently 'Roma' and Eastern European families. The second school (Northside Primary) is located in an area of socio-economic deprivation that has a large number of newly arrived families from different regions of Africa (Somalia, Republic of Congo), Pakistan and some children from families displaced from areas in the Middle East.[4]

The team consisted of practitioners and researchers working reflexively and collaboratively for approximately six months. The initial workshop played a key role in the formation of a close collaborative working partnership amongst all involved with university staff and teaching practitioners reviewing current policy on English as an additional language teaching and new arrivals. The second workshop served as quality assurance step to validate the data collected and research findings with the practitioners. During the project, the university team participated in several classroom tasks to support the teacher, including leading on some teaching and discussion sessions.

### The texts

*The Rabbits* (2000) by Marsden (illustrated by Tan) is an allegorical tale about colonization told from the perspective of native animals of a country, represented as bandicoots. This disquieting picture book offers a wealth of opportunities for discussion of immigration, colonialism, power and the destruction of the environment. Marsden and Tan play on the symbolic purchase that 'rabbits' hold for Australian colonial history. The subtlety of such references broadens the story's relevance, which is important since this type of cultural violence and dispossession is a common experience of indigenous and other marginalized people over the world.

*Gervelie's Journey A Refugee Diary* (2008), by Robinson and Young (illustrated by Allan) is one of a series of picture books about refugee children from different countries. They are based on real children's narratives and include photographs as well as mixed-media illustrations. Each spread is based on a particular stage of *Gervelie's Journey* from Brazzaville in the Congo to Norwich in the UK and describes the places and the people she meets as well as her fears and hopes. Her 'diary' describes her mixed feelings about Africa and also reflects her hopes for the future.

Gleitzman's *Boy Overboard* (2003) is a 'chapter' book and differs from the other books used in the project in that it contains no illustrations. Jamal and his sister, Bibi, are forced to flee Afghanistan with their parents. In their attempt to reach Australia they deal with smugglers, pirates and immigration authorities. The football theme and realistic characters make this a humorous, entertaining novel that does not shirk from the difficulties faced by those who experience forced resettlement.

All of these books highlight intercultural encounters between the characters, whether they be humans or animals, and the wide range of emotions that are involved in these encounters, from curiosity to fear or friendship. These encounters open a space for the emergence of generative themes about exchange, safety and threat and also about

Figure 1.   River of Reading.
An example of a visual 'River of Reading' which illustrates the different types and genres of reading one student did over a weekend and reflects the breadth and cultural significance of reading practices that include contemporary pop culture; a favourite comic strip and other personal interests such as fashion and favourite snacks.

supposedly 'neutral' encounters in 'no-man's lands' such as internment camps on Australian territory or UK Immigration Control at the airport. Some of the children in the project who had undergone the experience of forced migration told their own stories sparked by these fictional encounters, speaking of friends who had helped them escape or hide, of family left behind and of airport officials. While the books used in the enquiry provided some 'facts' and 'knowledge of the world', because they were literary texts, the readers acquired 'not so much additional *information* as additional *experience*. Literature provides a *living-through*, not simply *knowledge about*' (Rosenblatt, 1938, p. 38).

*Overview of visual strategies*

There were several innovative visual strategies used in the current project. The first one was 'River of Reading' (Bednall, Cranston, & Bearne, 2008) which was designed to create an inclusive classroom ethos through an investigation of the children's varied literacy practices. This is achieved by building a visual collage using the accessible metaphor of a river to represent children's reading outside of school, at home and in their local communities (see Figure 1).

The second strategy, 'Walk- and talk throughs', encouraged the children to 'enter the world of the book' by setting the context and allowing the space and time to look closely at the images and their relationship with the text, as well as co-constructing meaning, making personal links and testing hypotheses about the plot and characters.

In addition, we applied critical reading strategies and tasks that led to creative responses. 'Annotation of visuals' involved the comprehensive observation, analysis and interrogation of one particular image, thus allowing the children to undertake a deeper

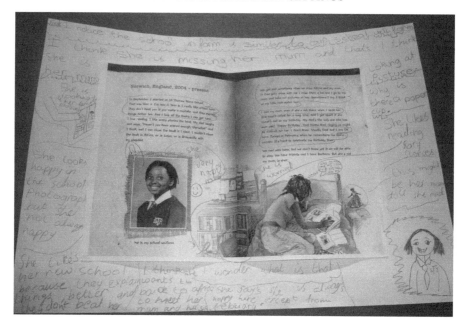

Figure 2. Annotated Image.
An example using a spread from *Gervelie's Journey* which demonstrates the 'interrogation' of the words in combination with real photographs and illustrations in order to construct meaning through the interplay between words and images. (Copyright © Annemarie Young and Anthony Robinson 2009. Reproduced with permission of Frances Lincoln Ltd.)

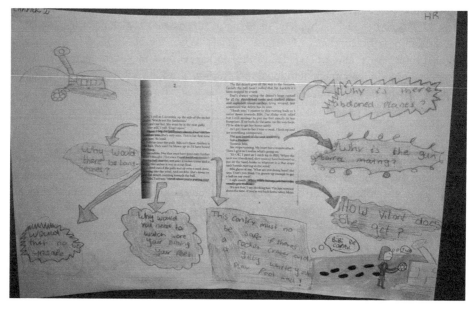

Figure 3. Annotated Text.
An example of an 'Annotated Text' for *Boy Overboard* which shows how this visual method can foster a deeper engagement with traditional text and enables students to visualise the words, think of questions and illustrate key parts of the text to enhance ideas, engagement and meaning-making.

Figure 4.   Photo-journal.
Part of a representative Photo-journal which included photographs of the student's family as well as places and items that were of great significance, with explanatory captions underneath.

'excavation' of meaning through the visual image and the addition of speech or thought bubbles, questions as to the plot or speculation about the unfolding story (see Figure 2).

Some of the written comments extracted from Figure 2 illustrate the depth of this student's empathy:

I notice the school uniform is like our school uniform.

She looks happy in the school photo but she is not always happy.

We also introduced the 'Annotations of text', which involved a close textual analysis that encourages a focus on figurative language and other structural aspects of the text. As in the case of the 'Annotation of visuals', it was made more accessible to the children by the addition of speech or thought bubbles, questions and illustrations (see Figure 3).

In keeping with the modes of representation used in *Gervelie's Journey*, we also introduced the construction of 'Photo-journals', another strategy that was inclusive as it provided the opportunity for the children to photograph elements of home life and organize them into collages in order to share events and stories in the classroom (see Figure 4).

In Figure 4, one of the students has written: 'This is our prayer mat. We always pray on this. This is very, very, very important to us'. The emphasis added by the repetition of the word 'very' in this example, gave classmates and teachers an insight into the significance of a cultural and religious artefact.

Finally, other flexible and reflective tasks, such as illustrating the text and drawing narrative graphic strips provided the opportunity for other creative multimodal responses to the texts (see Figure 5).

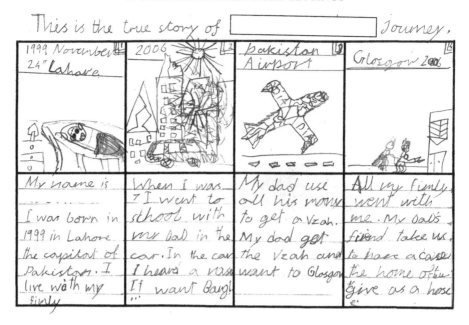

Figure 5.    Graphic journey narrative.
A representative example of one of graphic narratives in which some students offered to share their own real life journeys. This one shows the skilful combination of visuals and words which one student used to tell the story of their own personal journey from Lahore to Glasgow.

Between them, these strategies created a level playing field where students could construct meaning from the text and from their context by using their visual skills, home literacy practices and previous personal experiences. They therefore exemplify a pedagogy that is both critical and culturally responsive.

## Critical and culturally responsive pedagogy

I want to know more about why do they send people back to their country

I thought refugees were wrong, but I must have been wrong.

I learned that it's not all fighting in Afghanistan, there is love and family and school, football and friends

I want to campaign. Make a campaign for refugees and see how many people would join in.

Examples from P7 students' evaluations (from both schools) of the event that included talks by Morris Gleitzman (author of Boy Overboard), GRAMNet and the Scottish Refugee Council.

The above examples reflect the intercultural thinking that occurred in some students as a result of reading, reflecting and responding to difference and otherness. This can lead to a shift in thinking *(I must have been wrong)* and to the desire for transformative social action *(I want to campaign)*, confirming Short's (2009) argument:

Critically reading the word and the world involves students in thinking critically and questioning the way things are and the power relationships they observe in order to consider multiple cultures, perspectives, and ways of taking action. (p. 9)

Critical pedagogy builds on the knowledge and lived experiences of the learners to explore and understand and then to challenge the systems of oppression (which ignore, silence or dismiss) and move on to transformation through dialogue, exchange and creative practices (Giroux, 2011). Tavin (2003) asserts that critical pedagogy and 'visual culture' (which he understands as incorporating visual studies) are dialogical partners. From a pedagogical perspective, he argues, visual culture helps to analyse contemporary visual imagery and visual experiences, particularly popular culture which provides children and young people with many experiences in common which 'are invested with meaning and pleasure' (Tavin, 2003, p. 198).

Our approach built on the visual skills students brought from their experiences with familiar home and popular culture literacy practices. In this sense, their previous visual experiences performed the same role as past experiences of language and life through which, as Rosenblatt (1938) argues, a reader 'reorganizes' in order to 'attain new understanding' and these experiences 'serve as the raw materials out of which to shape the new experience symbolised on the page' (p. 26). At the same time, it also confronts them with new and challenging texts which encourage questioning of the familiar texts and the ideologies constructed within them. Each student is armed with a set of visual skills rooted in their lived experiences but, with a diverse student demographic in which each student has very different exposure to print and digital media as well as other modes of representation, these visual skills will vary. The exposure to particular forms of representation and the way language is represented in a text, as well as cultural approaches and/or social attitudes towards visual literacy, will be formative in each student's visual skill set. For instance, while reading the same text (*Gervelie's Journey*) some participating students could identify and engage with the emotional content being represented in an image and others could parse out small details that helped to develop plot complexities, while others focused on visual techniques used by the author to generate an aesthetic tone. Specificities in visual skills can cause confusion and 'translation problems' or can add richness (or a plurality of perspective) to a classroom setting. At times, the specificity can simply result in students taking different routes through the images to create congruent meaning with their classmates. All three routes are opportunities for intercultural learning By providing tools and a process to question and analyse images, teachers can help students understand 'how subjectivities are constructed through images and imaging' and how values and beliefs are interconnected with power (Tavin, 2003, p. 210), moving towards Freire's concept of 'critical consciousness' to arrive at a critique which increases agency in the face of social injustice and inequality, and empowers by valuing personal experience.

These experiences support the children when confronting 'specific and substantive historical, social and/or economic issues' such as migration and diversity, engaging 'in a democratic project that addresses real life issues regarding real life struggles' (Tavin, 2003, p. 200). Tavin concludes that this dialogic partnership has the power to challenge art education and we argue that equally it has the power to challenge literacy practices and turn them into transformative agency by including visual literacy as a tool for understanding and critique. However, because experience is at the heart of generative themes, the conventional teacher–student hierarchy is challenged, in this case, those who have lived through a migrant experience 'know' more than the teachers. Culturally responsive pedagogy like the one employed in this enquiry can help address this challenge (McAdam & Arizpe, 2011) by focusing on generative themes.

## Generative theme as an analytical tool

Generative themes are cultural or political topics that are of great concern or importance to participants which can be employed as educational tools to catalyse the meaningful engagement of often underrepresented or struggling populations. These themes reflect the lived experience of participants, which means that the participants have direct access to the material which may be tangible (i.e. a cultural artefact) or virtual and emotional (images and memories). The dispossessed individual learns that she is in possession of important experiential knowledge, and on this level, is empowered as a teacher as well as a student. At the heart of Freire's thinking about critical consciousness is literacy learning which begins with a series of codifications of these generative themes. Some of these codifications were in the form of visuals and were meant to prompt discussion, phrases and words which learners would then use to develop their decoding and meaning-making skills. However, Freire (1988) emphasizes that the process should not be carried out mechanically but through creatively 'awakening [the] consciousness' of the learner because for him literacy was a 'self-transformation producing a stance of intervention' (p. 404).

The codification of generative words into visual images stimulated people 'sub-merged' in a culture of silence to 'emerge as conscious makers of their own culture'. They participated in a 'culture circle', where new codifications were created and were aimed at transformative action (Goulet, 2002, p. viii; Souto-Manning, 2010). For Freire, the dialogue, or the expression of often-unheard voices, generated by these creative literacy practices constitutes transformative action in itself. In the same vein as Freire and in the celebration of the image as a transformative source, Boal (2006) suggests, 'Words are the work and the instruments of reason: we have to transcend them and look for forms of communication which are not just rational, but also sensory – aesthetic communications' (p. 15).

Themes can be generated from texts and/or images that resonate with the participants. In the case of this research, themes were generated from powerful images of migration and journeys. These generative themes became a catalyst for meaningful discussion because they were relevant to the readers. They were first represented in the form of 'codifications' (Freire, 1972) (either represented by a word or short phrase or a visual representation in a book) and then, through discussion, these initial codified themes were taken in and transformed by the readers/viewers into new 'codifications' – drawings, graphic strip, annotations, photographs, writing.

Returning to the example at the beginning of this article where the children are talking about communication between the rabbits and the bandicoots, we find the generative theme of 'the need for communication or understanding' during an encounter between different 'species' emerged. The words used by the children in this brief exchange between the species included: 'talk', 'write', 'read', 'language', 'sign (language)', 'gift', 'book' and 'draw', and the progression of the exchange reveals reflection about communication, not only verbal and textual, but also material and visual. The question of literacy ability and 'difficulty' also arises, with literacy being linked to the more human-like rabbits. During the group discussions and the annotations there was a focus on the consequences of this literacy – and numeracy – in the observation about the scientific instruments, maps and records being used by the rabbits (many of which lead to the destruction of the natural environment). An analysis of the annotations based on *The Rabbits* revealed the use of other words related to generative themes relevant to intercultural encounters: 'power', 'trust', 'symbols', 'flags' and 'culture'. Negative connotations were apparent in the use of words such as 'evil', 'poison', 'guns' and 'destruction'. Other themes such as displacement, colonization and oppression were evident in the discussions. At the end, one of the boys summed up the story, putting himself in the position of the indigenous species, 'There was peace until the rabbits came... they studied our land. I thought they became selfish about our land, so they took and conquered our country'.

The generative themes that emerged from the activities around *Gervelie's Journey*, in particular through the written annotations of the visuals, reflected both the awareness of the refugee's situation and empathetic and comparative observations around the children's own life experiences (Figure 6).

In Figure 6, this student has imagined what Gervelie's father must be feeling, 'He is feeling very sad because they have to leave their home'. The comment represents the strong sense of empathy and awareness of the family's plight evidenced by many of the students and also a sense of causality and an interpretation of the father's facial expression.

Some annotations also revealed a more in-depth understanding of the term 'refugee', pointing out, for example that these were, 'People who *have been made* into refugees' (our emphasis); in other words, it refers to the external circumstances that have forced them into this role, some of which appear in the images but were also discussed in the 'Walk- and talk throughs'. This understanding was extended to what it means for the people caught up in a situation of conflict, inferred from the visuals and evoked through the children's own words: 'People have died. People burned'; 'Fear, confusion'.

As in the responses to *The Rabbits*, certain words and images in *Gervelie's Journey* were infused by readers with intellectual and emotional meanings and they were interpreted as symbols which channelled their own thoughts and feelings (Rosenblatt, 1938). For example, some students commented on the name of the group of soldiers and

Figure 6.    Annotated Image.
Part of an Annotated Image from *Gervelie's Journey* (Copyright © Annemarie Young and Anthony Robinson 2009. Reproduced by permission of Frances Lincoln Ltd.)

one student made this strong symbolic link as he wrote: 'Cobra militia, [a] snake is a negative thing'. Other comments reflected the emotive, 'lived-through' experience of the reader, such as 'I would not like to be there.' Finally, the annotations for an image near the end of *Gervelie's Journey* demonstrate an insight into gains and losses of reaching a secure place, as well as the mixed feelings it implies, through the use of words like 'safe', 'happy', 'friends' and 'learning', set alongside others such as 'sad', 'missing' and 'memories'.

The generative themes in the three texts resulted in students communicating and sharing some of their lived experiences. The refugee children who drew and wrote about their journeys also included many of these words: 'terrible', 'sad', 'happy' and 'together'. Through the dialogue, participants were able to gain a greater awareness and understanding of what migration experiences might mean for others. The strategies described here allowed them to do this, inviting the dual response of involvement and detachment, going beyond the experience and moving from more literal to more inferential meanings.

While picture books are an ideal medium to represent particular generative themes, it is not the case that there is a movement from the coded image 'towards' the word, or that words reflect more refined, higher order thinking. Freire (1972) was careful to refute the popular notion that visual literacy was a 'primitive', or lesser form of education and communication. We interpret the movement towards the word as simply a way of engaging in a manner that extends beyond what is present on the page. The images are useful because they act as cues and also have intrinsic value in themselves. This approach also fits within school expectations which have to do with words and traditional language development while opening a space for consideration of visual elements.

As the project progressed, there was a gradual emergence of home languages and cultures in the discussions and creative responses as well as a realization that these were valued in the classroom context. This helped build bridges between the school and the home community literacies together with the display of student's work and their presentations to families, carers and the school community. It was a source of pride to the participating children and situated migration and race relations in a central role. Teachers noted that newly arrived students began to participate more fully in the ongoing work of the class as they felt they had valuable contributions to make to the community of learning using texts they found appealing and relevant and using strategies designed to take better account of their prior knowledge and experience. New arrival students were excited and engaged by the possibilities of storying their own journeys after encountering varied model texts, and unique stories emerged together with stronger voices.

## Conclusion

While current scholarship on literacy widely recognizes the influence of changes in visual culture on reading practice, this article has suggested that it is also essential to turn a focus towards the influence of migration on literacy practices. We have considered how visual methods can be employed to address some of the impact of the experience of migration for education, and at the heart of our image-based approach is the use of picture books and/or visual responses to text. We have suggested that the visual content of a book can itself be a generative theme, since the medium reflects experiences of students from varied backgrounds and provides many 'points of entry'. In addition to generating empowering dialogue with the students, we have used activities that offer students creative avenues for representation. This process of creating aesthetic works is an emancipatory and self-actualizing activity, which allows an exploration of new realities or possibilities (Boal, 2006). While it seems inevitable that new arrivals will be positioned on the 'outside' of their transplant cultures, placing a focus on the experience of displacement in the classroom means that these students are actually positioned as bearers of valued knowledge and experience, which echoes Freire's (1972) vision for a pedagogy of the oppressed.

As we apply and expand these methods, there are many ethical considerations and practical issues we continue to ruminate upon. For instance, many new arrivals involved in these projects have undergone serious trauma, or may need to keep their migrant experiences very private for their protection. What is intended to be an inclusive project may run the risk of further alienating these particular students who feel unable to engage, which emphasizes the need to find new ways of developing tailored, sensitive pedagogical approaches. Similarly, it is important to find new ways to explore the varied forms of displacement that do not arise simply from migration, but perhaps also unstable living arrangements experienced by many host children. Making the generative themes non-threatening and accessible to a range of students' experiences is a challenge we continue to navigate. While generating discussion of migration in the classroom is vital, a conscious effort must also be made to avoid treating new arrivals as ambassadors of a coherent, essentialized culture. This runs the risk of cementing their alterity by valuing migrants for their ability to represent difference, instead of valuing them for their more realistic, hybrid identities.

Vertovec (2011) notes that there is a common-place understanding 'which regards national cultures, ethnic cultures, and religious cultures as finished objects […] In this view, culture, whether national, ethnic, or religious, is something one has and is a member of' and this is contrasted with 'making culture' which is described as 'a dynamic, antiessentialist conception or processual view of culture that acknowledges how values and practices are continuously reshaped by renewing activity, dialectically from above and below' (p. 250). In Boal's (2006) estimation, 'making culture' is not just a symbolic or figurative concept, but one that involves representing ourselves aesthetically, or making images, which has been a central component of our image-based approach. Using critical pedagogical approaches, we have found that reading texts and images on themes of migration can generate the creative engagement of students, who appropriate and create texts and images and in doing so, participate in a meaningful process of making culture through intercultural literacy.

## Notes

1. *Journeys from Images to Words*: Examining the efficacy of visual meaning-making strategies in the development of inclusive communities of critical readers was funded by the Esmée Fairbairn Foundation, 2011–2012 and based at the School of Education, University of Glasgow. http://journeys-fromimagestowords.com/
2. *Visual Journeys*: Exploring children's visual literacy through intercultural responses to wordless picture books was funded in the UK by the UK Literacy Association 2009–2010. See Arizpe et al. (2013).
3. According to United Nations, approximately 191 million individuals (3.0% of the world population) were living outside of their native countries as of 2005 (United Nations 2008). http://esa.un.org/migration.index.asp?panel=1
4. Ethical approval was obtained from the Local Authority and the School of Education (University of Glasgow) to conduct the present study. We have used pseudonyms to protect the anonymity of participants. All the examples that appear in this article are taken from students' work in both schools, which was found to have more commonalities than differences. We have not specifically attributed the children's quotes because these exemplify the emerging themes presented by the students in keeping with the use of the Freirian culture circles employed in the methodology.

## References

### *Primary sources*

Gleitzman, M. (2003). *Boy overboard*. London: Puffin.

Marsden, J. (S. Tan ilus). (2000). *The rabbits*. Sydney: Lothian.

Robinson, A., & Young, A. (J. Allan ilus). (2008). *Gervelie's journey. Diary of a refugee girl*. London: Frances Lincoln.

### *Secondary sources*

Anstey, M. (2002). "It's not all black and white": Postmodern picture books and new literacies. *Journal of Adolescent and Adult Literacy, 45*, 444–458. doi:10.1598/JAAL.45.6.1

Arizpe, E. (2009). Sharing visual experiences of a new culture: Immigrant children in Scotland respond to picturebooks and other visual texts. In J. Evans (Ed.), *Talking beyond the page: Reading and responding to picture books* (pp. 134–151). London: Routledge.

Arizpe, E., Colomer, T., & Martínez-Roldán, C. (2014). *Visual journeys through wordless narratives: An international inquiry with immigrant children and the arrival*. London: Bloomsbury Academic.

Arizpe, E., Farrell, M., & McAdam, J. (2013). Opening the classroom door to children's literature: A review of research. In K. Hall, T. Cremin, B. Comber, & L. Moll (Eds.), *International handbook of research on children's literacy, learning and culture* (pp. 241–257). London: Wiley-Blackwell.

Arizpe, E., & Styles, M. (2003). *Children reading pictures*. London: Routledge.

Banks, J. A. (2001). Citizenship education and diversity: Implications for teacher education. *Journal of Teacher Education, 52*(1), 5–16. doi:10.1177/0022487101052001002

Banks, J. A., & Banks, C. A. M. (Eds.). (2001). *Handbook of research on multicultural education*. Francisco: Jossey-Bass.

Bearne, E. (2004). Multimodal texts: What they are and how children use them. In J. Evans (Ed.), *Literacy moves on* (pp. 16–30). Portsmouth: Heinemann.

Bednall, J., & Cranston, L., Bearne, E. (2008). 'The most wonderful adventure … going beyond the literal'. *English Four to Eleven, 32*, 19–26.

Boal, A. (2006). *Aesthetics of the oppressed*. New York, NY: Routledge.

Botelho, M. J., & Rudman, M. K. (2009). *Critical multicultural analysis of children's literature: Mirrors, windows, and doors*. New York, NY: Routledge.

Brice-Heath, S., & Wolf, S. (2004). *Visual learning in the community school*. Kent: Creative Partnerships.

Crouch, C. (2008). Afterword. In J. Elkins (Ed.), *Visual literacy*. London: Routledge.

Cullingford, C. (1998). *Children's literature and its effects: The formative years*. London: Cassell.

Ee Loh, C. (2009). Reading the world: Reconceptualizing reading multicultural literature in the English language arts classroom in a global world. *Changing English: Studies in Culture and Education, 16*, 287–299. doi:10.1080/13586840903194755

Fransecky, R. (1969). 'Visual literacy and teaching the disadvantaged'. *Audiovisual Instruction, 28–31*, 117–118.

Freire, P. (1972). *Pedagogy of the oppressed*. Harmondsworth: Penguin.

Freire, P. (1988). The adult literacy process as cultural action for freedom and education and conscientizacao. In E. R. Kintgen, B. M. Kroll, & M. Rose (Eds.), *Perspectives on literacy* (pp. 398–409). Carbondale: Southern Illinois University Press.

Freire, P. (2008). *Education for critical consciousness*. London: Continuum.

Giroux, H. (2011). *On critical pedagogy*. London: Continuum.

Gonçalves, M. A. (2012). *Literary texts and intercultural learning*. Bern: Peter Lang.

Gopalakrishnan, A. (2011). *Multicultural children's literature: A critical issues approach*. London: Sage.

Gopalakrishnan, A., & Ulanoff, S. (2003). *Making connections to cultural identity: Using multicultural children's literature and storytelling to explore personal narrative*. Paper presented at the meeting of Hawaii International Conference on Education, Honolulu, September.

Gough, N. (1998). Reflections and diffractions: Functions of fiction in curriculum inquiry in curriculum. In W. Pinar (Ed.), *Curriculum: Toward new identities*. New York, NY: Garland.

Goulet, D. (2002). Introduction. In P. Freire, *Education for critical consciousness* (pp. vii–xiv). New York: Continuum.

HMIe. (2009). *'Count us in. A sense of belonging'. 'Meeting the needs of children and young people newly arrived in Scotland'*. Livingstone: Author.

Iser, W. (1978). *The act of reading: A theory of aesthetic response*. London: Routledge and Kegan Paul.

Kenner, C., Mahara, R., & Gregory, E. (2010). Teacher partnerships between mainstream and complementary schools: From parallel worlds to connected curricula. *NALDIC Quarterly, 7*(2): 46–48.

Kiefer, B. (1995). *The potential of picturebooks: From visual literacy to aesthetic understanding*. Englewood Cliffs, NJ: Merrill.

Kornfeld, J., & Prothro, L. (2005). Envisioning possibility: Schooling and student agency in children's and young adult literature. *Children's Literature and Education, 36*, 217–239. doi:10.1007/s10583-005-5971-2

McAdam, J., & Arizpe, E. (2011). Journeys into culturally responsive teaching. *Journal of Teacher Education and Teachers' Work, 2*(1), 18–27.

McGonigal, J., & Arizpe, E. (2007). *Learning to read a new culture: How immigrant and asylum-seeking children experience Scottish identity through classroom books*. Project Report. Edinburgh: Scottish Government.

Pantaleo, S. (2008). *Exploring student's response to contemporary picturebooks*. Toronto: University of Toronto Press.

Perkins, D. (1994). *The intelligent eye: Learning to think by looking at art*. Los Angeles, CA: The J. Paul Getty Trust.

Phipps, A. (2013). Intercultural ethics: Questions of methods in language and intercultural communication. *Language and Intercultural Communication, 13*(1), 10–26. doi:10.1080/1470 8477.2012.748787

Reedy, D., & UKLA. (2010). Agenda for action: UKLA's vision for future literacy education. Available from: http://www.ukla.org/download.php?file=/.../UKLA_Agenda_for_Action.pdf.

Rosenblatt, L. M. (1938). *Literature as exploration*. London: Routledge and Kegan Paul.

Rosenblatt, L. M. (1978). *The reader, the text, the poem: The transactional theory of the literary work*. Carbondale, IL: Southern Illinois University Press.

Scottish Executive. (2004). *A curriculum for excellence*. Edinburgh: The Curriculum Review Group. Available from: http://www.scotland.gov.uk/Resource/Doc/26800/0023690.pdf.

Scottish Government. (2009). *Statistical bulletin: Pupils in Scotland, 2008*. Edinburgh.

Scottish Government. (n.d.). *Curriculum for excellence: Literacy across learning: Principles and practice*. Edinburgh. http://www.educationscotland.gov.uk/images/literacy_across_learning_-principles_practice_tcm4-540108.pdf

Short, K. G. (2009). Critically reading the word and the world. *Bookbird*, (2), 1–10. doi:10.1353/bkb.0.0160

Sipe, L. (2008). *Storytime: Young children's literary understanding in the classroom*. New York, NY: Teachers College Press.

Sleeter, C. E., & Grant, C. A. (2002). *Making choices for multicultural education: Five approaches to race, class and gender*. New York: John Wiley & Sons.

Souto-Manning, M. (2010). *Freire, teaching, and learning: Culture circles across contexts*. New York, NY: Peter Lang.

Suárez-Orozco, C., & Suárez-Orozco, M. (2001). *Children of immigration*. Cambridge, MA: Harvard University Press.

Tavin, K. M. (2003). Wrestling with angels, searching for ghosts: Toward a critical pedagogy of visual culture. *Studies in Art Education, 44*, 197–213.

Vertovec, S. (2011). The cultural politics of nation and migration. *Annual Review of Anthropology, 40*, 241–256. doi:10.1146/annurev-anthro-081309-145837

Young, L., & Barrett, H. (2001). Adapting visual methods: Action research with Kampala street children. *The Royal Geographical Society, 33*, 141–152.

# The social and symbolic aspects of languages in the narratives of young (prospective) migrants

Giovanna Fassetta

*School of Education, University of Strathclyde, Lord Hope Building, Glasgow, UK*

When talking about language in the context of research regarding children and migration, the focus tends to be on proficiency in the receiving country's language as an indicator of successful integration and/or for its role in educational achievement. This article explores the social and symbolic aspects of language in the narratives of young Ghanaian migrants to Italy at several levels: that of global hierarchies of power as expressed through the prestige offered by different languages; that of the expectations for linguistic assimilation and linguistic maintenance which centre around migrant children; and that of young people's challenging of adult rules through the instrumental use of different languages.

Parlare di lingua nel contesto della ricerca su ragazzi e immigrazione significa generalmente focalizzare la discussion sulla padronanza della lingua del paese ricevente, spesso come indice di integrazione e/o in relazione al successo scolastico. Questo articolo si propone di esplorare gli aspetti sociali e simbolici della lingua nelle narrative di giovani migrant Ghanesi in Italia a vari livelli: quello delle gerarchie globali di potere espresse attraverso il prestigio offerto dalle varie lingue; quello delle aspettative di assimilazione linguistica e di mantenimento della lingua di cui i giovani migrant sono al centroe quello dell'uso strumentale delle diverse lingue da parte dei ragazzi, al fine di sfidare alcune delle regole imposte dagli adulti.

## Introduction

Eleven-year-old Jackson thought he knew what the problem was: 'You don't understand because you are white', he told me. His friend Marty, however, had a different explanation: 'No. White has nothing to do with it' he replied, '[The problem is that] she doesn't understand our language'. For a brief moment I was forgotten, the two boys pondering over this insight. 'True' agreed Jackson, thus settling the issue: the problem was that I did not understand *their* language.

For the past hour, I had been conversing with the group of young people in Italian, my mother tongue, and the language that Marty and Jackson (born in Italy of Ghanaian parents) had been speaking as far back as they could remember. During the focus group conversation (of which Marty and Jackson were part), the young participants had raised the issue of Ghanaian witchcraft beliefs, one that would later recur in other, similar focus groups with Italian-born children. This was a topic that appeared to alarm and fascinate the young people in equal proportions, and the group had been discussing it at length, wavering between scepticism and awe. I had done all I could to maintain a non-judgemental attitude towards this unexpected subject, while the young people patiently tried to explain to me the principles of witchcraft and of its geographically bounded nature. I had been keen to understand, careful not to show surprise and not to appear disapproving or unconvinced. However, Jackson and Marty clearly knew – or at least suspected – that on a topic such as this we were not speaking 'the same language', and that there was a possibility that we may not (could not) understand each other, even though we recognised each other's words.

Bourdieu (1991) observes that all social relations are symbolic interactions, relations of communication that imply cognition and recognition. However, he adds, '[...] one must not forget that the relations of communication *par excellence* – linguistic exchanges – are also relations of symbolic power in which the power relations between speakers or their respective groups are actualized' (Bourdieu, 1991, p. 37). The young participants recognised the asymmetry in our exchange: while we were all speaking Italian, our relative positions (the white, adult, middle class woman and the black children of unskilled labour migrants), and underlying frames of reference, meant that although the sounds of the words were shared, our understanding of them might not be. It also meant a somewhat blurred, but nevertheless perceived, realisation of the scorn and disapproval with which the receiving society, incarnated in my person, regarded witchcraft beliefs and those holding them.

Thinking back on this short exchange, I cannot help wondering how often, in their daily lives, migrant children and the children of migrants confront the feeling of speaking a language that the majority population can comprehend but not (truly) understand. Recognising each other's words, as the young participants pointed out, does not necessarily mean sharing meanings and frames of references. However, as I shall argue later, the opposite is also true: individuals do not need to speak the same language in order to communicate acceptance, empathy and respect.

The young people in the opening vignette were participants in a study that aimed to investigate how children[1] make sense of migration. The project looked specifically at the Ghana–Italy migration nexus, focusing on the following: the imaginings and expectations of Italy (and of life in Italy) held by children left in Ghana by unskilled labour migrants; the imaginings and expectations of Ghana held by children born in Italy of Ghanaian parents and the experience of moving between the two countries as recounted by young people who had eventually bridged the gap between imagined and lived lives.

I start this article by outlining the theoretical framework that supports the subsequent discussion, concentrating in particular on the sociology of childhood and the importance of adding children's perspectives to the conversation on migration; I also briefly discuss the dynamics of intercultural communication in a context of migration, and the colonial echoes that shape the perceived status of different languages by young Ghanaians. I then outline in further detail the study from which this article draws, in order to contextualise the findings. The core of the article consists of the exploration of the emotional, symbolic and pragmatic aspects of language and communication through the children's own understanding: the emblematic (perceived) value of different languages in expressing global hierarchies of countries; the social role and relevance of these languages before, during and after migration; and, finally, the way in which young migrants navigate the plurality of languages that migration entails.

## Childhood in a context of migration

As Mayall (2000) observes, 'children are those whom adults have defined as non-adults' (p. 245), and what children are understood to need and what they are expected to be able to do, as well as the policies and regulations of which they are the objects, are usually decided for them by adults. The arbitrary line legally separating adults from non-adults means that young people live their lives within discrete – and historically determined – social, economic and spatial spheres. The boundaries created by adults are, however, not passively accepted: they are challenged, resisted and thus at least partly shaped by the young people themselves (Corsaro, 2005; Holloway & Valentine, 2000; James & James, 2004; James & Prout, 1990).

Research on migration has for a long time centred on the choices of adults as lead agents, motivated (and justified) by economic interests. The role and influence of their dependants have often been downplayed, in particular when these are minors with no direct economic influence (Dobson, 2009). However, family reunion visas play an increasingly important role in keeping immigration to OECD countries[2] stable, despite the recent financial crisis (Castles & Miller, 2010). As a consequence, a growing number of young migrants need to contend with – and adjust to – choices about which they may not have been consulted, towards which they may have had little or no input, but which impact on them in direct, powerful and inevitable ways.

Leaving to settle in a different country is, in many cases, a decision taken by adults *for* the children, to improve their future prospects, but one seldom taken *with* them (Faulstich Orellana, 2009). Young people may try to influence their parents' choice by actively voicing their disagreement or by putting in place challenging patterns of behaviour (Dreby, 2010). However, once the decision to leave is taken, they have no other option but to follow their parents. Some of them will move with their family, but significant numbers are left in the country of origin, in the care of kin, while their father and/or mother settle abroad and start the (often unexpectedly lengthy) procedures for a family reunion visa.

Once migration is under way, young people will inevitably endeavour to make sense of, and adapt to, changed circumstances that may bring with them unforeseen material and emotional costs (Suàrez-Orozco & Suàrez-Orozco, 2001). Moreover, children often act as a link between members of the transnational (extended) family (Dreby, 2006; Levitt, 2001), being the shared focus of affection, hopes and concerns for adults who live in different countries. Many young people actively engage in the crucial preservation of these transnational ties, which constitute vital social capital for migrant families (Leonard, 2005), participating in the various forms of long-distance communication that are essential in order to maintain familial relations (Faulstich Orellana, Thorne, Chee, & Lam, 2001; Yeoh & Lam, 2006). For some children, as I discuss later, this can mean engaging with the features of a language (that of their parents' sending country, or of the country they left when still quite young) whose 'terrain' is known but not entirely familiar (anymore), and one over which they may, at times, trip and stumble.

## Moving languages

Language plays a central role in the maintenance of transnational relations (Rumbaut, 2002), and migrant children can find themselves pulled between the contrasting demands for linguistic assimilation made by the receiving country and those for linguistic preservation made by the ethnic community and the extended family (Phinney, Romero, Nava, & Huang, 2001). As they enter the education system in the receiving country, young migrants usually learn the new language and social norms more quickly than adults (Faulstich Orellana, 2009). For some families this may result in what Portes and Rumbaut (2001) term 'dissonant acculturation', with children and parents growing increasingly estranged from each other, and with the family language, customs and traditions becoming a source of embarrassment and annoyance for the younger generation.

Linguistic assimilation is generally expected (often vocally demanded) of migrants. Several destination countries have made proficiency in the official language(s) a requirement of visa regulations (Hogan-Brun, Mar-Molinero, & Stevenson, 2009; Piller, 2001). A degree of fluency in the new language is undeniably important for communication and self-sufficiency. However, the prominence that language proficiency is progressively acquiring to control the entry of migrants[3] also assumes a symbolic function (Portes & Rumbaut, 2001), and competence in the receiving country's language(s) is quickly becoming the arena within which power dynamics between majority and minority groups are played out (Harison, 2009; Piller, 2012). As Bourdieu (1991) argues, while the faculty to speak is a biological trait common to all human beings, what is rare is '[…] the competence necessary in order to speak the *legitimate* language which, depending on social inheritance, re-translates social distinctions into the specifically symbolic logic of differential deviations […]' (Bourdieu, 1991, p. 55, emphasis added). The demand for linguistic conformity plays a far greater part than the immediately practical one. It asserts the power of the dominant group to define as legitimate the language its members speak, and to demand that minority groups make appropriate efforts to demonstrate acceptance of their linguistic demands, or risk marginalisation and exclusion (Sayad, 2004).

The majority's call for linguistic assimilation has, in more recent years, gone hand in hand with official narratives and policies that emphasise the benefits of linguistic and cultural diversity (Piller, 2012). However, integration and inclusion are still predicated upon a monolingual and monocultural vision of society (Philippou & Theodorou, 2014), and celebrations of diversity in educational settings are still often limited to tokenistic events in which 'exotic' foods are shared, and posters with greetings in a range of languages and scripts are displayed (Kymlicka, 2003).

Nation-states, languages and cultural values (usually conflated and often simplistically portrayed as uniform, unchangeable and 'natural') remain at the centre of demands for unilateral adaptation that are commonly made of young migrants (Piller, 2001). Migrant children and the children of migrants are under greater pressure than adults to comply with the demands for conformity the receiving society makes of them. As Sayad poignantly notes, in order to avoid being permanently relegated to the position of outsiders, children will strive:

> […] to assimilate thanks to a subtle game of bluff that is designed to conceal the stigma, or at least to mask its more obvious external signs. They therefor promote a self-image that is as close as possible to a legitimate identity: the dominant identity. (Sayad, 2004, p. 256)

Performing the legitimate identity means primarily being able to speak the legitimate language, one of its most apparent external signs. The fact that the standardised form is spoken by a minority of even the indigenous population does not detract from the rhetoric that links migrants' successful integration to linguistic proficiency in the receiving country's standard language (Phinney et al., 2001).

**Overview of the study**

As briefly illustrated in the Introduction, this article is based on a study that looks at the specificities of young people's imaginings, expectations and experiences in relation to migration. In line with the tenets of the sociology of childhood, this qualitative study brings children's points of view into the debate on migration. In order to achieve this, it explores the imaginings of Italy (the country, the people and everyday life) shared by Ghanaian children left behind by migrant parents. It further investigates migrant children's own assessment of their previously held expectations in the light of the experience of moving. Finally, it looks at the imaginings of Ghana held by children born in Italy of Ghanaian parents.

The participants in the study were a total of 41 children (30 girls and 11 boys) between the ages of 10 and 15 years, with direct or indirect experience of migration from Ghana to Italy. The total sample consisted of three groups of similar size: a group of 15 children who had recently left Ghana to join one or both parents in Italy; a group of 13 children who were born in Italy of Ghanaian parents and a group of 13 children who were left in the country of origin by migrant parents.

Fieldwork was multi-sited. I gained access to the participants, both in Italy and in Ghana, through the schools they attended, collecting the data using a multiple-technique approach, chosen primarily as a means of maximising children's active participation (Catts, Allan, & Smyth, 2007; Kesby, 2007; Punch, 2002). I first met the young people in focus groups to discuss shared expectations and imaginings in relation to the country they only had indirect experience of, as well as the reflections of the participants who had recently made the transition from imagined to lived. At the end of each focus group, the participants were offered a disposable camera, and asked to photograph anything they would miss, or be keen to leave behind, were they to move. The group of children who had recently migrated was asked to take pictures of anything that had surprised them, positively or negatively, upon arrival in Italy. I then met again each young participant individually, to discuss the photographs taken and to collect more subjective narratives. The conversations were carried out in Italian and/or English, depending on the language in which the children were more proficient and on their preference. The exchanges were audiotaped and then transcribed, the Italian parts translated into English concurrently. The transcripts were analysed through a progressive process of coding and categorising, the categories eventually grouped into major analytical themes (Rubin & Rubin, 2005).

While the research did not focus primarily on the issues connected to language differences and language learning, the young participants made constant references to languages and to their social relevance. In the following sections, I discuss the expectations held by the children left behind in Ghana; I then illustrate the difficulties experienced by the children who had recently migrated from Ghana to Italy to join their parents; finally, I discuss the way in which the children born in Italy of Ghanaian parents articulated their understanding of the role of different languages.

**Language and expectations**

A former British colony, Ghana was the first African country to gain independence in 1957, and the present Ghanaian school system is rooted in colonial history, as missionaries set up the first formal educational institutions in what was formerly the Gold Coast (Graham, 1971). The aim of these schools was to educate the children of local chiefs into the religion, language and cultural norms and values of the colonisers, in order to produce a pool of mediators between newly introduced and existing social structures, who would simultaneously act as agents of 'civilisation' (Coe, 2002). English remains Ghana's official language and the medium of instruction in schools[4] and, while the local variation of English appears to be gaining status[5], the country's vernacular languages[6] are generally confined to the realm of private, day-to-day exchanges.

The young participants I interviewed in Ghana all attended state-run boarding schools. As children of labour migrants whose earnings enjoy highly favourable exchange rates, the young people could be educated and looked after in institutions that are at the upper end of the Ghanaian publicly funded education system. These are primary and secondary 'residential schools'[7] that were set up under British rule and that still hold a degree of prestige (albeit very much diminished in recent years) amongst the Ghanaian population, thus justifying parental sacrifices.

The 13 participants I visited during my stay in Ghana all spoke English as well as one of the local languages; they all had one or both parents in Italy and were, without exception, expecting to join them in the near future. Some young participants talked about younger siblings, born in Italy, whom they had never met; all of them had regular contact with their migrant parent(s) and sibling(s), generally through phone conversations, and mothers and/or fathers appeared to make fairly regular visits, bringing presents, pictures and stories with them.

Visits also brought with them the sounds of the new language, as was the case for 13-year-old Wendibel:

**Researcher:** and… this younger brother… does he live with you?

**Wendibel:** no. He came from Italy

**Researcher:** were your brothers born there?

**Wendibel:** yes they were both born there

**Researcher:** so they must speak Italian well… Have you heard them speaking Italian?

**Wendibel:** yes, they speak Italian to each other

**Researcher:** can they speak Twi?

**Wendibel:** no, they don't understand Twi

**Researcher:** so if you wanted to talk to them, how would you speak?

**Wendibel:** English

[Wendibel, female, age 13 – School X, Ghana]

The fact that her little brothers could not speak Twi meant that Wendibel had to communicate with them through the public language of school and education rather than the private language of home and family. English was Wendibel's second language, and the fact that her brothers conversed in Italian suggests that English was an additional language for them too. While a direct link between first language and intimacy is not generalizable, speakers maintain significant emotional ties to their first language (Pavlenko, 2004), a language that, nevertheless, Wendibel was unable to use to interact with her brothers. It also shows how her parents had opted not to speak the vernacular to her Italian-born offspring, strategically choosing instead to speak English at home while they were learning Italian at school, something which, as I shall discuss further below, appears to be a relatively common practice amongst Ghanaian families in Italy.

Invariably, when asked, the children in Ghana stressed their wish to go to Italy, and their excitement at the prospect. The motives for looking forward to moving to Italy, however, appeared to have less to do with being reunited with their parents and siblings and more to do with their desire for adventure, travel, getting to know new places, getting to explore a new culture and, generally, improving both personally and socially. This was not surprising, as separation was something the young people were quite used to (indeed, a few could not remember otherwise) and the median age was 14, an age when most young people start to consider their futures as independent beings, as was evident in some of the questions about Italy that were asked by a few of the older participants. Having given them a chance to exploit my knowledge of the country in order to satisfy any curiosity they may have harboured, several questions focused on jobs and the costs of further education.

Almost all participants told me how much they were looking forward to going to school in Italy, even though they seemed to realise that language could be a potentially powerful barrier. Italian schools were imagined as 'better', in rather broad terms: they would be better decorated; they would have better grounds. Many remarked on the fact that there would be lots of young people, potential friends they were eager to meet. However, their concern about not being able to communicate was quite apparent in our conversations, as the following extract exemplifies:

> **Researcher:** what do you think you would find more difficult? What do you think may be a bit hard for you there?
>
> **Chantal:** the language. Only the language
>
> [Chantal, female, age 11 – School Y, Ghana]

However, the young people also expressed curiosity for the new language, and even indicated learning Italian as one of the reasons why they were looking forward to moving to Italy.

Different languages have different degrees of prestige in the global arena and are symbolic of hierarchies of power that different countries hold. English (British or American) is a language which holds great prestige internationally (Baugh & Cable, 2002; Piller, 2011) and which reflects both the historical weight of British colonialism and the present-day power of US cultural dominance. Some of the children in Ghana were aware of these differences or, at least, aware that English and Italian held different status in the eyes of their parents.

Ten-year-old Sheila is a case in point. Born in Italy, she had started school there, but had been sent to boarding school in Ghana at the age of six, while her parents had remained in the destination country:

> **Sheila:** when I came here it was 2005
>
> **Researcher:** so you were... you said, six?
>
> **Sheila:** yes
>
> **Researcher:** right. Did you know you would be staying here?

**Sheila:** yes

**Researcher:** your mother had explained to you that you would be staying here?

**Sheila:** yes. She was speaking Twi to me so that when I came here it would be easy for me to understand the language

**Researcher:** ok. And so you can speak Twi as well?

**Sheila:** yes

**Researcher:** was it difficult at the beginning? Do you remember?

**Sheila:** yes, the English.

[Sheila, female, age 10. School Y, Ghana]

It is interesting to notice the instrumental teaching of the Ghanaian language that Sheila recounts: her mother had elected to speak only Twi to her daughter so that she could, one day, take her to Ghana to be educated in the more prestigious English. Sending children (back) to Ghana so they can be taught in English is not unusual for Ghanaian migrants. This allows them to ensure their children have linguistic capital (Yosso, 2005) that may grant them access to better jobs or that will ensure their offspring have better chances for moving to an English-speaking country, a wish that was apparent, as I shall discuss, for many of the Ghanaian children in Italy.

## Italian, from imagined to real language

While the children left in Ghana showed awareness of the fundamental role that language would have in the new social environment when they finally moved to Italy, for the children born in Italy of Ghanaian parents and children who had recently migrated, Italian played an essential and 'lived' role as the language of everyday social exchanges and, crucially, the one they needed to master in order gain access to their peer group (Penn & Lambert, 2009; Zuppiroli, 2008). In the schools they attended, most children received (or had received) some linguistic support, as the Italian education system makes provision for a professional figure (the 'cultural and linguistic mediator') to aid young people's adaptation process, and it also allocates some time for the learning of Italian. However, the support to which immigrant children in Italian schools are entitled is generally sparse, short term and lacking sufficient financial backing (Balboni, 2008; European Commission, 2013). As a consequence, the social and linguistic inclusion of immigrant children is often left to the organisational skills of individual institutions and to the chance availability of the necessary human resources (e.g. English-speaking teachers), and while some of the young participants appeared to have enjoyed systematic support, for most newly arrived children help was limited and piecemeal.

The Ghanaian children who had recently migrated to Italy were all very keen to discuss the issue of language and, more generally, to talk about the school environment. The first few days in the new school were recollected by the vast majority of the young participants as emotionally very demanding. Not being able to communicate in Italian, not understanding what was happening and what they were expected to do were occasions of anxiety and frustration that the migrant children still remembered vividly:

**Researcher:** but do you remember the first days?

**Philly:** [laughs] yes, yes

**Researcher:** how was it?

**Philly:** when the… the… teacher was saying something… it annoyed me, 'I don't understand anything!' when [the other children] got up, I said… ah… the teacher said 'Get up!' and I was…when I saw that others…

**Researcher:** were getting up

**Philly:** yes, I got up too [laughs]

[Philly, female, age 12. Born in Ghana. School C, Italy]

As Piller (2011) argues, being rendered 'speechless' by being placed in a situation in which they cannot communicate is an infringement of an individual's human rights that too often fails to be adequately acknowledged. Philly reported being upset enough by the experience of isolation that she had endured not to want to go to school anymore. At the time of our interview, over two years after her arrival, Philly's use of Italian in a social situation still came across as rather uncertain. She was repeating a class, not having been deemed able to move on with the rest of her original group because of her language difficulties, something that had not just academic repercussions, but social and emotional ones too. As a consequence of being made to repeat a class she had lost touch with a good friend, something that still appeared to pain her considerably.

Rebecca, who had been in Italy only for two weeks at the time of our interview, described her on-going struggle with language in school, one that was clearly a subject of conversation between her and her mother:

**Rebecca A.:** in my class… I don't understand the language, so everyday they insult me, but I don't care…

**Researcher:** very good

**Rebecca A.:** I know that God…

**Researcher:** you need to be strong

**Rebecca A.:** yes! So they laugh at me… so I don't care. My mother says that 'When God permits I will understand the language'

[Rebecca, female, age 14. Born in Ghana. School B, Italy]

The girl's conviction that she was being regularly insulted may have been due more to perception than an accurate description of her classmates' attitude. In any case, it was a clear indication of the feeling of exclusion and hostility the girl constantly experienced, and of the disempowerment that being left alone to cope with the new language meant for her. She spoke English well enough to communicate with me (she also spoke Twi to the other participants) but this appears to have made no substantial difference to her experience, despite the fact that the Italian curriculum places great emphasis on the learning of English as a foreign language. In all our conversations, never once did the children refer to their linguistic skills in languages other than Italian (nor to their knowledge of other cultural practices) as beneficial or as an advantage. Their 'foreign' status was exclusively spoken about in deficit terms (Eksner & Faulstich Orellana, 2005; Turner, 2004), as a hindrance to their achievement or inclusion rather than as added experience and skills to be shared with others.

Experiencing isolation and powerlessness is not inevitable, however. School should be the place where newly arrived children can get to know other people (both children and adults), where they feel welcome and have their skills valued. The social nature of schools means that they can offer an important source of friendship and companionship, as well as the help and care of empathetic people, as Slatan recalled during our conversation:

> **Researcher:** ok. And... the first... the first days in school, how were they? How did you feel? Do you remember?
>
> **Slatan:** only one friend talked to me, then on the second day I started to get to know them better...
>
> **Researcher:** right. And did the teachers help you?
>
> **Slatan:** yes. Especially one teacher... she helped me a lot!
>
> **Researcher:** right? Ok. So she was nice?
>
> **Slatan:** yep!
>
> **Researcher:** what did she help you with?
>
> **Slatan:** ah... subjects... then... subjects... She was saying... 'Relax, here you have new mates, they will not do anything to you...'
>
> **Researcher:** and how did she say that, in English?
>
> **Slatan:** no, in Italian, but... I didn't understand... I said... I kept saying 'yes, yes'
>
> [Slatan, male, age 12. Born in Ghana. School C, Italy]

Since, as he pointed out, he did not understand Italian when the exchange took place, the words Slatan reported might not be the actual ones the teacher used on those first days of school. However, they were what he 'remembered' her saying. Slatan was putting into words his perception of the teacher, translating her tone of voice, her body language and, generally, the interest, concern and empathy she was managing to convey. As in the vignette that opens this article, where the Italian-born children were evaluating the possibility that we may not be speaking the same language, Slatan's comments demonstrate that understanding each other's words is not an indispensable condition for communication to take place (Fassetta, 2013).

The power of the majority to impose rules and to demand conformity, however, is often present even in exchanges between peers, and the imposition of forms of 'verbal hygiene' (Cameron, 1995) aimed at eradicating 'different' languages can take very direct forms:

> **Linelle:** in our class Theresa and I speak Ghanaian. Everyone... everyone stares at us and then they say 'But what sort of language are you speaking? Look, here we speak Italian, right!'
>
> [Linelle, female, age 15. Born in Ghana. School D, Italy]

The request for linguistic conformity Linelle encountered rests on the assumption that speaking a different language threatens the cohesion of the group, whether this is the group of the peers, as in this case, or the national community, as implied by the policies of language testing for aspiring immigrants (Hogan-Brun et al., 2009). The children who demanded the use of Italian were actually objecting to the use of a language they could not understand and which they felt excluded them. As members of the majority group, they felt entitled to object to the use of 'Ghanaian' and to demand that the Ghanaian children spoke Italian to each other, regardless of the actual reality of the region in which they live, one which, bordering as it does Austria and Slovenia, has a long and complex history of multilingualism and multiculturalism.

## A hierarchy of languages

When deciding which country to move to, migrants often have to settle for the best option amongst those available to them. Different countries hold different degrees of potential for the fulfilment of aspirations (Pajo, 2007), and the country of settlement may not be (as is indeed the case for many of the Ghanaian migrants in Italy) the one they would have chosen as the ideal destination, but rather the one that was more accessible and/or where they could enjoy more support and practical help.

Potential destination countries are not equally desirable, and migrants appear to share a hierarchical view of the different nation-states, with some countries holding more potential for the fulfilment of ambitions and hopes than others. For the Albanian migrants to Greece in Pajo's study, as well as for the young participants in mine, the country at the top of the list, the one where many of them dream to be, is the USA. In the USA, the young Ghanaians in Italy claimed, everything is possible; the 'American Dream' means that everyone has an opportunity for success and prosperity, and to become, as a consequence, respected and admired.

Several of the Ghanaian children in Italy illustrated Italy's inferior status by referring to the lack of value of the Italian language. The language to know, they pointed out, is English, that of the former colonisers and also Ghana's official language, as well as the language of the country that holds the highest place in the global hierarchy. The following conversation with a group of children who were born in Italy of Ghanaian parents exemplifies the way in which languages underline perceived hierarchies:

**Researcher:** what's there in America that is special? What makes you want to go there?

**Erica:** because here in Italy, I mean... Italian cannot help you in the...

**Researcher:** the language, you mean?

**Erica:** yes, the language

**Researcher:** right...

**Erica:** In America you can go wherever and speak English

**Researcher:** ok, sure. And you said [you wanted to go] to London?

**Claire:** to learn English

[Erica, female, age 12; Claire, female, age 11. Born in Italy. School B, Italy]

The fact that several of the young Ghanaian participants stressed the greater importance of English over Italian arguably demonstrates a discourse that the wider Ghanaian community shares, one where their inferior position in Italian society as unskilled labour migrants of African origin can be offset by their coming from a country where a higher status language is spoken, something which can help, however partially, to compensate for the marginalisation experienced.

Besides English, some of the young Ghanaians born in Italy also spoke Twi at home, Ghana's lingua franca. This is also the language they needed to use in order to communicate with relatives in Ghana, something they said they were called to do quite regularly. Juggling between the different languages is not, however, without difficulties, and Twi seemed to be the language that many of the young participants had trouble with, as this extract illustrates:

**Researcher:** and when you speak to your relatives in Ghana, do you useTwi or do you use... English?

**Anastasia:** Twi

**Barak:** let's see... Twi is too hard. 'Pure' Twi without... without English, is too difficult

**Researcher:** do you speak Twi? Do you speak it?

**Barak:** yes, I... well... I... yes... I mix...

**Researcher:** ah, you can mix a bit of this and a bit of that?

**Barak:** yes, because [Twi] is too difficult

[Anastasia, female, age 12; Barak, male, age 12. Born in Italy. School D, Italy]

As appears from our conversations, many of the Italian-born participants had been raised speaking English in the home, the language their parents could speak to some degree as a result of having been schooled in Ghana. The Ghanaian vernacular had often been sacrificed to allow English to be passed on, while Italian was learnt outside the home, although the children had picked up some Twi through listening to their parents, hearing it spoken within the Ghanaian community and through phone conversations with members of the extended family.

The majority of the young participants were therefore proficient in at least two languages, but their linguistic competence appears never to have been considered a resource. Even the English many of the Ghanaian children spoke, and which the families strove to maintain, appeared to be undervalued, despite the great emphasis Italian education places on the learning of this language. Some of the teachers observed during our informal conversations about the project that the Ghanaian children's was not 'real' English. As a variety of English spoken by unskilled labour migrants from an African country it was not acknowledged as linguistic capital but rather as still one more element that hindered communication with the newly arrived children and their families.

However, at the intersection between their multiple linguistic belonging, the young people were also able to find a space in which they could resist and challenge adults' authority or restrictions, and to exercise a degree of autonomy. Being able to shift between languages and cultures allowed the children to choose amongst them strategically in order to achieve a specific goal, as the following excerpt illustrates:

**Anastasia:** One day we were in church and… it was [my friend's]birthday. The priest did not know this, and we were chatting and the people behind us were saying 'Stop chatting!' but we did not care, right…

**Researcher:** and…?

**Anastasia:**…and the priest called us. She went first, because I said 'You go first', and then he called me… I went quiet and… seen that he was speaking in English I pretended not to understand… I said 'Sorry, but I don't understand English' and he let us go, thanks to my intervention

[…]

**Researcher:** Is the priest strict?

**Anastasia:** no! They are all very nice. Only that… they talk a lot

[Anastasia, female, age 12. Born in Italy. School D, Italy]

Children are social agents who play a part in shaping their own childhood experiences (James & James, 2004). By playing on language difference, the girls managed to get away with chatting through the tedious service ('they talk a lot') and share in some fun amongst friends at the minister's expense. By pretending she could not understand English, thus exploiting her 'Italianness', Anastasia managed to create a zone in which she and her friend were able to bend and shift the adults' rules (to be still and quiet during services) and establish a complicity that would affirm and strengthen the social bond amongst peers.

## Conclusion

English, Italian and the Ghanaian vernacular spoken in the home come to acquire different connotations at different stages of the migration process, tied as they are to past histories, present global orders, transnational relations and personal biographies. While learning a new language is an exciting prospect before migration, once young people have moved they come under pressure to learn the official language of the receiving country.

Young people left behind by migrant parents are aware that learning the receiving country's language will be a challenge and that entering a new school system where the medium of instruction is one they will not understand could be very demanding. At the same time, however, the new language is seen as part of the new life the children are anticipating and the image of these Italian-speaking selves, immersed in a totally new social environment, was one they spoke about with a mixture of anticipation and apprehension. Moving to Italy, going to school, speaking Italian, making Italian friends: these would be challenges they would have to face, but they had no doubt that they would be successful in overcoming them.

The children who had recently moved to Italy, on the other hand, recollected the impact with the new language and social environment as a highly demanding, often upsetting and confusing period. At the time of our interview, most of the young Ghanaian migrants had settled into their new schools and could speak enough Italian to cope with everyday social interactions. However, for many of them this had come at the price of weeks and months of anxiety and isolation, an experience that none of them could forget and which still pained those who had arrived more recently. Several migrant children remarked on the lack of help and empathy on the part of peers, or about the (perceived) racism of teachers. The new language had proven a mighty barrier, one they had to face alone and with little support.

The children born in Italy of Ghanaian parents had all grown up exposed to at least three languages: the Italian of their country of birth, the vernacular language of their parents' area of origin (and of the extended family in Ghana or elsewhere) and the English of Ghanaian officialdom. While a very small minority were proficient in all three, most had received little encouragement to maintain the vernacular language, caught between their parents' wish to sustain their ability to speak and understand English and the Italian they spoke outside the home. While their multilingualism proved useful at times to avoid complying with adults' requests or in order to maintain privacy, it appears not to have been acknowledged as a valuable skill by the educational institution.

Moreover, as children of African unskilled labour migrants, they were never allowed to forget their inferior position within Italian society. Moving to an English-speaking country, the USA or the UK, signified for the children reaching a country that is, by virtue of speaking the powerful language of colonial collective memory, higher up in an assumed global hierarchy. The English the children had been taught by their parents was carefully preserved as linguistic capital that would allow them access to the realisation of ambitions and that would finally lead them to social advancement.

As the study focused on children's expectations and experiences, adults' voices are not included and this is undeniably a limitation for this discussion. Nevertheless, the migrant children's narratives highlight the expectation on the part of the receiving country's educational institutions and of the majority group that young people will adapt unilaterally and effortlessly; these same narratives also criticise the undue pressure young people are put under and expose a general lack of awareness of the emotional costs the process of adaptation required of them.

This article does not wish to be dismissive of the linguistic needs of immigrant children. Human beings share a necessity to communicate and a common language is important not just for practical purposes but also as a conductor of shared meanings and as a vehicle for socialisation. However, migrant children need appropriate linguistic support and adequate resources must be allocated towards this in order to minimise the consequences of a process that can be long and painful and which can leave lasting consequences. The goal of speaking a common language should not come at the price of months, even years, of loneliness and apprehension that can impact directly on the children's attainment and, crucially, on their perception of their own value as learners and as individuals.

## Notes

1. As defined by Article 1 of the 1989 UN Convention on the Rights of the Child, in this article the word 'children' will be applied to refer to individuals under the age of 18 years. The terms 'young people' and 'young participants' will be used as synonymous of children.
2. OECD refers to the Organisation for Economic Cooperation and Development, which has 34 member countries. They include many of the world's most advanced countries but also emerging countries like Mexico, Chile and Turkey. See http://www.oecd.org/about/membersandpartners/ (Accessed 25 February 2013).
3. These tests are aimed to covertly exclude people who, for a variety of reasons (which can include costs of language courses, availability of language classes, age, ability to learn, etc.), do not meet linguistic standards set by the prospective destination country (Hogan-Brun et al., 2009).
4. Ghana has a history as regards the language used in its public schools, and the medium of instruction in the first few years of primary education has alternatively been one of the local

languages (depending on the geographical area), and English (Owu-Ewie, 2006). In secondary schools, universities and colleges, the language of instruction is English.

5. Hirsh's (2012) Ghana calls an end to tyrannical reign of Queen's English. See http://www. guardian.co.uk/world/2012/apr/10/ghana-calls-end-queens-english?CMP=twt_gu (Accessed 25 April 2012).

6. The exact number of languages spoken in Ghana is disputed because of the lack of a clear-cut distinction between languages and dialects. Different scholars put the number of languages spoken between 45 and 80 (Bodomo, Anderson, & Dzahene-Quarshie, 2009).

7. Primary and secondary schools are part of Universal Basic Education, which comprises the compulsory stages of education. Basic Education lasts for a total 11 years, which include 2 years of kindergarten, 6 years of primary school and 3 years of junior high school

## Notes on contributor

Giovanna Fassetta has a Masters in Education (Applied Linguistics) and a Doctorate in Sociology. She has taught for over 20 years in Italy, Eritrea and the UK. Since being awarded her PhD in 2012, she has been a researcher at the University of Strathclyde. She is a member of Glasgow Refugee and Migration Network (GRAMNet) and part of the Diverse Teachers for Diverse Learners (DTDL) international research network. She is the current chair of the charity Scottish Detainee Visitors (SDV), who regularly visit Dungavel Immigration Removal Centre to offer emotional and practical support to people in detention.

## References

Balboni, P. E. (2008). Italiano L2: Una via italiana. *Studi di glottodidattica* [Italian L2: An Italian Route], *2*, 17–31.

Baugh, A., & Cable, T. (2002). *A history of the English language* (4th ed.). London: Routledge.

Bodomo, A., Anderson, J. A., & Dzahene-Quarshie, J. (2009). A Kente of many colours. Multilingualism as a complex ecology of language shift in Ghana. *Sociolinguistic Studies, 3*, 357–379. doi:10.1558/sols.v3i3.357

Bourdieu, P. (1991). *Language and symbolic power.* Cambridge: Polity Press.

Cameron, D. (1995). *Verbal hygiene.* London: Routledge.

Castles, S., & Miller, M. J. (2010). *Migration and the global economic crisis: One year on.* Update to *The Age of Migration.* Retrieved from www.age-of-migration.com

Catts, R., Allan, J., & Smyth, G. (2007). Children's voices: How do we address their right to be heard? *Scottish Educational Review, 39*, 51–59. Retrieved from http://ser.stir.ac.uk/pdf/190.pdf

Coe, C. (2002). Educating an African leadership: Achimota and the teaching of African culture in the gold coast. *Africa Today, 49*(3), 33–44. Retrieved from http://muse.jhu.edu/login?auth=0& type=summary&url=/journals/africa_today/v049/49.3coe.pdf

Corsaro, W. A. (2005). *The sociology of childhood* (2nd ed.). Thousand Oaks, CA: Pine Forge Press.

Dobson, M. E. (2009). Unpacking children in migration research. *Children's Geographies, 7*, 355–360. doi:10.1080/14733280903024514

Dreby, J. (2006). Honor and virtue. Mexican parenting in the transnational context. *Gender and Society, 20*, 32–59. doi:10.1177/0891243205282660

Dreby, J. (2010). *Divided by borders. Mexican migrants and their children.* London: University of California Press.

Eksner, J. H., & Faulstich Orellana, M. (2005). Liminality as linguistic process. Immigrant youth and experiences of Language in Germany and the United States. In J. Knörr (Ed.), *Childhood and migration. From experience to agency* (pp. 175–206). London: Transaction.

European Commission. (2013). *Study on educational support for newly arrived migrant children. Case study report: Italy.* Brussels: European Commission – Education and Training.

Fassetta, G. (2013). Communicating attitudes: Ghanaian children's expectations and experiences of Italian educational institutions. *Childhood*, OnlineFirst, 1–16. doi:10.1177/0907568213512691

Faulstich Orellana, M. (2009). *Translating childhoods. Immigrant youth, language and culture.* London: Rutgers University Press.

Faulstich Orellana, M., Thorne, B., Chee, A., & Lam, W. S. E. (2001). Transnational childhoods: The participation of children in processes of family migration. *Social Problems, 48*, 572–591. Retrieved from http://www.jstor.org/stable/10.1525/sp.2001.48.4.572

Graham, C. K. (1971). *The history of education in Ghana. From the earliest times to the declaration of independence*. Abingdon: Frank Cass.

Harison, G. (2009). Language politics, language capital and bilingual practitioners in social work. *British Journal of Social Work*, *39*, 1082–1100. doi:10.1093/bjsw/bcm153

Hirsh, A. (2012). *Ghana calls an end to tyrannical reign of the Queens English*. Retrieved from http://www.guardian.co.uk/world/2012/apr/10/ghana-calls-end-queens-english

Hogan-Brun, G., Mar-Molinero, C., & Stevenson, P. (Eds.). (2009). *Discourses on language and integration*. Amsterdam: John Benjamin.

Holloway, S. L., & Valentine, G. (2000). *Children's geographies. Playing, living, learning*. London: Routledge.

James, A., & James, A. L. (2004). *Constructing childhood. Theory, policy and social practice*. Basingstoke: Palgrave Macmillan.

James, A., & Prout, A. (Eds.). (1990). *Constructing and reconstructing childhood. Contemporary issues in the sociological study of childhood*. London: Falmer Press.

Kesby, M. (2007). Methodological insights on and from children's geographies. *Children's Geographies*, *5*, 93–205. doi:10.1080/14733280701445739

Kymlicka, W. (2003). Multicultural states and intercultural citizens. *Theory and Research in Education*, *1*, 147–169. doi:10.1177/1477878503001002001

Leonard, M. (2005). Children, childhood and social capital: Exploring the links. *Sociology*, *39*, 605–622. doi:10.1177/0038038505052490

Levitt, P. (2001). *The transnational villagers*. Berkley: University of California Press.

Mayall, B. (2000). The sociology of childhood in relation to children's rights. *The International Journal of Children's Rights*, *8*, 243–259.

Owu-Ewie, C. (2006). *The language policy of education in Ghana. A critical look at the English-only language policy of Education*. Selected Proceedings of the 35th Annual Conference on African Languages. Somerville, MA: Cascadilla Proceedings Project. Retrieved from http://www.lingref.com/cpp/acal/35/paper1298.pdf

Pajo, E. (2007). *International migration, social demotion, and imagined advancement*. New York: Springer.

Pavlenko, A. (2004). 'Stop doing that, *Ia Komu Skazala!*' Language choice and emotions in parent–child communication. *Journal of Multilingual and Multicultural Development*, *25*, 179–203. doi:10.1080/01434630408666528

Penn, R., & Lambert, P. (2009). *Children of international migrants in Europe – Comparative perspectives*. Basingstoke: Palgrave Macmillan.

Philippou, S., & Theodorou, E. (2014). The 'Europeanisation' of othering: Children using 'Europe' to construct 'others' in Cyprus. *Race, Ethnicity and Education*, *17*, 264–290. doi:10.1080/13613324.2012.759923

Phinney, J. S., Romero, I., Nava, M., & Huang, D. (2001). The role of language, parents, and peers in ethnic identity among adolescents in immigrant families. *Journal of Youth and Adolescence*, *30*(2), 135–152. doi:10.1023/A:1010389607319

Piller, I. (2001). Naturalization language testing and its basis in ideologies of national identity and citizenship. *The International Journal of Bilingualism*, *5*, 259–277. doi:10.1177/13670069010050030201

Piller, I. (2011). *Intercultural communication. A critical introduction*. Edinburgh: Edinburgh University Press.

Piller, I. (2012). Multilingualism and social exclusion. In M. Martin-Jones, A. Blackledge, & A. Creese (Eds.), *The Routledge handbook of multilingualism* (pp. 281–296). London: Routledge.

Portes, A., & Rumbaut, R. G. (2001). *Legacies. The story of the immigrant second generation*. Berkeley: University of California Press.

Punch, S. (2002). Research with children. The same or different from research with adults? *Childhood*, *9*, 321–341. doi:10.1177/0907568202009003005

Rubin, H. J., & Rubin, I. (2005). *Qualitative interviewing: The art of hearing data*. Thousand Oaks, CA: Sage.

Rumbaut, R. G. (2002). Severed or sustained attachments? Language, identity and imagined communities in the post-immigrant generation. In P. Levitt & M. C. Waters (Eds.), *The changing face of home. The transnational lives of the second generation* (pp. 43–95). New York: Russell Sage Foundation.

Sayad, A. (2004). *The suffering of the immigrant*. Cambridge: Polity Press.

Suárez-Orozco, C., & Suárez-Orozco, M. M. (2001). *Children of immigration*. Harvard University Press.

Turner, J. (2004). Academic literacy in post-colonial times: Hegemonic norms and transcultural possibilities. In A. Phipps & M. Guilherme (Eds.), *Critical pedagogy. Political approaches to languages and intercultural communication* (pp. 22–32). Clevedon: Multilingual Matters.

Yeoh, B. S. A., & Lam, T. (2006). *The costs of (im)mobility: Children left behind and children who migrate with a parent. Perspectives on gender and migration*. Bangkok: United Nations. Retrieved from: http://e.unescap.org/ESID/GAD/Publication/Perspectives_on_Gender_and_Migration_FINAL.pdf#page=128

Yosso, T. J. (2005). Whose culture has capital? A critical race theory discussion of community cultural wealth. *Race, Ethnicity and Education, 8*, 69–91. doi:10.1080/1361332052000341006

Zuppiroli, M. (2008). Migrare in adolescenza Aspetti psicosociali del ricongiungimento familiare in Italia [Migrating in adolescence. Psychosocial aspects of family reunion in Italy]. *Ricerche di Pedagogia e Didattica, 3*, 1–26. Retrieved from http://rpd.unibo.it/article/viewFile/1537/910

# Learning across borders – Chinese migrant literature and intercultural Chinese language education

Yongyang Wang

*Melbourne Graduate School of Education, The University of Melbourne, Carlton, VIC, Australia*

Chinese migrants have been a rich source of influential international literature, represented by key works such as *Eat a Bowl of Tea* by Louis Chu in 1961 and *The Joy Luck Club* by Amy Tan in 1989. Cultural differences and conflicts, stereotypes and other complex issues regarding the diasporic lives of the Chinese sojourners are revealed vividly in those stories. In the intercultural language teaching of Chinese in USA, Australia and Europe, a central and pressing task is to improve students' intercultural sensitivities and develop the capability to communicate efficiently with China and Chinese people. In light of critical literary studies that treat literature as a kind of 'cultural artefact' and recent analysis of Hay and Wang which advocates 'migratory' literature as a 'third place' for intercultural communication, this paper takes a step further. It does so by expanding the spectrum into Chinese norms, stereotypes and some core values that are significant in intercultural communication with Chinese and explores interdisciplinary approaches to linking studies of Chinese migrant literature and the intercultural education of Chinese at university level.

世界各地的海外华人创作了诸多反映其海外生活经历的文学作品，比如说雷霆超的《吃碗茶》和谭恩美的《喜福会》。这些作品体现了东西方文化上的差异、文化固见和诸多复杂的、因为文化差异引起的话题或问题。同时，在世界各地的汉语教学中又有一个迫切的任务——提高汉语学生的跨文化敏感性和与中国人有效交际的能力。本文将移民文学与国际汉语教学相结合，探讨移民文学在提高汉语学生跨文化敏感性和跨文化交际能力等方面的作用和意义。

## Chinese overseas migrants and migrant literature[1]

Literature, the literary canon in particular, has played an important role in language education in throughout history. In recent years, under the influence of transcultural literary studies, critical and cultural studies, social semiotics and communicative language teaching, a broader range of literary genres and more innovative methodologies of literature teaching have been employed and developed in second/foreign language education. For example, Kramsch (1993) argues for the use of literature as a pedagogical tool for exploration of various levels of meaning in language teaching. Lau (2002) applied literature in the primary language classroom in Hong Kong. Carroli (2008) explores the application of literature in Italian language class. A number of literary texts are examined by Wang and Hay (2011) for the purposes of intercultural education when teaching Chinese as a second language (CSL). To take a step further, Hay and Wang (2010) define a specific 'genre' – 'migratory' literature as a 'third place' (Kramsch, 1993, 1999; Liddicoat, Lo Bianco, & Crozet, 1999) for intercultural education in CSL. 'Migratory' literature embraces a wide range of literary texts, including those written by Chinese writers who have experience of living outside of China and by non-Chinese writers with experience of living inside China. By so doing, the authors argue for a corpus of literary texts as a 'third place' for intercultural exploration of dialogues between China and the West and provide a comparative perspective in viewing Chinese language and culture, in which meanings are negotiated amongst themselves and between insiders and outsiders. Rather than treating literature as a stable product of an epoch, the authors emphasize the status quo and consequences of their mobility across time and space. While following the basic principles proposed by the above-mentioned researchers, this paper focuses on a particular group of Chinese migrant writers who live in English-speaking countries, for the purpose of teaching Chinese language and culture to native English learners. It also adopts the term 'overseas Chinese migrant/literature' in contrast to Chinese internal migrant/literature resulting from China's urbanization in recent decades.[2]

China has a long history of overseas migration due to political, cultural and social economic reasons. Since the early nineteenth century in particular when China forcibly opened its door to the West after the First Opium War (1839–1842) and the Taiping Rebellion (1851–1864), a growing number of residents, especially those in the coastal regions, who suffered from constant wars, poverty, famine and epidemic disease, frequently ventured overseas, seeking a better life. By the 1860s, significant populations of Chinese immigrants were established throughout much of North America, Peru, the West Indies, Australia, New Zealand and Southeast Asia (Voss, 2005). The discovery of gold in San Francisco (Jiu Jinshan/Old Gold Mountain) and around Melbourne, Australia (Xin Jinshan/New Gold Mountain), triggered two major overseas migrations in the history of modern China. Most of the early years' diaspora Chinese suffered greatly from discrimination, and sometimes hostility in the host societies, along with nostalgia, isolation, illness, culture shock and injustice. Literature became the media through which they shared feelings, empathy, experience, support and communication with each other. A large number of overseas Chinese writers contributed to this literary 'genre' which has usually been neglected by mainstream literature anthologies. To list a few, *Eat a Bowl of Tea*, 1961 by Louis Chu explores Chinese masculinity and patriarchal cultural traditions in the setting of a 1940s' Chinatown in America. The popular novel by Amy Tan (1989), *The Joy Luck Club*, upon which a movie is based, reveals a number of intercultural themes in relation to overseas Chinese women, and cross-cultural differences and conflicts between mothers and daughters. The dialogues between different generations, rich in linguistic significance and intercultural underpinnings, form a vivid 'third place' that opens possibilities for further interpretation for intercultural communication and Chinese language education. This will be illustrated in the following sections.

Since Deng's 1980s economic reform and open door policy, a new tide of Chinese overseas migration has emerged, usually in the form of seeking overseas education and exporting labour. New migrants (*xinyimin*; Liu, 2005) exhibit some different character-istics from old-generation migrants. In general they do not usually suffer from financial difficulties and poverty as the old-generation Chinese migrants did, and they also have higher literacy levels in general. With the growing power of China economically and socially in the world in recent years, the overseas Chinese have gained new status in the host societies. Their encounters with their host cultures have fashioned a complex tapestry, sometimes blending and sometimes contrasting with aspects of culture in the

Western host societies. One of the most influential works in the beginning of the post-Deng era is the *Beijinger in New York* by Cao and Wang (1993). The novel, based upon Cao and his wife's sojourner life in pursuit of their 'American dreams', grew in popularity, especially after it was turned into a TV soap opera. *A Concise Chinese-English Dictionary for Lovers* by Xiaolu Guo (2007) depicts a love story between a white British man and Z – a young female Chinese overseas student. The novel starts deliberately with pidgin English which reflects vividly the English level of Z as a new overseas student at a British university. It also explores themes such as feminism, privacy and family relationships that are significant in China–West intercultural dialogues.

However, despite the existence of migrant literature in Chinese, English or bilingual versions, its application and significance in Chinese language education have remained under-examined and thus demand closer inspection. Wang (2008) suggests a new reading practice – 'intercultural thematic reading approach' that is based upon a view of literature as a cultural sign system, on principles of intercultural communication competence, and on the kind of multiplicity of interpretation, perspective and voice that are the subject of much theoretical debate in critical and cultural studies. This new 'reading practice' is not just a matter of different content, or an expanded repertoire of sources, but also a matter of integrating cultural awareness and language learning in a form of pedagogy that is derived from appreciation of a non-Chinese learner's needs and perspectives. This paper, following this new reading approach, selects four literary texts and attempts to interpret the pedagogical meanings and to suggest applications in the intercultural teaching of Chinese for the 'intercultural speakers' of the twenty-first century.

## A social semiotic reading approach

Several methodological paradigms contribute to the approach that is taken in this paper, culminating in a method of interpreting 'text' and narratives based on the developing area of critical and cultural studies now referred to as 'social semiotics'. This is essentially a way of treating texts as 'cultural documents', but then going beyond this to read them as 'signs' of cultural practices. As Culler (1981) points out 'cultural studies can be seen as the heir to semiotics in its interest in understanding cultural practices'. The task of semiotics is to understand the conventions and the functioning of the sign systems that make up the human world (Culler, 1981). Lewis (2002) also draws our attention to the idea of 'cultural documents' or texts:

> Rather than consider meaning to be something immanent in the text or something which elevates art over all other aspects of life, cultural studies has treated texts as cultural documents. These documents cannot be separated from the circumstances and conditions of their production and consumption. Thus cultural texts are fundamentally and inescapably embedded in social practices, institutional processes, politics and economy. The meanings of texts cannot be treated as independent of the broader flows and operations of the culture in which the text exists. (p. 35)

Thus, reading a 'text' in a narratological way involves contextual analysis of meanings (Kostera, 2006). Readers play a critical role in the study of sign systems. In the social semiotic sense, the study of signs involves the study of how meaning is constructed and understood for and by the readers. It is rooted in the hermeneutic tradition which stresses that the interpretation of a text must always be undertaken from the readers' perspective (Scott, 2006). Texts are culturally marked and open to interpretation in terms of their denotations, connotations and effects on their readers or hearers (Culler, 1997). Barthes

(1967, 1973, 1974) suggested that the ideal text is one that is reversible, or open to the greatest variety of independent interpretations and not restrictive in meaning. It is precisely the issue of meanings for readers that I will emphasize in this study.

Culler (2002) observes that cultural studies include and encompass literary studies, examining literature as a particular cultural practice and suggests:

> Semiotic investigation is possible only when one is dealing with a mode of signification or communication. One must be able to identify effects of signification – the meanings objects and events have for participants and observers. Then one can attempt to construct models of signifying processes to account for these effects. A semiotics of literature is thus based on two assumptions, both of which can be questioned: first, that literature should be treated as a mode of signification and communication, in that a proper description of a literary work must refer to the meanings it has for readers; second, that one can identify the effects of signification one wants to account for. (p. 53)

Exploration of meanings for readers will obviously require adequate recognition of who the readers are and what perspectives they bring to the act of reading. In the study of Chinese literature for non-Chinese learners, Wang (2008) argues that this whole dimension is currently missing from the selection of literary texts in the CSL curriculum, and nor is it considered in terms of pedagogy due to the influence of China's literary tradition of hagiography and historicity. Semiology or semiotics – a general science of signs – opens up the possibility of the study of literature as cultural text in language education through the interpretation for the particular readers of language learner. It also allows inclusion of non-canonical literary genres such as 'beauty writers'[3] and migrant writers into the language curriculum. Diverse interpretations of literary works become possible according to the perspective of the readers, in contrast to traditional 'insider' and author-oriented 'reading' practices in CSL (Wang, 2008).

This approach to meaning has been explored by Hodge and Louie in a series of books (Louie, 1986, 1987, 1989, 2000, 2002), especially *The Politics of Chinese Language and Culture, The Art of Reading Dragons* in particular (Hodge & Louie, 1998) and Hay (2008) on the narrative structure of Cultural Revolution theatre. According to Hodge and Louie (1998), 'semiotics itself is basically a simple concept. It refers to the study of all sign systems, all the media and means by which humans and other animals communicate or have communicated with each other' (p. 8). In this way, a semiotic approach encompasses a wide range of 'texts', popular or elite, visual or verbal, practices, customs, greetings, rituals, ways of eating, dressing, photographs, films, posters and paintings. Thus, in addition to verbal language, the traditional connotation of 'text', 'a mug and a robe can be readable texts as much as books or paintings' (p. 9). Hodge and Louie (1998) argue that we should:

> Apply social semiotics, and critical linguistic and discourse theory to the teaching and learning of the Chinese language and culture to build up a repertoire of ways of reading China through many kinds of cultural texts. (xi)

They also argue that such texts include 'traditional and contemporary fiction, literary criticism, journalism, film and popular culture, comics and the customs of everyday life' (xi). Louie (2000) suggests that the new way of 'reading' literary texts could provide insights into intercultural communication. He has provided a convincing example in his interpretation of *The Chess King* (Qiwang) written by a Chinese contemporary writer, Ah Cheng, in 1990. *The Chess King* has been analyzed as a 'text' that reveals the social life and subtle social relationships between two protagonists, Ni Bin and Wang Yisheng. Their relationship indicates social competences through which one can negotiate and communicate with people within the particular culture. Louie analyzes in detail the relationship between these two characters through their greeting ritual and self-introduction. The dialogue reveals rich social codes including the building of social solidarity between these two men, based on their social identity and educational level. Hodge and Louie conclude that:

> By supplementing the language textbooks, with their artificially controlled dialogues and pattern drills, with more lively models, literary works like Ah Cheng's *The Chess King* can play a vital role in a language-learning programme. (p. 30)

Similarly, Kramsch (1993) has rightly pointed out the doubtful dichotomy between language teaching and literature, and argued for a new pedagogy that helps students in searching for various levels of meaning of literary texts. I stated in my book *Reading Chinese Literature or Reading China* (Wang, 2008) that CSL literature selection is a 'sign', a 'display' (Hay, 2008) that has its own dynamic, its own meaning, its own narrative, beyond the discrete meanings contained in the works selected to represent Chinese literature to foreigners. This display is encapsulated in the memorable phrase, 'golden ages and outstanding exponents' (Lai, 1964) along with any number of other things such as China's Four Great Inventions,[4] or porcelain and calligraphy. However, a CSL curriculum should distinguish between what is necessary to understand the special place of literature in history and what is necessary to learn Chinese language and culture effectively. This suggests, not the abandonment, or even dilution, of the literary canon, but the use of a variety of 'texts' that will permit it to be reread, including contemporary texts written by marginalized, avant-garde and diasporic writers.

In recent decades, the concept of national literature has been challenged by more recent research paradigms that explore hybridity, colonization and regional literatures (Porter, 2011). The advocates of world literature for world civilization challenge the Eurocentric canonical literary curriculum and teaching in recent years, which also sheds light on second language (L2) language education. The absolute dichotomy between 'self' and others, mother culture and target language culture, 'first place' and 'second place' in intercultural communication has become even more problematic. In the study of Hay and Wang (2010), literature – 'migratory' literature in particular – is not only considered as an 'intertextual' but also an intercultural phenomenon, a heavily populated site for directions to a 'third place' for intercultural education. It is a discourse which goes beyond that of individual works and looks at the literature of China–West interchange as a 'signifying practice'. This new reading practice is a means of linking cultural studies and the teaching of languages and cultures in pedagogy for a 'third place' – a place of restlessness, shifting identity and hybridity (p. 127).

Kramsch famously discussed language study as 'a kind of social practice that is at the boundary of two or more cultures', and posited a 'third place' for language learners. She explained that:

> what is at stake is the creation, in and through the classroom, of a social, linguistic reality that is born from the L1 speech environment of the learners and the social environment of the L2 native speakers, but is a third culture in its own right. (Kramsch, 1993, p. 9)

And she indicated that at this critical intersection:

the major task of language learners is to define for themselves what this 'third place' that they have engaged in seeking will look like, whether they are conscious of it or not. .... For most, it will be the stories they will tell of these cross-cultural encounters, the meanings they will give them through these tellings and the dialogues that they will have with people who have had similar experiences. In and through these dialogues, they may find for themselves this third place that they can name their own. (Kramsch, 1993, p. 257)

A number of scholars have also noted the strengths of literature in intercultural language education (Berwitz-Melzer, 2001; Kehrer, Hunter, & McGlynn, 1990; Louie, 1987; Luchtenberg, 1989; Matos, 2005; Schewe, 1998). Literature provides authentic materials for teaching and the delivery of contextualized knowledge is therefore more friendly to the learner/reader's psychology of learning. For their aesthetic merits and artistic literary features, literary texts are a powerful stimulus for classroom discussion, task or drama-based learning and for fostering a more interactive classroom atmosphere (Wang, 2008; Wang & Hay, 2011). Migrant literature, in particular, forms a 'third place' in intercultural communication in which the dialogues take place between mother language culture and target language culture, self and the other, and within the migrants themselves (Hay & Wang, 2010). In the narratives of Chinese sojourners, Chinese language and culture have been placed in the host culture society – a 'foreign' environment in which Chinese traditional values and behaviours are challenged, contrasted and transferred through conflicts, culture shock and negotiation with the host society. Because of these dramatic contrasts, Chinese language and culture become more prominent and visible to its readers/learners in CSL. In addition, with the migrant literature usually situated in the familiar cultural environment of the language learners, this in turn brings closeness and provides a kind of rapport with the learners which is expected to be an advantage in learning. In the following section, this paper will position and read Chinese migrant literature – a marginalized literary 'genre' as a cultural document/practice in order to interpret its meaning in the intercultural education of non-Chinese at university level.

## Chinese tea culture

Important components of Chinese migrant writers are their nostalgic retrospection and contemplation of their former life in their home country, China before or during their sojourn journey. A vivid, old and yet new China is encapsulated in their narratives which in turn make powerful teaching materials with great potential in L2 teaching. In the following section, I will exemplify this through the book that may well be one of the most read by non-Chinese readers – *Wild Swans – Three Daughters of China* (1992) by a Chinese contemporary female diaspora writer, Jung Chang.

Jung Chang is arguably a former Red Guard in Mao's China now living in London with her husband Jon Holliday who is also the coauthor of their book *Mao The Unknown Story* (Chang & Halliday, 2005). *Wild Swans* depicts the lives of three generations of Chinese women throughout modern China's major social movements and events. It has been translated into 30 languages and sold multi-millions of copies throughout the world. Images and cultural meanings about Chinese culture, themes such as masculinity, feminism and revolution, and values such as filial piety, collectivism, patriarchy and hierarchical family relationships are richly and vividly depicted in Jung Chang's narrative. Some sections can be directly incorporated into teaching of Chinese language and culture. For example, tea plays a significant role in Chinese people's daily life and in history, along with silk and porcelain that are exported overseas and as a theme is included in some textbooks for non-Chinese learners. However, the contents are usually tedious factual introduction of the types, history and statistics about its region and production. In fact, tea in China is not merely a daily consumption item, but has embedded humanistic meanings, a social semiotic worth close examination. Chang's description of a teahouse in Sichuan is particularly rich:

> A Sichuan teahouse is a unique place. It usually sits in the embrace of a bamboo grove or under the canopy of a large tree. Around the low, square wooden tables are bamboo armchairs which give out a faint aroma even after years of use. To prepare the tea a pinch of tea leaves is dropped into a cup and boiling water is poured on top. Then a lid is sunk loosely onto the cup, allowing the steam to seep through the gap, bringing out the fragrance of the jasmine or other blossoms. Sichuan has many kinds of tea. Jasmine alone has five grades. (p. 289)

> Teahouses are as important to the Sichuanese as pubs are to the British. Older men, in particular, spend a lot of time there, puffing their long-stemmed pipes over a cup of tea and a plateful of nuts and melon seeds. The waiter shuttles between the seats with a kettle of hot water which he pours from a couple of feet away with pinpoint accuracy. A skillful waiter makes the water level higher than the edge of the cup without it spilling over. As a child I was always mesmerized watching the water fall from the spout. (p. 290)

> Like European cafes, a Sichuan teahouse provides newspapers on bamboo frames. Some customers go there to read, but it is primarily a place to meet and chat, exchanging news and gossip. There is often entertainment – storytelling punctuated with wooden clappers. (p. 290)

> The teahouse, like all the others in Sichuan, was shut for fifteen years – until 1981, when Deng Xiaoping's reforms decreed it could be reopened. In 1985 I went back there with a British friend. We sat under the scholar tree. An old waitress came to fill our cups with a kettle from two feet away. Around us, people were playing chess. It was one of the happiest moments of that trip back. (p. 291)

As teaching materials for intercultural education of Chinese, the narration of Jung Chang is learner-friendly in the sense that not only is it human with personal affections but also because of its comparisons with learners' familiar Western cultural icons such as the café and pub. Based upon the above-mentioned paragraphs, the potential for teaching can be further explored and expanded to Chinese regional culture and Deng's 1980 reform according to available teaching hours.


## Gender roles – historical perspective

Undoubtedly, one of the greatest values of *Wild Swans* for Chinese intercultural education lies in its revealing the fates of three generations of Chinese women. Grandmother unwillingly accepted an arranged marriage with General Xue arranged by her father, because traditionally to question a parental decision was considered unfilial:

> General Xue had said that she could stay in Yixian, in a house which he was going to buy especially for her. This meant she could be close to her own family, but even more important, she would not have to live in his residence, where she would have to submit to the authority of his wife and the other concubines, who would all have precedence over her. In the house of a potentate like General Xue, the women were virtual prisoners, living in a state of permanent squabbling and bickering, largely induced by insecurity. The only security they had was their husband's favor. General Xue's offer of a house of her own meant a lot to my grandmother, as did his promise to solemnize the liaison with a full wedding ceremony. This meant that she and her family would have gained a considerable amount of face. (p. 30)

It is widely accepted that in the 1000-year-old feudal system, Chinese women were subordinate to men in both family and public life. Men had economic power and were entitled to have both a wife and concubines when their financial circumstances permitted. Women had no rights to education or to hold any public office. Lack of economic independence resulted in the reliance of women on men. However, this tradition that has been officially condemned since the 1949 revolution appears to be more complex in contemporary writer Guo Xiaolu's (2007) *A Concise Chinese-English Dictionary for Lovers*. The stereotyped image of Chinese women in its modern era as the 'holders of half sky' is challenged by a story that took place in a non-Chinese context, London.

Guo is a former international student in London and now a writer living in London. *A Concise Chinese-English Dictionary for Lovers* tells the story of a female Chinese international student (Z) and her lover, a British man. This novel is deliberately written in 'bad English'. However, native English speakers would not have a problem understanding it. This novel illustrates that understanding culture is not exclusively a matter of acquiring fluency in reading or speaking. On the contrary, this 'bad English writing' provides an alternative way of understanding Chinese language (e.g. syntax and morphology) and ultimately Chinese patterns of thought (Wang, 2008).

The narrator is Z, a Chinese girl who finds herself in a Western cultural environment in which her characteristics and identity as a Chinese become more prominent, and problematic, especially in her relationship with a British man. Their relationship starts from a misunderstanding and ends as the result of not understanding each other properly – which are in fact, two different things. As the blurb suggests, this book is a whole 'dictionary' of possible misunderstandings. Z asks her new British friend whom she has bumped into in the cinema if she can see where he lives. The man looks into her eyes and says 'be my guest'. Z thinks that he has asked her to move in with him, and he is happy enough to go along with it, in spite of his surprise. This is the start of continuing confusion and misunderstanding in their relationship, marked by separate entries, in the style of a thematically organised 'dictionary'. For Z, as an alien in British society, her experiences form a stark contrast between her own culture and that of the surrounding environment. Her misunderstandings, culture shock and confusions reveal the differences between the two cultures. The Chinese cultural heritage becomes more prominent when it is placed in the context of an alien territory. The relationship between males and females provides a rich and painful context in which cultural differences can be fully exposed. The understandings of, and expectations within, a relationship may reveal social norms and rituals, ethics, diet, sexuality, customs, perceptions of woman's status in a family or society, understandings of privacy, the gender roles in the relationship, independence, dependence and the like. The individual is a social and historical agent that carries some particular cultural and historical assets. The following dialogue between Z and her lover after they have been to a restaurant reveal the complexities:

You take out twenty pounds, put on the bill book. I don't move. I look at you, wondering.

'Half!' you say.

'Why? I don't have twenty pounds with me!' I say.

'You've got a debit card.'

'But why?'

'I'm always paying for you. In the West, men and women are equal. We should split food and rent.'

'But I thought we lovers!' Loudly, I argue...

'It's not about that. You are from China, the country with the most equal relationship between men and women. I'd have thought you'd understand what I'm talking about. Why should I pay for everything?'

I say: 'Of course you have to pay. You are man. If I pay too, then why I need to be with you?'

Now you're angry: 'Are you really saying you're only with me to pay your living costs?'

'No, not that! You are man and I am woman, and we are live together. When couple is live together, woman loses social life automatically. She only stays at home do cooking and washing. And after she have kids, even worse. So woman can't have any social position at all. She loses ... what is that word ... financial independence?' (pp. 173–174)

Z is in fact illustrating a complexity in examining the gender role of women in contemporary China. She has come to London in search of independence and a means of securing a livelihood, but her thinking does not keep pace with her own behaviour in a social situation. Vividly depicted in the novel, she reverts to feudal thinking. Literature of this kind is an incomparable resource to reveal these complexities vividly to the learners/ outsiders of Chinese culture.

Migrant literature, placing Chinese values and beliefs in a contrasting context, reveals differences prominently and provides a more comprehensible means for Western learners. The stereotyped view with regard to particular Chinese social groups, Chinese women in this case, can be explored. Understanding of the diversity of Chinese culture is readily developed through this kind of critical reading. Related scenarios are also applicable in language classes for group discussions, dramatization, role-play and other kinds of creative pedagogy.

## Social norms

Migrant literary texts can also be used to teach Chinese social norms and therefore can provide a contextualized learning for L2 learners. Lao She (1899–1966) was an outstanding Chinese novelist and dramatist and best known for his novel *Rickshaw Boy* and the play *Teahouse*. Based upon his life in London, his novel, *Ma and Son* (Lao, 1980), depicts the life of old-generation Chinese father Mr. Ma and his son Ma Wei in Britain. The following short paragraph illustrates the power of literary text as a form of social semiotics in illustrating and revealing the differences between China and the West in the perception and behaviours of face, politeness and hospitality:

Reverend Evans looked round at Mr. Ma with his little brown eyes, and then said to Ma Wei, 'Are you hungry?' 'Not...' Mr. Ma started to say hurriedly. In the first place, to arrive in England and promptly clamor for food couldn't help but be utterly lacking in decorum. In the second place, to make Reverend Evans spend money entertaining them made him very uneasy. Reverend Evans didn't wait for him to say 'hungry,' he just said, 'Come along, have a little something. Not hungry? I don't believe it?' It went against the grain for Mr. Ma to be impolite. In a low voice he said to Ma Wei in Chinese, 'he wants to be host. We mustn't insult him by disagreeing.'

when they had finished, Reverend Evans asked Ma Wei to take away the plates and glasses, then said to Mr. Ma, 'A shilling each. No, that's not right, you and I each had two beers. Ma Wei pays one shilling, you pay one shilling and six pence. Do you have enough change?' (p. 27)

As a conventional Chinese scholar who first came to Britain without any knowledge of Western individualism and social protocols, Mr. Ma applies naturally typical Chinese norms in which the hosts will be obliged to show their hospitability by buying guests a meal, especially the first meal upon guests' arrival. However, this convention is also complicated with other dominating social conventions – face and politeness. Blunt rejection of hosts' hospitality can be considered an insult to the hosts and thus make the hosts lose face and this alone is an impolite thing to do. After thinking through the dilemma carefully, Mr. Ma decides to accept the 'invitation' so as not to insult the host. It turns out to be a surprise to Mr. Ma that his hesitation appears to be completely unnecessary in this context. Evans displeases Mr. Ma by applying, also naturally, his Western social norms and therefore appears to Mr. Ma as stingy in his later comments to his son Ma Wei. Lack of awareness of each other's cultural conventions caused this embarrassment between Mr. Ma and Evans. The vivid revelation of insiders' and outsiders' perspectives in this story can be very powerful teaching material for Chinese L2 learners. It also provides a good story base for further interactive learning such as role-play and dramatization (Wang, 2011).

## Conclusion

This kind of reading for intercultural language education is not mere interpretation of meaning. It is a boundary-free journey through the meanings of texts for learners/readers in CSL. Chinese migrant literature, as a global phenomenon, continues to grow in recent years with the increasing number of Chinese people studying, living overseas or migrating in and out of China. There are a number of influential overseas Chinese newspapers, magazines, websites and blogs that publish their stories and provide rich sources for the exploration of intercultural themes for Chinese language education. To list a few, *World Newspaper*, the *Sing Tao Daily*, *Ming Bao*, *Southern Chinese Daily News*, *China Times* and *World Journal* in North America. In Europe, there are literary magazines *Olive Tree*, *Forum on the East and the West* and *Zhenya*. From a pedagogical point of view, migrant literature is significant in providing the perspectives of 'others' and revealing dialogues for in-between cultures. Inclusion of migrant literature in language courses would increase learners' intercultural sensitivities and intercultural awareness which in turn would enable them to 'step out' of their own cultural space and gradually build up a 'third place' in which different cultural views coexist harmoniously. As discussed in the previous chapters, literary texts such as *The Chess King* can bring specific, otherwise opaque Chinese social relationships into the view of non-Chinese learners. On their second encounter with a similar situation, they would be able to understand the subtleties and to respond in a socially acceptable manner. This is a process of learning from 'others' and through critical reading and 'thirding' – in search of a 'third place' in cross-cultural communication.

This kind of literature based on a social semiotic reading approach is more applicable to intermediate and advanced language learners who have developed a certain level of linguistic competence. Some of the migrant literature is written in English, such as Amy Tan's *Joy Luck Club*. Some of the works have bilingual versions. This paper suggests bilingual texts be provided to the students where available. Undoubtedly this will be decided according to students' language capability, especially reading capability, and the objectives of the class. By arguing for the potential, strengths and possibility of migrant literature in intercultural learning, this paper also raises a number of questions for further research – for example, what are the criteria for selection of migrant literature? How might migrant literary texts be incorporated into the language classroom within limited teaching hours? Are there conflicts between the learning of vocabularies, syntax and grammar and the appreciation of literary texts for intercultural learning? If so, what are they and what techniques may be applied to cope with them?

## Notes

1. 'Migratory' literature (Hay & Wang, 2010) exists in various languages to which the literature-based 'reading' approach discussed in this paper applies equally.
2. Under some circumstances, the term 'Chinese migrants' is used interchangeably to refer to Chinese internal migrants who uproot from the countryside and adopt a new life in urban cities such as in Magistad (2006). This paper uses 'overseas Chinese migrants' to differentiate from Chinese internal migrants.
3. 'Beauty Writers' refers to a group of young Chinese female writers, represented by Wei Hui – the author of *Shanghai Baby*, 2002 and Mianmian – the author of *Candy*, 2003. As Lu (2008) points out, 'their writings are characterized by an unabashed, unprecedented foregrounding of female sexuality. The parading and pandering of female subjectivity via a body politics have become a major literary fad in contemporary mainland China' (p. 167).
4. The Four Great Inventions of ancient China refer to Compass, Gunpowder, Papermaking and Printing that are celebrated in Chinese culture as symbols of ancient China's advanced science and technology.

## Notes on contributor

Dr Wang Yongyang is a research fellow, and executive director in the Australian federal government funded research project, 'Intercultural Approaches to Teaching Chinese: A Basis for Pedagogical Innovation' and recipient of Guizhou Education Bureau 'Migratory Scholar Grant'. She is the author of an academic book 'Reading Chinese Literature or Reading China' in which she proposes a creative and intercultural thematic reading approach for teaching Chinese as a foreign/second language. Her research interests include second language acquisition, sociolinguistics, critical and cultural studies, process drama for Chinese and intercultural communication.

## References

Barthes, R. (1967). *Elements of semiology*. London: Cape.
Barthes, R. (1973). *Mythologies*. London: Paladin.
Barthes, R. (1974). *S/Z*. New York, NY: Hill and Wang.
Berwitz-Melzer, E. (2001). Teaching intercultural communicative competence through literature. In M. Byram, A. Nichols, & D. Stevens (Eds.), *Developing intercultural competence in practice*. Clevedon: Multilingual Matters.
Cao, G., & Wang, T. (1993). *Beijinger in New York*. San Francisco, CA: Cypress Book.
Carroli, P. (2008). *Literature in second language education – Enhancing the role of texts in learning*. London: Continuum.
Chang, J. (1992). *Wild swans – Three daughters of China*. New York, NY: Anchor Books.
Chang, J., & Halliday, J. (2005). *Mao: The unknown story*. London: Jonathan Cape.
Cheng, A. (1984). *The Chess King*. Shanghai Literature, vol. 7.
Chu, L. (1961). *Eat a bowl of tea*. New York, NY: Kensington Lyle Stuart.
Culler, J. (1981). *The pursuit of signs: Semiotics, literature, deconstruction*. London: Routledge & Kegan Paul.
Culler, J. (1997). *Literary theory. A very short introduction*. Oxford and New York, NY: Oxford University Press.

Culler, J. (2002). *The pursuit of signs*. London and New York, NY: Routledge.

Guo, X. (2007). *A concise Chinese-English dictionary for lovers*. London: Chatto & Windus.

Hay, T. (2008). *China's proletarian myth: The revolutionary narrative and model theatre of the cultural revolution*. Lambert Academic.

Hay, T., & Wang, Y. (2010, August). *'Migratory' literature: A 'Third Place' for intercultural teaching and learning of Chinese as a second language?* The International Conference on the Development and Assessment of Intercultural Competence: Aiming for the "Third Place", Tucson, AZ, USA.

Hodge, B., & Louie, K. (1998). *The politics of Chinese language and culture, the art of reading dragons*. London and New York, NY: Routledge.

Kehrer, G., Hunter, J., & McGlynn, H. (1990). Internationalizing freshman composition I and Ii through literature and film: A cross-cultural approach. *Community/Junior College*, *14*, 359.

Kostera, M. (2006). The narrative collage as research method. *Storytelling, Self, Society*, *2*, 5–27.

Kramsch, C. (1993). *Context and culture in language teaching*. Oxford: Oxford University Press.

Kramsch, C. (1999). Thirdness. The intercultural stance. In T. Vestergaard (Ed.), *Language, culture and identity* (pp. 41–58). Aalborg: Aalborg University Press.

Lai, M. (1964). *A history of Chinese literature*. London: Cassell.

Lao, S. (1980). *Ma and son*. (Jean M. James, Trans.). San Francisco, CA: Chinese Materials Center.

Lau, G. (2002). The use of literary texts in primary level language teaching in Hong Kong. *Journal of Hong Kong Teachers' Centre*, *1*, 172–179.

Lewis, J. (2002). *Cultural studies – The basics*. London: Sage.

Liddicoat, A., Lo Bianco, J., & Crozet, C. (1999). *Striving for the third place: Intercultural competence through language education*. Melbourne: Language Australia.

Liu, H. (2005). New migrants and the revival of overseas Chinese nationalism. *Journal of Contemporary China*, *14*, 291–316. doi:10.1080/10670560500065611

Louie, K. (1986). *Inheriting tradition: Interpretations of the classical philosophers in communist China 1949–1966*. Hong Kong: Oxford University Press.

Louie, K. (1987). *Teaching the cultural components of Chinese*. Sydney: Centre for the Study of Australian-Asian Relations.

Louie, K. (1989). *Between fact and fiction: Essays on post-Mao Chinese literature and society*. Wild Peony Pty.

Louie, K. (2000). Constructing Chinese masculinity for the modern world: With particular reference to Lao She's The Two Mas. *The China Quarterly*, *164*, 1062–1078. doi:10.1017/S0305741000019305

Louie, K. (2002). *Theorising Chinese masculinity: Society and gender in China*. Cambridge and Oakleigh: Cambridge University Press.

Lu, H. S. (2008). Popular culture and body politics: Beauty writers in contemporary China. *Modern Language Quarterly*, *69*, 167–185. doi:10.1215/00267929-2007-030

Luchtenberg, S. (1989). Migrant literature in intercultural education. *Journal of Multilingual and Multicultural Development*, *10*, 365–381. doi:10.1080/01434632.1989.9994384

Magistad, M. K. (2006). Chinese migrants: Refreshing reporting about a longtime trend. *Nieman Reports*, *60*, 17–18.

Matos, A. G. (2005). Literary texts: A passage to intercultural reading in foreign language education. *Language and Intercultural Communication*, *5*(1), 57–71. doi:10.1080/14708470508668883

Porter, D. (2011). The crisis of comparison and the world literature debates. *Profession*, *15*, 244–258. doi:10.1632/prof.2011.2011.1.244

Schewe, M. (1998). Culture through literature through drama. In M. Byram & M. Fleming (Eds.), *Language learning in intercultural perspective* (pp. 204–221). Cambridge: Cambridge University Press.

Scott, J. (2006). Textual analysis. In V. Jupp (Ed.), *The sage dictionary of social research methods* (pp. 297–298). London: Sage.

Tan, A. (1989). *The Joy Luck Club*. New York, NY: G. P. Putnam's Sons.

Voss, B. L. (2005). The archaeology of overseas Chinese communities. *World Archaeology*, *37*, 424–439. doi:10.1080/00438240500168491

Wang, Y. (2008). *Reading Chinese literature or reading China – An intercultural thematic reading approach in the teaching of Chinese literature in the teaching of Chinese as a second language (TCSL) curriculum*. Guiyang: Guizhou University Press.

Wang, Y. (2011). Drama-in-education and teaching Chinese as a second language – Introduction and case study. In Y. Wu (Ed.), *Chinese language globalization studies* (pp. 129–143). Beijing: The Commercial Press.

Wang, Y., & Hay, T. (2011). Application of literary texts to intercultural education of Chinese. *Yunnan Normal University Journal* (Version of Teaching Chinese as a Second Language), *9*(3), 66–75.

# Constructing the 'rural other' in post-soviet Bishkek: 'host' and 'migrant' perspectives

Moya Flynn[a] and Natalya Kosmarskaya[b]

[a]Central and East European Studies, University of Glasgow, Glasgow, UK; [b]Russian Academy of Sciences, Institute of Oriental Studies, Moscow, Russia

This article takes as its focus post-Soviet Bishkek and explores the arrival to the city of a Kyrgyz migrant population and the perceptions of and reactions to this migrant population on the side of long-term residents (predominantly ethnic Kyrgyz [Russian-speaking], ethnic Russian, and other Russian-speaking communities). The article explores the way migrants are constructed and represented in the language of long-term residents. The data reveals an anti-migration discourse on the side of the long-term residents as the migrants are identified as culturally (e.g. not 'urban'); linguistically (e.g. Kyrgyz speaking having poor Russian); and behaviourally (e.g. uncivilised) as not being part of their past, present or future vision of Bishkek. The article looks also at the ways in which migrants themselves perceive their position in Bishkek. Their narratives highlight the diversity present amongst the migrant population, and demonstrate a counter-representation of themselves and their place within a changing city, which in its very pragmatism and realism, contests the simplistic representation favoured by the long-term residents. The article reveals important insights into emerging notions of both urban identity and Kyrgyz identity in the post-Soviet period, where linguistic and ethnic boundaries become blurred and moveable and new categories of inclusion and exclusion are constructed.

В центре внимания данной статьи – миграция киргизов из разных частей Киргизской республики в столицу, город Бишкек, и отношение к этим мигрантам со стороны старожилов города (это так называемые городские, русскоязычные киргизы, а также собственно русские и представители других русскоязычных этнических групп). Для авторов особенно важно показать, как ситуация вокруг мигрантов и сами мигранты представлены в дискурсе старожилов. Анализ собранных эмпирических материалов свидетельствует о том, что этот дискурс носит анти-мигрантский характер: 'приезжие' видятся как люди, не принадлежащие ни прошлому, ни настоящему, ни будущему города, поскольку они 'другие' культурно (не городские), лингвистически (в основном киргизоязычные и плохо говорят по-русски) и с точки зрения поведенческих моделей ('нецивилизованные')

В статье также уделяется важное внимание тому, как сами мигранты видят свою жизнь в городе. Их нарративы показывают, как разнородны мигранты и траектории их адаптации к городским условиям, хотя всё это воспринимается старожилами в едином ключе. Прагматично-реалистичная картина выживания и постепенного 'движения вверх' ставит под сомнение упрощённые представления старожилов о 'приезжих'. Авторы также выявляют важные грани собственно городской и киргизской идентичности в постсоветский период, когда этнические и языковые границы расплываются, уступая место новым формам социального исключения и адаптации.

## Introduction

From the late Soviet period onwards, the number of migrants arriving in Bishkek, predominantly from rural areas, significantly increased.[1] The migrants' arrival and presence have contributed to and partially shaped the considerable socioeconomic, political and cultural changes which are under way within the urban space of the capital. In this article, we explore the arrival and presence of the migrant population and the perceptions and reactions to them amongst long-term residents (*starozhily*) through focusing upon the predominantly antagonistic discourse which has developed. Turning our attention to the migrants' perspective, we also explore their perceptions of arriving to Bishkek, the way they place themselves in the city and how their self-representation may challenge that which is applied to them by the long-term residents. Through this, we identify the divisions that exist amongst the migrant population where some migrants are seen as 'other' and 'not urban' along cultural and linguistic lines. Through its dual analysis the paper reveals important insights into notions of urban identity in post-Soviet Bishkek, often related to Soviet rooted discourses about what is 'urban/civilised', but also related to new understandings of what is 'Kyrgyz', where socioeconomic, linguistic and ethnic boundaries become blurred and new categories of inclusion and exclusion are constructed.[2]

## Migration and the changing cultural-linguistic space of Bishkek

During both the Soviet and post-Soviet periods, migration has been an important factor in shaping the urban character of Bishkek, in a linguistic, ethnic and cultural sense. During the Soviet period Bishkek (Frunze at the time) was very much a 'Russian' city. As with other urban centres in Central Asia it experienced the arrival of large numbers of Russian and Russian-speaking settlers, who were central to the expansion and consolidation of the Soviet state, and its forms of economic and industrial production. Non-Kyrgyz residents in fact made up the majority of the city's population until 1991. In the late Soviet and post-Soviet period the situation shifted dramatically due to the large out-migration of Russians[3] and the arrival of Kyrgyz from other regions of the country. By 1989, the percentage of ethnic Kyrgyz had risen to 22.9, whilst the percentage of ethnic Russians had fallen to 55.7 (Svodnyi tom, 1992, p. 6). By 1999, the corresponding figures were 52.2% and 33.2% (Naselenie Kirgizstana, 2000, p. 78), and in 2009, 58.6% and 26%.[4]

The make-up of this migration movement during the Soviet period shaped the urban space of Bishkek as the arrival and relative dominance of Russian and Russian-speaking settlers led to the consolidation of a Soviet/Russified culture and lifestyle. The majority of the Kyrgyz population continued to live in rural areas, and where movement did occur, this was primarily for higher education. Kyrgyz young people who remained in the city entered the local bureaucracy and intelligentsia, and formed the basis for the present day Russified Kyrgyz urban population. Gradually, these Kyrgyz (often now 'second generation' urban) moved closer to the Russian and Russian-speaking population in terms of language, social status, lifestyle and cultural norms. The Kyrgyz people are one of the most Russified ethnic groups in the FSU and the most Russified in Central Asia.[5] These new residents became known as 'urban Kyrgyz', where the most relevant and important component of their (self)-identification was this 'urban-ness'. As one of our respondents, son of Soviet era migrants and a university teacher stated when asked where are you from: 'I am from the city. I am an urbanite (*gorodskoi*)'.

Increased levels of Kyrgyz migration occurred to Bishkek from rural areas in the later period of the Soviet Union, due to an increase in the size of the rural population and rising unemployment in the agricultural sector (Anderson, 1999, p. 67). In 1990, as restrictions on the movement of people were reduced, a new wave of rural youth arrived to the city. Unlike previous migrants, the newer group of migrants became culturally and economically marginal in what was still a predominantly Russified linguistic and cultural environment. This new group of migrants, arriving to the city amidst the context of the nationalist uprising and revival of the early 1990s, as Kolstoe (1998) suggests 'soon formed a reservoir of restiveness and frustration of great value to the Kyrgyz nationalists' (pp. 234–235). Although the migrants identified the city as 'alien' and 'other' in a sociocultural rather than a strictly ethnic sense, their discontent, in the first instance, was directed against Kyrgyzstani Russians.

The 'discomfort' that was felt by long-term Russian residents regarding the ways in which the urban environment was changing with the arrival of rural migrants, began to be experienced also by Kyrgyz 'urbanites'. Furthermore, the friction that started to emerge between 'urban' and 'migrant' Kyrgyz furthered the closeness of the relationship between urban Kyrgyz and Russians. Kosmarskaya's research (2006), conducted between 1994 and 1998, primarily points to the distinction being made between rural and urban Kyrgyz by Russians, which at this point they more vehemently expressed than did Kyrgyz 'old residents'. This was due to the heightened levels of Kyrgyz nationalism existing at the time and appeals for 'Kyrgyz' unity. The way in which Kyrgyz 'old residents' increasingly began to identify with their Russian neighbours[6] sheds light on the emerging 'Kirgiz' – 'Kyrgyz' divide. Kirgiz (in Russian) are usually Russified urban dwellers. 'Kyrgyz' (in Kyrgyz) are Kyrgyz-speaking people, although they might have some knowledge of Russian, who are frequently rural, and/or from regions with a negligible presence of Russians. These terms have become part of everyday communication in Kyrgyzstan, and were present in our respondents' narratives. Their evolution, which transgresses ethnic and linguistic boundaries, emerges in more detail in our empirical analysis below.

From 2000, a further change in the nature of migration movements impacted upon the urban mosaic of Bishkek. In the 1980s and early 1990s, the majority of migrants were from the North.[7] However, by the mid 2000s, the numbers of people moving from the South rose significantly, connected with the 'Tulip Revolution' of March 2005, the change in the presidency from Askar Akaev to a Southern president, Kurmanbek Bakiev, and a shift in the political elite and personnel at all levels of the state bureaucracy and in business from Northern to Southern.[8] The migration movements described above, from the late 1980s onwards,[9] were accompanied by the construction of 'new settlements' (*novostroiki*) around Bishkek.[10] This 'migration belt' is closely associated with the 'illegal' seizure of land by migrants, which has occurred to ensure access to land and settlement in the city.[11] Although the idea of '*nakhalovka*' – districts made up of slums, constructed on the outskirts of Soviet and post-Soviet cities – is not specific to Kyrgyzstan,[12] it is unusual in Bishkek due to the mass nature of the phenomenon, its repetitive character, the inadequate state response, and the correlation of each new wave of seizures and subsequent 'illegal settlements' with social upheaval and popular unrest in the country.

Central Asia, and Kyrgyzstan, have long been affected by the movement of people, yet, as suggested above, with the end of the Soviet Union in 1991, and the mass political, economic, and social change this engendered, migration has taken new forms. There is significant movement out of Central Asia, particularly from Uzbekistan, Kyrgyzstan and

Tajikistan, to Russia and Kazakhstan. Research exploring this external labour migration from Kyrgyzstan has focused on its nature, consequences, and on the situation of migrants in the destination countries (Abashin, 2013; Doolotkeldiyeva, 2009; Olimova & Olimov, 2010; Ruget & Uzmanalieva, 2008; Reeves, 2009, 2011b; Schmidt & Sagynbekova, 2008; Thieme, 2012). Similar to what has been described above with regards to Bishkek, internal labour migration has dominated across the wider post-Soviet region due to economic decline, ineffective reform of the rural economy and rising unemployment particularly in rural areas.[13] Some research has been conducted on the internal labour migration going on within Central Asian states (Alymbaeva, 2006, 2008; Ilkhamov, 2001; Schroeder, 2010; Yessenova, 2005).

Bishkek, however, presents a particularly interesting and specific case in terms of its experience of internal migration for a number of reasons: the present day migration taking place is primarily from the South to the North of the country, reflecting the striking disparity in economic development between the two regions; Bishkek, compared to other urban centres in Kyrgyzstan, is the main destination for internal migrants from all regions of the country; and the close relationship between political uprisings and subsequent social upheaval and increased migration and the construction of new settlements around the city. This context is significant for understanding the narratives of both long-term residents and migrants below.

## Constructing the 'rural other'

Our analysis of the narratives of both long-term residents and migrants is based upon empirical data, gathered during fieldwork carried out in 2008 and 2011 in the city of Bishkek. The empirical data was gathered by three researchers, two Russian and one British, and comprises 80 in-depth interviews carried out in the city and new settlements with long-term residents (including Russians, Kyrgyz, Koreans, Uigurs and Ukrainians) and migrants (Kyrgyz). Informing the analysis is data from ethnographic observations of life in the city and new settlements, and analyses of the local press, although this is not presented in this article. The majority of the interviews were carried out in Russian, reflecting respondents' choice and their ability in speaking Russian. A number of the interviews in the new settlements were carried out in Kyrgyz, through an interpreter. These interviews were then fully transcribed and translated into Russian, and together with the other transcribed interviews, analysed in Russian, using NVivo 10 sofware. Codes were based upon recurring and emerging themes. The analysis below is structured around the key themes which emerged from the detailed process of coding of the gathered data, thus prioritising our respondents' perspectives.

The interrelated themes in the narratives of long-term residents,[14] 'South-North'; *novostroiki* (new settlements) and *samozakhvaty* (self-seizures of land); and *beskul'tur'ye* (lack of culture) are woven together in the predominantly anti-migrant discourse which emerges. Through the language used when talking around these themes migrants are constructed as the 'rural other'.[15]

In Bishkek, we saw how long-term residents primarily associated migrants with those people arriving from the South, and then attributed to them particular negative characteristics. This is despite the fact that there was very little, if any, contact between long-term residents and migrants, especially those migrants living in the new settlements. This suggests a much deeper reason for the enmity. In this case, the question of 'where are you from' is clearly much more important that the fact of being a migrant per se. The placing according to 'region', 'clan' and 'kin' in Kyrgyzstan, particularly in more rural areas, is an important way of positioning oneself and others, in relation to place, but often in a positive sense (Beyer, 2011; Reynolds, 2012, p. 288). Yet, in the language of the city's long-term residents, it appears to be a way of marking those that 'don't belong'. Respondents spoke of how differences in the Kyrgyz nation can be defined according to particular characteristics of those from the North and South. Amongst our respondents, the characteristics of people from the North were seen as 'good' (reliable; strong; honest) whereas those from the South were seen to possess the opposite 'bad' features (unreliable; weak; dishonest). This characterisation was more prevalent amongst urban Kyrgyz long-term respondents (see also discussion on page 8 below), whereas Russians tended to primarily see 'all migrants' as coming from the South.

The difference between new migrants from the South and long-term residents is constructed by the latter in an essentialist way as something that is unchanging, and will not shift over time. This is reflected in comments such as '…those from the Northern regions of the republic and those from the South, they are from the beginning, through blood, somehow made to be hostile to one another'. The stereotype of 'Southerner' frequently exists alongside a comparison with Uzbeks, who are often viewed negatively. Statements like '*Oshskie* (people from Osh)…it is as if they are Uzbeks' were made.[16] Attitudes towards 'Southerners' and their persistent association with Uzbeks reflect the complicated and sensitive issue of the relationship between Kyrgyz and Uzbeks in the South of Kyrgyzstan.[17] Southern Kyrgyz are not Uzbeks; nevertheless, as evidenced through our research, the transmission of negative stereotypes from one group to another (from Uzbeks to Southern Kyrgyz, by Northern Kyrgyz) is clearly operating.[18]

Another common tendency is for long-term residents to discuss the arrival of migrants using phrases such as: *ponaekhali* (they descended upon us),[19] *zapolonili* (they flooded us), *naplyv* (influx); *nashestvie* (invasion), etc. This use of 'aquatic' and other pejorative language has been identified in studies of migration, particularly those which explore the significance of discourse (popular, media and academic) on the construction and perception of migrants and refugees, and the ways in which these discourses both serve to exaggerate the impact of migration and to hide the individual stories behind such migration (De Haas, 2006, p. 6; Crush & Dodson, 2007, p. 444; Pulitano, 2013, p. 3). From our observations, these terms seem to be used unconsciously and easily by the long-term residents.[20]

The presence of 'Southern' migrants and *novostroiki* and *samozakvaty* are firmly linked in the minds of long-term residents.[21] The statements made point to the wider concerns of long-term residents connected with living in the city during a period of social upheaval: a lack of acceptance of the way in which the city is changing and an identification of the newcomers as not urban:

> And who is grabbing the land? Southerners are grabbing the land. You know, when it was the revolution, when they all arrived here, they were told, go ahead, take the land… and now this ring is all around the city…but it is not the urbanites (*ne gorodskie*). (female, Russian, 1941, higher education, researcher)[22]

Migrants are seen by long-term residents as having constructed the 'ugly new settlements' through illegal means, which, as Sanghera and Satybaldieva (2012) suggest, serves to 'delegitimatise their legal and moral status as citizens and persons' (p. 103). Furthermore, the new settlements are identified as being detrimental to the city landscape, where the migrant residents are not 'making an effort' to fit in with what is seen as urban:

> R: It is becoming more 'Southern', they build such awful houses, from adobe bricks (*saman*). There is no gas there, no electricity.

I: So why does it worry you, you don't live there, you don't go there?

R: Because of the general image it gives – it is the capital after all. With time people stand on their feet, they have to develop, to improve themselves. Here, it is the other way around, everything is getting worse. (female, Kyrgyz, 1984, student)

The final theme, 'lack of culture' (*beskul'tur'ye*), which emerged from the narratives of long-term residents, is interwoven with the themes above, but strongly reflects the expectations of the city rooted in the late Soviet period, and Soviet ideas of 'culturedness' (*kul'turnost'*).[23] Claims against migrants focus on concerns about the standards of culture and education of those 'coming down from the mountains', *kolkhozniki* (workers from a collective farm, used here in a derogatory way) who are turning the city into a 'huge countryside', into a 'chaotic city' – '*bardachnyi gorod'*. There are different expressions of this sense of an encroaching 'lack of culture' and its impact upon Bishkek: a fixation on the worsening psychological climate in the city; the decline in everyday culture; the growth of aggressiveness and loutishness (on the side of migrants); complaints about (migrant) neighbours; migrants not respecting their surroundings, untidy, not knowing how to behave in an urban environment and not knowing how to use modern facilities (e.g. toilets, lift, etc); claims that migrants drop rubbish, urinate in public places, spit and so on.

These changes to the city, perceived to be brought about by migrants, conflict with understandings and expectations existing amongst long-term residents about what to expect from the city, that is, an idea of the city as representing 'progress and culture', rooted in Soviet ideology and practice (Crowley & Reid, 2002; French & Hamilton, 1979). This understanding includes accepted ways of how the city should look, that is in terms of its state of cleanliness and order, the regulation of its building and other commercial activity, and also expectations regarding the behaviour, standards and morals of its residents. Both the way migrants are perceived to look and behave, and also the presence of the 'ugly new settlements' where they are resident, are not in keeping with this past idea of a city. In a study of rural-urban migration in Kazakhstan this tendency was also identified. Claims of rural versus urban identity reflect the inequalities between the urban and rural worlds which existed under socialism. Yessenova (2005, p. 662) argues that the legacy of this inequality now allows urban populations to exercise power over arriving rural populations and what they represent. This desire to protect the known intellectual and cultural order of an urban space from often rural migrants has also been identified in other post-socialist contexts. A study of young urban intellectuals in Belgrade demonstrated how they 'protect' their city through a discourse which 'others' newly arrived rural residents (Volcic, 2005). Similarly in a study of Hungarian labour migration from Romanian Transylvania to Hungary, these co-ethnic migrants were identified as uneducated, Romanian, rural people (Brubaker, 2006, pp. 321–332).

A word used by long-term residents about the migrants from the South is the derogative word '*myrk*' (*myrki, pl*), implying 'country bumpkin'. Schroeder (2010) elaborates about the meaning of the term '*myrk*'; someone recognisable principally by their language, behaviour and appearance. Reflecting the findings above, he highlights the perceived uncultured or uncivilised nature of '*myrki*', their inappropriate forms of dress, and tendency towards aggressive and rude behaviour (Schroeder, 2010, pp. 455–456; see also Sanghera & Satybaldieva, 2012, p. 104). With regards to language, Schroeder makes the point that *myrki* are seen as lacking in Russian language skills (in his study of Russian speaking Kyrgyz), due to their use of Kyrgyz phonetics to pronounce Russian words. Overall, as

Schroeder states, 'these stereotypes most explicitly designate the *myrki* as intruders into the urban life-world'.[24]

'*Myrk*' however, also reveals another nuance in the stance of old residents. The 'North'–'South' divide, specific ethno-cultural and ethno-psychological stereotyping, comparisons to Uzbeks, and so on is much more an intra-Kyrgyz discourse. Russians, who more often use the term '*yuzhane*' (Southern), perceive the migrants as 'unwanted newcomers', but without a specific emphasis on their language, accent, appearance, or morals. However, in comparison to the initial post-Soviet period, when Russians feared the arrival of Kyrgyz migrants due to the wider context of everyday nationalism, in the later post-Soviet period their perception of newcomers has become broader and more socially and politically rooted. Similar to the Kyrgyz long-term residents they identify migrants as bringing about urban disorder, increasing social stratification and cultural decay. The label '*myrk*' is now used both by Kyrgyz and Russian long-term residents in relation to migrants from the South and, in broader terms, in relation to anybody lacking good manners and intellectualism,[25] (although Russians do not use the pejorative word '*oshmyak*' implying 'a person from Osh, from the South').

The theme 'lack of culture' demonstrates an attempt to show migrants 'their place', and also illuminates the feelings of humiliation, experienced by urban educated Kyrgyz, who believe that they have been forced to give up their positions (e.g. work places) to those, whom they do not hold in great regard, in many respects.[26] The dividing line between '*kyrgyzy*' and '*kirgizy*' in a culturally linguistic sense already existed (see above), but it has gained greater sociopolitical significance and, as we found in our respondents' narratives, is being more explicitly verbalised. However, there are also cases where Russian-speaking Kyrgyz are seen as somehow 'lacking' by Kyrgyz-speaking Kyrgyz. An urban Kyrgyz journalist told us about a disagreement with a colleague who was himself a migrant from the South:

> He said 'You don't understand the Kyrgyz language, you are a Russian speaker and you do not understand our grammar, etc...' He doesn't consider me Kyrgyz but a Kirgiz woman, not good enough for them. (Female, Kyrgyz, 1965, higher education, journalist)

## Migrant narratives of settlement in Bishkek

The quote above serves as a useful link to our exploration of narratives of settlement in Bishkek amongst migrants. These are perspectives which exist amongst different migrants in Bishkek, their view of the city and their place in it, and their views of and relations with different types of people they might meet with or have contact with in the different city spaces of Bishkek. An important point to emphasise is that the 'migrants' are not a homogeneous group. Although, all of them were not born and brought up in Bishkek, they moved at different points in time to the capital, and had a range of different experiences. Some were more established in the city, having managed to attain a good socioeconomic position and adapted well to life in Bishkek; others were experiencing more difficult and uncertain processes of adaptation. Investigation of these different experiences allows us to explore in more depth who is identified as a 'migrant' and on what basis and further, the presence of various boundaries not only between migrants and long-term residents, but also amongst migrants themselves, related to where you are from, to your perceived socioeconomic, cultural, linguistic, educational and class status, and ultimately your place in the city.

Analysis of the narratives of migrants who were more established in the city reflect how they felt able to assert their position; first, how they resist and counter the anti-migration discourse which exists in Bishkek amongst long-term residents through the identification of other social demarcations present within the city, and secondly, how they distinguish themselves from other migrants who they identify as 'other' and, in their understanding, as not 'urban'. These migrants included those who had recently arrived to Bishkek but were already equipped with cultural and social capital (education, social connections, skills, experience) and/or were relatively well off. The majority of these respondents were not from villages, but from different cities in Kyrgyzstan. Some of them had experience of working and/or studying abroad in China, Russia or in the West. They had come to Bishkek not just 'to survive', or, as in the Soviet period, to gain higher education and settle in the city, but with the more purposeful aim of climbing the property and social ladder. They do not face significant difficulties in adapting to city life, due to the fact that they have often grown up in and lived in an urban environment, however, this sense of belonging did not engender an automatic loyalty to Bishkek. One respondent, who clearly felt very comfortable in Bishkek, reacted with great surprise when asked whether he considered himself a '*Bishkekchanin*' (Bishkekian). 'No', he responded, 'Osh is my native city'. However, having come from Osh he logically took his 'urban-ness' for granted.

Another migrant who was a successful businessman and had studied and worked in China, also considered himself a genuine 'urbanite', and persistently rejected all that he felt was 'not urban', 'rural', 'uncultured'. In his view, these traits were being brought to Bishkek by 'other' rural migrants, whom he labelled as 'petty criminals' and 'provincial losers'. Such a tendency can be compared to findings from a study which took place in Buenos Aires, where middle class residents of the city, themselves 'old' immigrants of European origin, demonstrate resentment against new 'intruders', who due to their behaviour, work ethics, moral values, and so on, are identified as alien within the protected European space of 'la Boca' (Guano, 2003).

With regards to the regional division of the country into 'North'–'South', these established migrants did not notice this difference in their work environment. Instead 'professional achievement' was the key indicator of difference. However, regional difference mattered at the level of everyday life. Migrants from Northern regions did not talk about regional difference due to the fact they were not identified in these terms; furthermore they are living in the 'Northern' city of Bishkek. However, the complexity of social boundaries within the city could be seen in the narratives of migrants from the South, whose appearance and accent were remarked upon, regardless of their socioeconomic position. One respondent, with higher education, who worked in a bank, related an incident which demonstrates the dominant attitude of Bishkek residents towards anybody from the South:

> Recently, they even called me '*Sart*'. Have you heard this word? ... *Sart*, here is used to describe Uzbeks, *Oshskii*. We have a dialect, if I was to talk with a Kyrgyz person here in Bishkek, a local would straight away work out that I was from Osh... I live on the first floor, and these housewives ... until one o'clock, two o'clock at night... they just stay at home, and in the day they do nothing, sleep, sleep, and at night they don't sleep, they go out and chat on the bench outside. I asked them, 'Excuse me please, girls, but tomorrow I have work'. They were silent, then they shouted at me, and reacted very aggressively to me: '*Sart*, we'll force you to leave here!'. (Male, Kyrgyz, 1982, higher education, economist)

However, the multiplicity of this respondent's identity was also apparent. When talking about recently arrived migrants from the South, he stressed his 'urban' identity and his social-educational status. The respondent was critical of the behaviour and lifestyles of migrants living in some of the new settlements and those recently arrived to the micro-district where he lives, particularly regarding the dirt and rubbish surrounding the homes in the new settlements. He was also dismissive of the level of education of migrants living in his neighbourhood with whom he could not find a 'common language', likely meaning in terms of outlook, lifestyle and cultural values. For example, he said he would never throw litter down like they did; that he was educated; and significantly that he did not identify himself as *'priezzhii'* (newly arrived) but as 'urban'.

Amongst the more established migrants were those who had arrived in the capital often during the late Soviet period. These migrants were from rural areas or small towns, and came to the city with the aim of gaining a higher education degree, or of working in industry, reflecting Soviet patterns of upwards social mobility. Their social capital and material wealth increased very gradually, and adaptation to the city was a long and difficult process, securing housing being the most difficult problem. The majority of these respondents now have decent housing in one of the more established new settlements, but this is the result of many years of effort.

These respondents had different perceptions about their place in the city. Those who had been in Bishkek for twenty to thirty years, and who had worked hard to achieve their present relatively well-off status, answered in the affirmative when they were asked if they considered themselves 'urban'. They firmly linked their futures with Bishkek. Others, however, who from time to time left Bishkek to live in the provinces for professional and personal reasons, and also families whose material position had been affected by the loss of a family member (for example the death of a husband), appear somewhat distanced from the city. This is evidenced by their wish to eventually move to a quieter place, a district centre or neighbouring region:

> On the whole, I'm not really a lover of…lots of people, where there are cafés. I'm not really a fan. I'd like to go and live where there are less people, it's better there. I want some peace. It would be better to go to Issyk-Kul', or to Kant. (Male, Kyrgyz, higher education, 1960, businessman)

The lifestyle of these respondents appeared more traditional. Although they might adopt some urban norms, these are infused by rural habits. For example, they will go to cafes to celebrate 'life-cycle' events: birthdays; weddings; the birth of a child; circumcision. Others said they prefer to avoid public spaces, and celebrate these events privately. One respondent spoke of how he would organise celebrations at his house in a manner reflecting the way it would be done in his home village.

In relation to the 'North'–'South' divide, those who were originally from the North recognised the existence of these differences, but did this as 'outsiders', not being involved in or affected by these disputes. One respondent from the North claimed that it is the migrant populations in the new settlements who are divided in terms of 'North'–'South', by 'tribalism', whereas for him and the city population it is not of any concern where someone is from, stating 'tribalism amongst intellectuals doesn't exist, those that live in the centre of the city are "normal", whereas those who are uneducated, they have one concern – tribalism'.[27] Those migrants from the South complained about personal difficulties they experienced connected to these regional differences. For example, a taxi driver from Osh complained that although he had lived in Bishkek for more than twenty years, he was still considered (by long-term residents) as a stranger, and was considering returning 'back home'. This reflects how markers of distinction can continue to identify someone as 'Southern' and not belonging to the city, despite long-term residence in the city.

Significantly, a theme which appeared in conversations with all of the more established migrants, both those who had arrived in the late Soviet period and more recently, is the way they stressed the centrality and importance of being able to speak Russian to a high standard. This appeared to be a marker of belonging and a requirement for living in the city. Such a perspective is in many ways representative of the linguistic environment which existed in the past in the city, but equally demonstrates that despite the increased use of Kyrgyz, the legacy of a predominantly Russian-speaking space in the past persists (Florin, 2011; Kosmarskaya, 2014; Mamedov, 2012; Nasritdinov, no date given, p. 15).[28] Nasritdinov in fact identifies language as one of the biggest obstacles for integration of migrants (those who speak Kyrgyz only) in his study of discrimination of internal migrants. Here this discrimination is echoed in the criticism of the language 'failures' of newer, primarily rural migrants, residing in the new settlements, which we found amongst our established migrants.[29]

Those migrants we spoke with residing in the least developed new settlements appear to be less integrated into the urban space, and face significant problems linked to housing, employment and official status (possession of a residence permit), which then impacts upon access to health care, education and social benefits (Sanghera & Satybaldieva, 2012, p. 103). These migrants have recently arrived in Bishkek from rural areas and small towns which have been most affected by the economic crisis following the transition from socialism. Their main aim upon arriving in the capital is 'to survive', and to ensure the possibility of education and ultimately a better future for their children. Some of the children of these migrants were studying in Bishkek, while others had left to work in Russia. It was interesting to note that, amongst the migrants we spoke with, many were single mothers. Although some were widowed or divorced, many of the women's husbands had left to work in Russia. This vulnerable category of migrants does not receive any targeted support from the state. One of our respondents, in response to a question about benefits for single mothers, reflected on this rise of female headed households:

> Why would I get help, you mean as a single mother? They told me that 'single mothers' don't exist anymore. Half of Bishkek, half of Kyrgyzstan, they are all single mothers.
> (Female, Kyrgyz, 1970, secondary education, kiosk vendor)

The living conditions of these women were very difficult. They lived in 'shacks' which though they had electricity, had no water or heating, and were located on an unmaintained road a distance from the *marshrutki* (minibus taxis) which served as a link to the city centre. The journey to the city centre could take a great deal of time and the women seldom made the journey. One respondent, who worked at a small kiosk at one of the markets nearer to the city centre, would stay overnight there with her young daughter rather than making the arduous journey back to the new settlement.

However, despite their extremely difficult lives, and relatively imposed isolation from the city, these women clearly gained a great deal of support from those living nearby and a strong sense of local communal identity was apparent. Rather than the chaotic and disorderly picture painted by long-term residents and some longer or more established migrants of life in particular new settlements, one respondent talked about the strong relations which existed between herself and her neighbours. Many of the women we spoke with belonged to a 'cooperative' who were putting money together with the aim of establishing some form of business, and in the words of one woman 'we are learning how to live in the new settlements, what people need to do in order to achieve a better life here'.

In relation to the division of 'North' and 'South', for the respondents we spoke with in the new settlements, this did not seem significant. One respondent said:

> I get on well with everyone. Here, despite the fact that we haven't long arrived, we have good relations with one another, we are almost like relatives. Here, although it is the city, at the same time it isn't the city, it is like the countryside, where everyone knows one another, if you don't have any tea at home you can go and ask next door for tea, bread, butter or salt. (Female, Kyrgyz, 1963, secondary technical, part-time market trader)

Another respondent, one of the NGO activists involved in setting up the cooperative described above, similarly talked about the strong connections which existed between herself and her neighbours, and again, the North–South divisions did not appear as significant. She spoke about her neighbours in the following way:

> They are from Issyk-Kul' (in the North), from Naryn (in the North), from Osh (in the South). They are all arrivees. All from different places…we live like brothers and sisters, we are used to one another…. (Female, Kyrgyz, secondary technical, canteen owner)

Although research has pointed to the significance of North–South divisions in certain *'novostroiki'*, and the divisions this creates amongst the residents (Alymbaeva, 2006), this was not evident amongst the respondents we spoke with. The new settlements vary in terms of the length of time they have been established, the wealth of their residents, and the level of infrastructure (roads, water, electricity, gas). In those newer settlements with poorer conditions, numbers of migrants from the South are higher. Our research pointed to new forms of identification appearing in these settlements, which did not prioritise the North–South divide, instead foregrounding a sense of belonging to the locality. One of our respondents, speaking about the residents in the city, was more critical of their way of life, seeing 'city people' as more egotistical. Here, the respondent is framing the closeness of the ties which exist at the new settlement in a positive way, and is critical of the lifestyles of those who live in the city. Another respondent spoke of going to the city, for example, to the theatre or a café, or going to parks for celebrations, such as Independence Day. However, she strongly defended life in her 'new settlement', and said she would not want to live in the city, become a 'Bishkekian' or 'urban'. When she did spend time in the city, she expressed feeling of discomfort and 'otherness', particularly after the events of 2010 (see above). She firmly identified herself as a *'priezzhie'*, however, she also talked about how this was a negative label given to internal migrants from the South by those living in the city:

> On the street, on the bus, 'see the *priezzhie* have arrived, everywhere is dirty'. That's what they say, in the school it is the same…. (Female, Kyrgyz, 1969, secondary specialist, canteen owner)[30]

Insights from these less established migrants provide a way to unpick the stereotypes which underpin the anti-migrant discourse prevalent amongst long-term residents, and the views held of the new settlements both by long-term residents and those more established migrants living 'in the city'. The respondents above represent their lives in the new settlement as different, but significantly in some ways as preferable to life in the city, pointing to aspects which are missing from the city, and unconsciously stressing their rural

Kyrgyz 'roots' opposed to the lifestyles adopted by the urban residents of Bishkek. Although their engagement with the city is limited, they engage with it on their own terms, and shy away from divisive discourses, such as the 'North'–'South' divide, so prevalent amongst long-term residents.

## Conclusions

Through our analysis of the narratives of long-term residents and migrants, we have been able to unpick an anti-migrant/tion discourse present amongst long-term residents and to reveal a whole mix of contradictions relating to urban development in the post-Soviet period. It is possible to see the way in which a particular discourse emerges in relation to a group; a group which is seen to represent all that is negative about the 'new order' in Bishkek and which is seen to threaten the place of long-term residents within the urban environment. Migrants, primarily those from Southern rural areas become convenient scapegoats, who are blamed for the wider difficulties of post-Soviet contemporary life. Interestingly this is seen both amongst long-term residents, and other migrants who, due to their inclusion in the urban environment and more successful socioeconomic status, are often not identified as 'migrants' and align themselves with the long-term residents.

However, looking in detail at the themes which contribute to this discourse, it is often not actually about the migrants but reflects wider concerns about the society and environment in which the respondents live. It is undeniable that the arrival of migrants to Bishkek has affected the social, political and economic order of the city, particularly due to the scale of the migration processes in recent years and the growing number of new settlements on the outskirts of the city. Soviet ideas of what the city represented, and memories of this city, are yearned for and shape current perceptions. Yet, too easily, fears and complaints about this changed life in post-Soviet Bishkek are transposed onto the migrants, and specifically those from the South. When the discourse is unpicked, the wider concerns begin to take precedence, and the centrality of 'migrants' as those to blame recedes. Furthermore, the voices of the most marginalised migrants living in the least developed of the new settlements disproves the picture of them bringing disorder and chaos to the city, and being, for example, uneducated, uncultured and ill-mannered.

An interesting theme which has emerged is how ethnicity and language are being practised and demonstrated in new and different ways, and how this helps to explain the anti-migrant discourse. The cross-ethnic (urban Kyrgyz/Russian) allegiances which are apparent in this case have their roots in a Soviet past, where rural Kyrgyz men and women gradually became integrated into the Russified Soviet urban order – and became 'Kirgiz' and Russian-speaking. As the urban space occupied by the long-term residents is felt to be threatened by the arrival of 'rural migrants', this sense of allegiance is strengthened, as people try to protect what they identify as being urban. However, certain migrants are more easily accepted into the urban space, and are not identified as, and do not identify as, *priezzhie* (arrivees). Language, i.e. being able to speak Russian well, is a major part of this. However, the view from the new settlements demonstrates an attachment to a locally rooted communal identity. Thus, in broader terms, the new solidarities and divisions which are emerging point to the complexity of understanding urban identity in the post-Soviet space and highlight the need to look at how this intersects with factors of location, class, language and ethnic identification.

The discourse that has emerged amongst long-term residents and also some migrants tells us as much about what they perceive to be 'urban', acceptable, and the 'right path' for Kyrgyzstan, as it does about the real impacts of migration on the city. Urbaneness has become for the long-term residents a category of self-identification and a mechanism for defence against the unpredictability and chaos of the environment they are living in; for some migrants it is a label that has already been or wishes to be attained. For the most marginalised migrants, however, it is not necessarily the immediate priority.

## Funding

This work was supported by the Leverhulme Trust, under Grant no. [F/00179/AK].

## Notes

1. The numbers of migrants are hard to estimate due to the lack of a strict system of registration from the end of the 1980s. Schmidt and Sagynbaeva (2008, p. 117) discuss the difficulty of quantifying the scale of internal migration to Bishkek and adopt a much more qualitative, case study approach to investigating the nature of migration patterns in contemporary Kyrgyzstan. See footnote 10 for a discussion of the 'new settlements' around Bishkek where migrant populations are resident, and some estimation of their number and corresponding size of their populations.
2. The article is based on empirical data, gathered during fieldwork carried out in 2008 and 2011 in the city of Bishkek. The fieldwork was carried out as part of a collaborative project 'Exploring Urban Identities and Community Relations in post-Soviet Central Asia' (Leverhulme Trust Ref: F/00179/AK).
3. The term 'Russians' is used in the article not in the narrow ethnic, but in the broader sociocultural sense.
4. Figures from 2009, taken from unpublished census materials gained from informants in Bishkek. It is important to note that the character of urban settlement in Bishkek changed as a result of the outmigration of 'Russians' and other Russophones in the 1990s; however, this was in a quantitative rather than qualitative sense (see also Schroeder, 2010, p. 455). The flats left empty due to out-migration were primarily bought by urban Kyrgyz, by those Russians who remained in the city, and by Russians who had come to Bishkek from other towns and rural areas of Kyrgyzstan. Thus the population of the micro-regions of Bishkek remained 'mixed' although Russians were now often in the minority. In the 'new settlements' on the outskirts of Bishkek, the population is primarily made up of Kyrgyz from other regions of the country. Only a small minority of these new migrants eventually manage to buy property in Bishkek, or perhaps rent an apartment in the city.
5. For a more detailed analysis see Kosmarskaya (2006, pp. 190–198). In terms of language, although the last Soviet census of 1989 indicated that over 98% of Kyrgyz considered Kyrgyz their 'native language', many of them particularly in urban areas had very limited capabilities in it (Fierman, 2012, p. 1082).
6. Schroeder (2010) shows in his later research how, despite ethnic and other differences, Kyrgyz and Russian 'long-term inhabitants' of Bishkek (in his case young people) moved to co-identify as 'urbans' in opposition to newly arrived Kyrgyz migrants.
7. The migrants were mainly from Naryn and Talas region which had particularly difficult economic and climatic conditions. Southern Kyrgyz migrants primarily settled in Osh; one of the reasons for the bloody events in 1990 (see Brusina, 1995, p. 99, 102; Alymbaeva, 2008, pp. 71–72).
8. One of the driving forces of the Tulip Revolution was the rapid decline in living conditions in the South, which contributed to the sharp increase in migration from the South to Bishkek, and to Russia and Kazakhstan.
9. For a detailed overview of these waves of migration see Flynn and Kosmarskaya (2012, pp. 455–459); Kostyukova (1994).
10. Estimates of the number of 'new settlements' vary. At the start of the 1990s, they numbered 17 (Timirbaev, 2007, p. 1); towards the end of the 2000s, 41–47 (Alymbaeva, 2008, p. 67). Following the April 2010 events, there was talk of 50 settlements with populations of about 150,000 – 300,000 (Orlova, 2010, p. 1; Sanghera & Satybaldieva, 2012, p. 98).
11. The seizure of land began in the late Soviet period. The word 'samozakhvat' (self-seizure) appeared in everyday language in Kyrgyzstan at the end of the 1980s. Initially the movement

occurred with the appearance of Meskhetian Turk refugees from Ferghana, who came to Frunze where many relatives and fellow Meskhetian Turks lived. They erected tents on empty areas of land in the south-western outlying districts of the capital. In response, Kyrgyz people, living in Frunze and in nearby villages, began to seize land on outlying state and collective farms (Timirbaev, 2007, p. 1). For a measured and sensitive discussion of the reasons for 'land seizures' and their legal, political and social roots and implications see Sanghera and Satybaldieva (2012); Sanghera et al. (2012). In particular, see Sanghera (2010) for a discussion of the land seizures which followed the April 2010 uprisings, which explores their roots in poverty and social inequality.

12. For a description of the situation in Ulan-Ude, see Humphrey (2007, pp. 183, 199–200).

13. Countries across the Soviet Union had already experienced powerful internal population movements but this was as a result of mass industrialisation and urbanisation, particularly following Second World War.

14. By long-term resident, we mean a person who was born in the city of Frunze, who lived there during the Soviet period, and is still resident in what is now Bishkek.

15. For a fuller analysis of the anti-migration discourse which exists amongst long-term residents and a deconstruction of this discourse see Flynn and Kosmarskaya (2012). As the present article also includes migrant perspectives, the analysis of the anti-migration discourse amongst long-term residents cannot be covered in so much detail.

16. *Oshskie* is often used interchangeably with Southerners (*yuzhanie*) although there are three Southern regions with three different 'capitals'.

17. This issue is complicated due to the violent confrontations which occurred in Osh between Kyrgyz and Uzbeks in 1989 and which were repeated in June 2010. In-depth analysis of this issue lies beyond the scope of this article. Faranda and Nolle (2003, pp. 184–185) explored the ethno-cultural distance between ethnic Kyrgyz, ethnic Russians and ethnic Uzbeks and showed that the least preferred partner for contact (key out group), for both Russians and Kyrgyz in Kyrgyzstan were Uzbeks. In the South of the country Kyrgyz held a much more positive attitude towards Uzbeks than Kyrgyz in the North or East, or in Bishkek.

18. For a more detailed discussion of this association of southern migrants with Uzbeks, and its consequences, see Flynn and Kosmarskaya (2012, pp. 461–462). In her study of 'new settlements' in Bishkek, Alymbaeva also identifies the tendency amongst 'Northern' Kyrgyz migrants to identify 'Southern' migrants as being more related to Uzbeks than to Kyrgyz (2006, p. 89).

19. Interestingly '*ponaekhali*' was found to be one of the most common terms used with reference to migrants from the Caucasus and Central Asia coming to Moscow and Leningrad in the late Soviet period. As Ulinich (cited in Sahadeo, 2012, p. 348) suggests the word means 'they arrived over a period of time, in large enough masses to be an annoyance'.

20. Interestingly the use of these terms is hardly found amongst Kyrgyz politicians, who tend to stress the unity and completeness of the whole of the Kyrgyz nation, avoiding the 'north'-'south' division. However, such terms can be found in the Kyrgyzstani media, particularly in articles relating to the capital.

21. The generalisations are in many ways far from reality: most people from the South in recent years have moved not to Bishkek, but beyond Kyrgyzstan – in the first instance to Russia; 'self-seizures' are far from the most widespread means of receiving land for construction; and the 'new settlements' are diverse in terms of how well they are built, the social status of residents, and also in their social make up.

22. Each interview extract is followed by the gender, ethnicity, date of birth, educational status and profession of the respondents – this reflects sociodemographic data collected during the course of the field research.

23. '*Kul'turnost'* and '*beskul'turye*' are difficult to translate and the phrases 'culturedness' and 'lack of culture' does not completely encompass their meaning. The idea of '*kul'turnost'* that was prevalent in the Soviet period had a wide scope including characteristics related to work ethics, political engagement, personal cleanliness and intellectual self-improvement (see Kelly, 2002, p. 575).

24. Schroeder (2010, p. 456) adds that the term '*myrk*' is given primarily to recent migrants who are finding it hard to adjust to urban life, but that with time migrants may integrate more into city life, and avoid such stigmatisation.

25. See for example Kim (2011), a journalist and part of the Russian-speaking community (herself Korean) living in Bishkek, who describes the reasons for her enmity towards '*myrki*'.

26. In reality, there is no visible competition between migrants and long-term residents in terms of employment. More recent migrants in particular mainly find employment in low-skilled, low-paid sectors. Those migrants achieving higher status employment, are not visible to the receiving population.
27. The use of the term tribalism, in Russian '*traibalizm*', is interesting, as it can imply or allege corruption, not only clan cohesion or kin identification (Gullette cited in Beyer, 2011, p. 455).
28. Officially in Kyrgyzstan, the amended 2010 constitution states that Kyrgyz is the state language, but that Russian is 'used as an official language'. Russian is a compulsory school subject and Russian medium schools and classes are widespread (see Fierman, 2012, pp. 1083–1084 for more detail).
29. Nasritdinov suggests that the ability to speak Russian raises the personal status of a migrant and allows avoidance of discrimination in various areas of communication with official structures (p. 15). Similarly Kurbanova, in her study of rural youth in Bishkek, includes insights from a young rural migrant who stated that 'I felt discrimination with regards to language. If you speak Russian well, you are modernised' (2011, p. 33).
30. In their case study of a new settlement on the outskirts of Bishkek, Sanghera and Satybaldieva (2012) observed how migrants felt 'ashamed' to venture into the city due to the reaction of long-term, 'middle-class' residents (p. 104).

## Notes on contributors

Moya Flynn is Senior Lecturer in Central and East European Studies at the University of Glasgow. Her previous research has explored the return migration of Russians to the Russian Federation in the 1990s and the Russian 'diaspora' in Uzbekistan. Her current research concerns urban identities and community relations in Uzbekistan and Kyrgyzstan, and contemporary movements of migrants from Central Eastern Europe and the Former Soviet Union to Scotland, and their experiences of social security and settlement.

Natalya Kosmarskaya is Senior Researcher at the Institute of Oriental Studies, Russian Academy of Sciences (Moscow). She has published extensively on Russian-speakers' position in the New Independent States (especially those of Central Asia); diaspora formation in the NIS, and, more generally, adaptation of immigrant communities and conceptualization of their position under different ethnic/social milieus. Her current research concerns urban transformations in Central Asia and perception of international migration and migrants in the big cities of Russia.

## References

Abashin, S. (2013). Central Asian migration. *Russian Politics and Law, 51*, 6–20. doi:10.2753/RUP1061-1940510301

Alymbaeva, A. (2006). Kyrgyz ethnicity issues: North and South (in the Case of the Bishkek Peri-Urbans of Qelecheq and Qoq-Jar). *Politics and Society Journal under the Kyrgyz National University, 3–4*, 79–102.

Alymbaeva, A. (2008). K voprosu o urbanizatsii Kyrgyzstana [Questions relating to urbanisation in Kyrgyzstan]. *Voprosy istorii Kyrgyzstana, 1*, 65–77.

Anderson, J. (1999). *Kyrgyzstan: Central Asia's Island of democracy.* London: Harwood Academic.

Beyer, J. (2011). Settling descent: Place making and genealogy in Talas, Kyrgyzstan. *Central Asian Survey, 30*, 455–468. doi:10.1080/02634937.2011.605624

Brubaker, R. (2006). *Nationalist politics and everyday ethnicity in a Transylvanian Town.* Princeton, NJ and Oxford: Princeton University Press.

Brusina, O. (1995). Kirgiziia: sotsial'nie posledstvia agrarnogo perenaseleniia [Kyrgyzstan: Social consequences of rural migration]. *Etnograficheskoe obozrenie, 4*, 96–106.

Crowley, D., & Reid, S. (Eds.). (2002). *Socialist spaces: Sites of everyday life in the Eastern Bloc.* Oxford and New York, NY: Berg.

Crush, J., & Dodson, B. (2007). Another lost decade: The failures of South Africa's post-apartheid migration policy. *Tijdschrift voor economische en sociale geografie, 98*, 436–454. Retrieved from http://onlinelibrary.wiley.com/doi/10.1111/j.1467–9663.2007.00413.x/pdf.

De Haas, H. (2006). Turning the tide? Why development instead of migration policies are bound to fail. Working Paper, International Migration Institute, University of Oxford, Paper 2. Retrieved from http://

www.heindehaas.com/Publications/de%20Haas%202006%20-%20IMI%20WP2%20-%20Develop
ment%20Instead%20of%20Migration.pdf.

Doolotkeldiyeva, A. (2009). Kyrgyz migrants in the city of Moscow. *International Research,
Society, Politics, Economics, 1*, 80–93.

Faranda, R., & Nolle, D. (2003). Ethnic social distance in Kyrgyzstan: Evidence from a nationwide
opinion survey. *Nationalities Papers, 32*, 177–210. doi:10.1080/00905990307129

Fierman, W. (2012). Russian in post-soviet Central Asia: A comparison with the states of the Baltic
and South Caucasus. *Europe-Asia Studies, 64*, 1077–1100. doi:10.1080/09668136.2012.691722

Florin, M. (2011). Elity, russkiy yazyk i sovetskaya identichnost' v postsovetskoy Kirgizii [Russian
language and Soviet identity in post-Soviet Kyrgyzstan]. *Neprikosnovenny Zapas. Debaty o
Politike i Kul'ture, 6*, 225–233. Retrieved from http://www.nlobooks.ru/journals/neprikosno
vennij-zapas.

Flynn, M., & Kosmarskaya, N. (2012). Exploring 'North' and 'South' in post-Soviet Bishkek:
Discourses and perceptions of rural-urban migration. *Nationalities Papers, 40*, 453–471.
doi:10.1080/00905992.2012.685061

French, R., & Hamilton, F. (Eds.). (1979). *The socialist city: Spatial structure and urban policy*.
Chichester and New York, NY: John Wiley and Sons.

Guano, E. (2003). A Stroll through La Boca. *Space and Culture, 6*, 356–376. doi:10.1177/
1206331203257250

Humphrey, C. (2007). New subjects and situated interdependence. After privatization in Ulan-Ude. In
C. Alexander, V. Buchli, & C. Humphrey (Eds.), *Urban life in post-Soviet Asia* (pp. 175–207).
London: UCL Press.

Ilkhamov, A. (2001). Impoverishment of the masses in the transition period: Signs of an emerging 'new
poor' identity in Uzbekistan. *Central Asian Survey, 20*, 33–54. doi:10.1080/02634930120055442

Kelly, C. (2002). A laboratory for the manufacture of proletarian writers: The Stengazeta,
Kul'turnost and the language of politics in the early Soviet Period. *Europe-Asia Studies, 54*,
573–602. doi:10.1080/09668130220139172

Kim, M. (2011). *Sum'rki. Rassvet. Spasenie?* Retrieved from http://marinakim.taboo.kg/2011/10/
20/sumyrki-rassvet-spasenie/.

Kolstoe, P. (1998). *Russians in the former Soviet Republics*. London: Hurst and Company.

Kosmarskaya, N. (2006). *Deti imperii" v postsovetskoi Tsentral'noi Azii: adaptivnie praktiki I
mental'nie sdvigi (russkie v Kirgizii, 1992–2002)* [Children of the Empire in Post-Soviet Central
Asia: Mental shifts and practices of adaptation (Russians in Kyrgyzstan, 1992–2002)]. Moscow:
Natalis Press.

Kosmarskaya, N. (2014). Russians in post-Soviet Central Asia: More 'cold' than the others?
Exploring (ethnic) identity under different socio-political settings. *Journal of Multi-Cultural
and Multi-Lingual Development, 35*, 9–26.

Kostyukova, I. (1994). The towns of Kyrgyzstan change their faces: Rural-urban migrants in
Bishkek. *Central Asian Survey, 13*, 425–434. doi:10.1080/02634939408400872

Kurbanova, P. (2011). *Patterns of migration among rural youth in Bishkek: Modernity and different
forms of adaptation. American University of Central Asia Bishkek.* Unpublished manuscript.

Mamedov, G. (2012). *Russkiy yazyk v Kyrgyzstane: diskurs i narrativy* [Russians in Kyrgyzstan:
discourse and narratives]. Retrieved from http://www.art-initiatives.org/?p=3759.

Naselenie Kyrgyzstana. (2000). *Itogi pervoi natsional'noi perepisi naseleniia Kyrgyzskoi Respubliki
1999 roda v tablitsakh*. Bishkek: National Statistical Committee of Kyrgyzstan.

Nasritdinov, E. et al. (no date given). *Discrimination of Internal Migrants in Bishkek*. Social
Research Centre, American University of Central Asia Bishkek. Unpublished research report.

Olimova, S., & Olimov, M. (2010). Migranty v zone krizisa [Migrants in a crisis zone]. *Druzhba
Naradov, 7*. Retrieved from http://magazines.russ.ru/druzhba/

Orlova, T. (2010, May 21). *Bezzashchitnaia sobstvennost* [Unprotected property]. Retrieved from http://
www.24.kg/community/74589-bezzashhi..bstvennost.html.

Pulitano, E. (2013). In liberty's shadow: The discourse of refugees and asylum seekers in critical
race theory and immigration law/politics, identities. *Global Studies in Culture and Power, 2*,
172–189.

Reeves, M. (2009). Po tu storonu ekonomicheskogo determinizma: mikrodinamika migratsii iz
sel'skogo Kyrgyzstana [On the side of economic determinism: The microdynamics of migration
from rural Kyrgyzstan]. *Neprikosnovennyi zapas*. http://magazines.russ.ru/nz/.

Reeves, M. (2011a). Introduction: Contested trajectories and a dynamic approach to place. *Central
Asian Survey, 30*, 307–330. doi:10.1080/02634937.2011.614096

Reeves, M. (2011b). Staying put? Towards a relational politics of mobility at a time of migration. *Central Asian Survey, 30,* 555–576. doi:10.1080/02634937.2011.614402

Reynolds, R. (2012). Homemaking, homebuilding, and the significance of place and kin in rural Kyrgyzstan. *Home Cultures, 9,* 285–302. doi:10.2752/175174212X13414983522035

Ruget, V., & Uzmanalieva, B. (2008). Citizenship, migration and loyalty towards the state: A case study of the Kyrgyzstani migrants working in Russia and Kazakhstan. *Central Asian Survey, 27,* 111–127. doi:10.1080/02634930802355055

Sahadeo, J. (2012). Soviet 'blacks' and place making in Leningrad and Moscow. *Slavic Review, 71,* 331–358. Retrieved from http://www.jstor.org/stable/10.5612/slavicreview.71.2.0331.

Sanghera, B. (2010). *Why are Kyrgyzstan's Slum Dwellers So Angry? Open Democracy.* Retrieved from http://opendemocracy.net/od-russia/balihar-sanghera.

Sanghera, B., & Satybaldieva, E. (2012). Ethics of property: Illegal settlements and the right to subsistence. *International Journal of Sociology and Social Policy, 32*(12), 96–114. doi:10.1108/01443331211201798

Sanghera, B., Satybaldieva, E., Rodionov, A., Serikzhanova, S., Choibekov, N., & Sultanmuratova, K. (2012). *Illegal settlements and city registration in Kyrgyzstan and Kazakhstan.* Open Society Foundation, Occasional Paper Series, 5. Retrieved from http://www.opensocietyfoundations.org/sites/default/files/OPS-No-5-20120504.pdf.

Schmidt, M., & Sagynbekova, L. (2008). Migration past and present: Changing patterns in Kyrgyzstan. *Central Asian Survey, 27,* 111–127. doi:10.1080/02634930802355030

Schroeder, P. (2010). Urbanising Bishkek: Interrelations of boundaries, migration, group size and opportunity structure. *Central Asian Survey, 29,* 453–467. doi:10.1080/02634937.2010.537143

Svodnyi tom s nekotorimi itogami poslevoennykh perepisei naseleniia. (1992). Results of the post-war population census (collated volume). Bishkek: National Statistical Committee of Kyrgyzstan.

Thieme, S. (2012). Coming home? Patterns and characteristics of return migration in Kyrgyzstan. *International Migration,* 1–17.

Timirbaev, V. (2007). *Samozakhvaty zemli - sotsial'noe bedstvie Kyrgyzstana* [Self-seizures of land – The social disaster of Kyrgyzstan]. On-line project 'Open Kyrgyzstan'. Retrieved from http://www.open.kg/ru/day_subject_timirbaev. 17.03.2007.

Volcic, Z. (2005). Belgrade vs. Serbia: Spatial re-configurations of belonging. *Journal of Ethnic and Migration Studies, 31,* 639–658. doi:10.1080/13691830500109746

Yessenova, S. (2005). Routes and roots of Kazakh identity: Urban migration in Postsocialist Kazakstan. *The Russian Review, 64,* 661–679. Retrieved from http://www.jstor.org/stable/3664230.

# The migrant patient, the doctor and the (im)possibility of intercultural communication: silences, silencing and non-dialogue in an ethnographic context

Elsa Lechner[a] and Olga Solovova[b]

[a]Center for Social Studies, University of Coimbra, Coimbra, Portugal; [b]Centre for Social Studies, Coimbra, Portugal

This paper attempts to reflect on the impossibilities of intercultural communication implied in institutional medical encounters. Drawing from an ethnographic case study among patients of a transcultural consultation for migrants in Portugal, the analysis focuses on the contents and forms of the interaction observed by the anthropologist in the clinical setting. A repetitive pattern of communication between a refugee women patient and her psychiatrist foregrounded the unsaid within the interaction as well as the unwillingness of the refugee to speak about her life with the anthropologist. In this sense, we propose to understand silence as a form of communication pointing to both the condition of the patient but more significantly embedded in the institutional framework of the clinical setting, discursive positions of the participants, as well as their social statuses. Following the theoretical work of Jaworski, Wagner and Winter, our analysis of silence leads us to the critical examination of the question of privilege in intercultural situations pointing to a necessary deconstruction of post-colonial institutional object/subject positions. In practical terms, this challenge corresponds to the work of international cross-cultural psychiatry (in terms of clinical matters) as well as that of biographical research and research on memory among migrants and refugees.

Este texto propõe uma reflexão sobre comunicação intercultural num contexto institucional comprometedor da sua possibilidade efectiva. Partindo de um caso ocorrido no trabalho de campo na consulta do migrante num hospital psiquiátrico em Lisboa, é feita uma análise sobre as formas e conteúdos da comunicação entre os interlocutores envolvidos: paciente refugiada, médico e antropóloga. Tanto o caracter repetitivo da comunicação entre médico e paciente, como a recusa da refugiada em contar a sua história à antropóloga, trazem para o centro da análise a questão do silêncio que é aqui entendido como uma forma de comunicação substantiva. Neste sentido são aqui analisados também o peso institucional do contexto nas posições discursivas possíveis bem como o peso dos estatutos sociais dos diversos inter-venientes. Seguindo o trabalho teórico de Jarowski, Wagner e Winter, a nossa reflexão sobre o silêncio conduziu-nos a uma análise crítica da questão do privilégio nas relações interculturais indicando uma necessária desconstrução da 'dominação incorporada' nas nossas próprias posições de sujeito (médicos e cientistas sociais face a migrantes e refugiados). O trabalho da nova psiquiatria cultural, apelidada de internacional, traduz-se nisso mesmo na prática clínica, bem como o trabalho da pesquisa biográfica junto de migrantes e refugiados.

> History is the privilege that we should remember
> so as not to forget ourselves.
> (Michel De Certeau)

Encounters between migrants and public institutions in the host countries enact structural asymmetries within the very communicational contexts of interaction (Delory-Momberger, 2012; Giordano, 2008; Laacher, 2007; Portes, 2011). In such contexts, language and intercultural communication often slip into silences permeated by significant historical meaning which have been thoroughly addressed in scientific literature (anthropology, linguistics, cultural psychiatry and subaltern studies) film (documentary and fiction) and literary studies (comparative literature and feminist theories). Drawing from an ethnographic work in a migrant consultation at a psychiatric hospital in Portugal, this paper reflects upon the various analytical dimensions of silences and silencing in contexts marked by asymmetries between the interlocutors. Inspired by Jaworski's work, we consider it more productive to view silence not as the opposition to speech, but rather see both silence and speech as integral parts of communication (Jaworski, 1993). Silence is here understood as the non-enunciation of subjectivity before prevalent forms of power. However, we are interested in uncovering the symbolic potential this silence may imply. In our particular research these forms of power are embodied in the relations between doctors and migrant patients in clinical settings, between men and women, and between researchers and the researched. All the above reflect the larger structural inequalities that involve migrants, citizens and institutional experts.

Similarly to Roy Wagner, we focus our analysis on silences as forms of embodied action ('performatives', Wagner, 2012, p. 2) that may raise profound questions about the historical circumstances underlying the unequal relations between subjects and forms of knowledge in situations of inequality. In this sense, the unuttered or confiscated discourse of migrants can serve as a catalyst for the acceptance of the ambivalences and contradictions of institutional interculturality as a way to try to go beyond it. A further practical proposition is made by advocating biographical research as the relational kind of research.

## Fernanda's silences or the monologue of hegemonic knowledge

The case study presented here is based on Lechner's fieldwork in the 'Transcultural Psychiatry Consultations[1]' at the Miguel Bombarda Hospital in Lisbon, carried out between July 2004 and December 2007.[2] The project involved research in the domain of the psychopathology of migrations, medical anthropology and cultural psychiatry, situated in the Portuguese institutional context. Having been granted formal permission by the outpatients' administrative board and the hospital's ethics committee to do the ethnographic work at the migrant consultation (*Consulta do Migrante*), it consisted in: presence during the consultations between psychiatrists/psychotherapists and migrants; participation in team meetings; direct contact with the patients; individual interviews with the practitioners and patients. Research was focused on the migration and clinical backgrounds of the patients, their reasons for attending these consultations. Lechner was looking into the discourses of pain and resilience that could potentially be uttered, announced or revealed in the patient–doctor and patient–anthropologist relationship (Lechner, 2009).

This particular case study concerned a woman in her sixties (Fernanda will be a fictional name), who was attending weekly consultations with one of the psychiatrists of the 'transcultural group'. Fernanda lived in a reception centre for refugees, from where she had been referred to the hospital. The country she arrived from (not her country of origin, Cabo Verde) had been at war when she left (at gunpoint, she said), so she had been brought to Portugal by the Portuguese army. She had several children, each living in a different country, including the USA, Italy and Portugal. Before the refugee centre, Fernanda had lived in one of her daughters' houses in the outskirts of Lisbon but tensions between them subsequently resulted in the cease of communication.

The refugee centre administration had referred Fernanda to the specialist consultations because she had alleged feeling tired and confused while unable to establish good relations with the other refugees at the centre. Besides this, her legal status and accommodation needed to be taken care of, since Fernanda had no passport nor valid personal documentation.

Over the course of weeks and months, Fernanda, the psychiatrist and the anthropologist had met in the hospital, and every time, the interaction would follow a similar route. The doctor would ask Fernanda about her medication routines, about the legalisation progress and about the contacts with her son. Fernanda would repeat practically the same answers over and over again. Over the months, both the patient and the doctor seemed to have settled into a repetitive pattern of interaction. Given the therapeutic objective of the interaction, the unspoken may have been of more interest to the doctor yet he seemed to overlook it. In fact, in Lechner's anthropological view Fernanda's silence meant a lot, despite being influenced by the doctor's authority that clearly shaped, in its turn, what and how could or could not be said by Fernanda.

Despite Fernanda's consultations apparently going nowhere, she insisted on coming to talk to the doctor either to get the medication or for a break in her daily routine. At least nothing specific in her narrative of a woman who had migrated between various African countries and tried to settle as a refugee in Portugal could point to a possible explanation.

The psychiatrist had already arrived at Fernanda's diagnosis: he described it as a 'psychotic' state. The best treatment, in his opinion, relied on keeping the edifice of Fernanda's life intact, since any questioning might have unbalanced her fragile state. Lechner learned about this upon resuming Fernanda's consultation observation after a brief absence: Fernanda hugged and kissed the returning researcher with a broad smile, clearly pleased to see her back in the room. After Fernanda had left, the doctor observed: 'She hugged you. That sort of relationship with the body is not usual in a person who suffers with psychosis'.

It may appear that the doctor was questioning his own diagnosis. Yet that was not the case. He kept his diagnosis and continued to medicate the patient accordingly. One might also ask whether the doctor was opening his evaluation to discussion. But that was not the case, either. The doctor never questioned his diagnosis and went through Fernanda's behaviour without any change of position or transformation of ideas. There was no dialogue between the unquestioned knowledge of the doctor and Fernanda's manifest behaviour *in loco*, neither was there any medical discussion on the evidence of the indicated diagnostic feature. In our view, it is precisely this non-dialogue that may help understand Fernanda's repetitions and silences in that setting. As an outsider doing fieldwork in the hospital, Lechner was not meant to intervene, make comments or decide what to do. So, it led to a necessarily silent and 'neutral' position for the anthropologist position in that particular setting.

Prior to the described event of the psychiatric diagnosis and evaluation, Fernanda had been asked by the researcher to concede to an interview outside the hospital. She replied that her story was 'too sad', and that she did not want to talk about it. In this sense, her silence was not only replicated at the consultations with the doctor in the hospital, but also in her relationship with the anthropologist inside and outside that institution.

Such facts bring forth the question of the privilege of discursive positions of the psychiatrist and the anthropologist as compared to Fernanda's (refugee). The therapeutic setting represented an institutional space laden with power asymmetries which shaped the actions, words and practices of every person within it. Having been originally referred to the transcultural psychiatry consultation by the refugee centre, Fernanda was seen, spoken to and interacted as a patient, a foreigner, a low-qualified migrant refugee and a non-native speaker of Portuguese. In contrast, both the psychiatrist and anthropologist were seen, spoken to and interacted as educated Portuguese nationals, institutional actors of the host society and native speakers of Portuguese. Compared to the anthropologist's and the patient's, the psychiatrist's position within the setting was even further reinforced/legitimated by his alleged authority as a medical expert and the institutional licence to enact it as Fernanda's doctor. Besides this, the gender roles within the setting had to be acknowledged. Such a constellation of asymmetries had resulted in a very restricted space for Fernanda's communication; resulted in an 'abyss' requiring a post-abyssal thinking and post-colonial epistemology to bridge such great differences (Bhabha, 1983; Spivak, 1988; Sousa Santos, 2007). Differences deeply rooted in the privilege of 'the doctors' against the total disadvantage of the refugee patient.

In his thinking about the concept of privilege and how it is internalised by dominant groups, Bob Pease (2006) understands it as the other side of oppression. Following the work of feminist theory and critical reflection in human services (mostly social work but equally applicable to clinical work or social research), Pease indicates two ways of dealing with privilege in work positions and social life: (1) focusing solely on oppression and the oppressed or (2) by paying attention also to the domination contexts and dominant groups. In the first case, there is the 'reinforcement of the structure of invisibility of privilege' (Bailey, 1998, p. 17, apud), allowing the complex systems of domination to rely on the oppression to generate their privilege. The advantages and benefits of the privileged ones result from their membership in dominant groups with access to multiple kinds of resources (material, symbolic, intellectual and political), as well as institutional power.

In the second case – that of becoming aware of one's own privilege – there is a necessary deconstruction of self-incorporated social dominance. The author explains:

> people live their lives trying to attain certain valued aspirations associated with these statuses. Thus, rather than seeing the concepts of race, gender and class as reified categories, we should be more interested in the process of gendering, racialising and classing. (Pease, 2006, p. 17)

Critically exploring the concept of privilege, the author goes on to identify its key characteristics: not recognised by its protagonists, unconscious, naturalised and structuring the world through invisible mechanisms. On the contrary, oppression is directly recognised by those who suffer it, experienced in the body and soul and lived as a violence that does harm rather than mobilizes. For these reasons, privileged groups have become the model of the norm ('normative human relations'), that is, hegemony in person. This applies to social conduct, interpersonal behaviour, communication and intercultural communication. Even though privilege may be partial or relative, it functions as domination through its points of location (social class, gender and race) and its processes of reproduction (communication and non-reflexive acts). Internalised domination is the core challenge for critical reflection and social justice, since it blocks effective validation of the 'others'.

The way out from this invisible mechanism of domination, therefore, can be found in the emancipation of the privileged groups, along with that (old struggled) emancipation of the oppressed and subordinated. To address the potential for members of privilege groups to develop a critical distance from their privilege, Pease turns to feminist theory (Harding, 1995) and subaltern studies: if profeminist men can challenge patriarchal power, antiracist whites can challenge white privilege. In the same way, we can state that anticolonial Europeans can challenge European privilege, and white men practising human service can challenge white male institutional service, as white men doctors can challenge white men's medicine, like doctors *tout court* can challenge their inherited positions of power and knowledge. From the monologue of their self-convinced unquestionable knowledge, doctors can move forward towards a critical reflection and action aware of history and politics. That is what international psychiatry is about.

On the other hand, the silent position of the non-privileged might be interpreted as a form of resistance. In his work 'The weapons of the weak: everyday forms of peasant resistance', the anthropologist James Scott refers to silence as the most significant and effective form of peasant resistance (Scott, 1985, p. xvi). Much of the same view, adds Scott, is appropriate to the study of slavery in the New World. In our case study, silences not only reflected the constraints of the institutional discursive framework (refugee centre and the therapeutic setting) but may have also included projections of the long-acting colonial discourses, which positioned Portuguese nationals (the doctor and the anthropologist) and nationals of former Portuguese colonies in Africa (the patient). Silences reflected the hegemonies (white, European, scientific and medical) weighing upon someone in Fernanda's position, as did her personal life experiences and her traditional African culture, along with her female condition. Ashcroft et al. affirm, in this regard, that 'The "silencing" of the post-colonial voice to which most recent theory alludes is in many cases a metaphoric rather than a literal one' (Ashcroft, Griffiths, & Tiffin, 1995, p. 4). Besides this, Fernanda's silence underlines the materiality of the human body, which is vulnerable with its fears and desires (Lemke, 2008).

Cases like Fernanda's reflect the 'incommunicability' between the citizen and the foreigner, a documented person and one without papers, a migrant and a native, a refugee in a reception centre and a doctor in a state hospital, an illiterate and a representative of hegemonic knowledge. This 'incommunicability' results from the symbolic weight of all those discursive positions; Fernanda's identity had been 'objectified' – as Wagner (2012, p. 12) explains, it would 'not depend on responding to interpellation in given discursive situations'.

Even though Fernanda's account of fleeing the war-struck country 'at gunpoint' would suggest being subjected to torture, traumatic and painful experiences which may have led to such verbal 'incommunicability' (Caruth, 1996; Scarry, 1985), Lechner has no direct data about it. Fernanda never mentioned such topics, nor had the psychiatrist asked her about them. So the silence on these issues appears to be co-constructed. As mentioned above, the psychiatrist was explicit about the need not to ask too much. Fernanda seemed to be playing along. By going through the motions while leaving the traumatic experiences unstirred, Fernanda was performing her patient identity within the immediate therapeutic encounter. In a larger context, her silence provides her with a mechanism of suspending herself in the vulnerable position of a patient in need of medical attention. As long as the refugee centre institutional frameworks could afford to bring Fernanda to the psychiatrist, her unbroken silence may have entitled her to more medical visits to Lisbon.

Being part of communication (Jaworski, 1993), silence communicates meaning, which constitutes a social and dialogical accomplishment (Ashcroft et al., 1995). Hence we need to examine the silence of all the participants of the described therapeutic setting: the patient's, the psychiatrist's and the anthropologist's. Even though the reasons for these respective silences may be partly assigned to the respective discursive positions, it has been created by the interaction setting itself and the non-reflexive attitude adopted by the interlocutor in power.

Intercultural communication may be deemed possible when institutional actors assume and work from the symbolic asymmetries (an important part of cultural psychiatry work). This is called 'cultural competence' in psychiatry and requires the interdisciplinary dialogue between medical and social sciences and the humanities. Rather than essentialising the cultural identity of the patient and 'leaving it unstirred', Aschroft urges for a focus on cultural difference, which is discursively constructed and is always situated. In our case, the difference to be explored lies between Fernanda and the psychiatrist, between Fernanda and the anthropologist and between the psychiatrist and the anthropologist.

## Possible dialogues: deconstruction of incorporated dominance and the work of 'international psychiatry'

The history of cultural psychiatry, in itself, is a history of interdisciplinary reflexion and practice (Kleinman, 1980, 1985, 1995; Kirmayer, 2000, 2001; Littlewood, 2006; Rousseau, 2002), as well as a critique of the modern Western science and societies (Beneduce, 1998; Barker & Stevenson, 2000; Comelles, 2013; Fanon, 1952, 1961; Fernando, 2003; Littlewood, 1990). Doctors, anthropologists and philosophers, driven to the understanding of human behaviour and communication in cultural contexts, include their own professional activities and scientific knowledge in their situated inquiries, very much in the previously indicated movement of critical reflection and 'liberatory knowledge' mentioned by Pease (2006).

One of the features of cultural competence is contextual and historical depth of analysis. In this sense, silences can be understood as more than only a symptom of possible personal trauma. The very context of (non)encounter between a patient and a doctor is to be analysed in its plural dimensions for the sake of an accurate diagnosis: the encounter per se (motivations, institutional setting and subject positions) and the non-encounter *in amount* (repetitions, incommunicability and silences). Individual symptoms, as well as cultural languages of pain and resilience, are to be contextualised in the larger frame of institutional encounters. Thus, a culturally competent work enacts both the ethical and political dimensions of health care. By this enactment, the therapeutic relationship ends the 'colonialist appropriation of the word of the other' (Pandolfo, 1997) thus initiating a project of less formal interaction, understanding and communication. It invites dialogue and relational work. In the same direction, Bahktin (1981) suggested the concept of 'voice' to talk about the relational self, situated in space and time.

Much literature in cultural psychiatry has addressed the 'micro politics' of therapeutic relations and health care. In Finland, a network-based language approach to psychiatric care, termed *Open Dialogue*, has been pioneered at Keropudas Hospital in western Lapland. Seikkula and Olson (2003) reporting on the approach worked as members of the original team. Recent studies suggest that this model has improved the therapy of people suffering from first-episode psychosis by significantly reducing frequent hospitalisation, the relapse rate and the use of medication (Seikkula et al., 2003). This approach has gained widespread recognition in Northern Europe where Seikkula, together with Norwegian psychiatrist Tom Andersen, has fostered an international network of teams using open dialogue and reflective processes in acute-care settings in Russia, Latvia, Lithuania, Estonia, Sweden, Finland and Norway. Open Dialogue method integrates a bigger collaborative therapy trend that started in the 1970s (Andersen, 2007). Collaborative therapy is developed by a worldwide community of practitioners and scholars committed to humanise mental care.

Among migrant patients and asylum seekers in long-term immigration countries like the USA, Canada, the UK or France, transcultural psychiatry has been particularly aware of the political and historical ingredients of the therapeutic encounters. The work of Cécile Rousseau in Montreal, Marie-Rose Moro in Paris or Sumann Fernando and Shushrut Jadhav in London are good examples of that. A detailed analysis of such practices could lead us to an interesting discussion on the influence of cultural acknowledgement into creative therapeutic strategies such as collective consultations, interdisciplinary teams, use of indigenous concepts, art therapy, ethno medicine and cartoons (Jadhav, 2009; Moro, 2005; Rousseau et al., 2006). Such choices engage a counter hegemonic movement of transformation of doctor/patient relationships and scientific knowledge within the medical psychiatric practice and academia. All of the mentioned practitioners are also professors and editors in the fields of medical anthropology, ethno psychiatry and cross-cultural and international psychiatry. Their clinical practice is critically reflected in and by their academic endeavours. In its turn, the latter are informed by the former.

In this sense, a transcultural practitioner would reflect on Fernanda's silences by resisting the temptation to impose a meaning (deemed universal because legitimised) upon her experience. And the non-imposition of such universal meaning (or a diagnosis considered universal) implies the awareness of the structural violence implicit in the power position of the doctor (Farmer, 2004). The exercise of subtracting hegemonic culture from medical practice is basic to the new cross-cultural psychiatry. The proper attribution of a diagnostic feature to a foreign patient varies according to the patient's culture (Jadhav, 2009). In this sense, the same medical symptom can require opposite or different therapeutic strategies as a result of the different cultural meanings involved in the treatment of culturally different patients. Jadhav gives the example of expressed emotions among patients diagnosed with schizophrenia in India and the UK, and adds:

> The past decade of research in medical anthropology and cultural psychiatry has continuously argued that the discipline of psychiatry might benefit from a fuller re-examination of its own cultural premise, rather than focus on how cultural variations in constructs such as Expressed Emotions in different societies could be better explained. (Jadhav, 2009, p. 95)

So the challenge is to self-reflect about the cultural premise of psychiatry in itself, and not only to try to take into account the culture of the other.

This premise/conclusion is useful for the work of both psychiatrists and social scientists, as it allows us to acknowledge the extent to which the place from where we speak and ask our questions might be completely alien to our interlocutors. Likewise, the very language that we use might need an intercultural detour to get to a point of negotiation with the interlocutors. And a third dimension of the communication challenge between asymmetric object positions can be found in the inherited nature of the scenarios of interaction in official institutions (a medical consultation, an administrative interview at the Borders and Immigration Services of the State, at court and in a police department). Therefore, the possibility of inventing alternatives with a view to achieving possible dialogue requires the examination of: (1) the social status of each participant, (2) respective sites of locution and action and (3) history of the communicational setting.

## Memory and the embodied nature of object/subject positions

Trying to understand the available means (diagnosis and incorporated knowledge) that we see at the same time preventing our interlocutors from speaking (through their hegemonic status) leads us into a whole new dimension of the 'duty to know' (*devoir–savoir*): the duty of memory. In addition to the historical memory of the broader contexts of colonialism and post-colonialism, implicit above or of women's condition in societies, authors such as Michel de Certeau (1988) and Derrida (1995) have suggested that memory is a private archive of collective history. Thus, it is material and cultural, even when it has been obliterated by forgetting or fragmentation. Each person's private archive is tangibly stored in his/her body, which is both the source and record of the deposit, presented in the form of *impressions*. Though it might not speak, sing or dance those impressions, each body transports the silences (whether imposed, guarded or carried voluntarily) of those same impressions. Thus, a tangible document of forgetting and obliteration may be encountered in the silences of our interlocutors. In the case of many undocumented immigrants, silence can be a passport to unique possibilities that open up on the margin of the law or in the gaps that exist in it.

In his work about the refugees in African camps (2011), Michel Agier analyses the situation of the refugee, and that of the foreigner, not as an identity but rather as a *place*. The territorial nature of this existential condition of the refugee corresponds to a political status of extra-territoriality and dependency that determines the terms and contents of possible communication with non-refugees. Agier posits his work as a fundamental critique of what he calls 'the partial globalisation' since foreigners, refugees and the exiled of our time are externalised (or internally marginalised) from a possible 'common world'. The same idea was suggested by Zygmunt Bauman in the late 1990s, when the Polish sociologist highlighted the fact that globalisation processes are promoted by globalizers in detriment of the globalised (Bauman, 1998). In this context, borders are no longer points of contact and exchange, but rather insurmountable barriers and walls of inequality, where the unforeseen foreigner becomes the object of 'managing the undesirables' (Agier, 2008). This is true in the Mediterranean Sea, as it is in the Mexican/ US border or the south-eastern European territorial border in Greece, or north-western French/British frontier (cf. Documentary Film 'The Wall' and fiction 'Welcome'). But a consequently metaphorical wall also exists in official communication happening in institutional settings, such as refugee centres, camps and general public services in host countries (cf. documentary film by Fernand Melgar, 'La Forteresse'), such as police departments, courts, medical consultations and schools. Here, we can observe a 'daily-life politics of silence' used by the refugees as a way to survive individual and collective memory. Jay Winter's idea of the life cycle of silence (Winter, 2010) may apply to such strategy in the sense that refugees in retention centres or camps live suspended lives in search of future solutions. So, there are times when only silence can speak, and times when, eventually, 'liberation' becomes possible. Jay Winter highlights, in this regard, that the fact of becoming capable of telling one's story makes people authors of their lives (Winter, 2010), which means that they become entitled and (literally) authorised, emancipated subjects. The stage for such emancipation cannot be found in the over-determined institutional settings of the state for the reasons previously analysed.

Silences, amnesias and fragmentations are traces of that memory which also serves the function of mourning: mourning for the words that cannot be uttered, mourning for the stories that cannot be told and mourning for the amnesia of whoever has been deprived of their subjectivity and thus becomes alienated from themselves. These subjectivities have been rendered invisible through forgetting or historical obliteration. They deserve to be recognised, known and expressed in the tangible form of silences that are heard. Thus, by naming Fernanda's silences, like those of her interlocutors, as we have seen, acknowledging them as embodied, we can go some way towards curing the individual and collective amnesia that has underpinned them from the outset. As in Marlene NourbeSe Philip's (2008) work into the restoration of the memory and dignity of victims of slavery, here too the unspoken past re-enacted/revived in the transcultural consultation needs to be told and revisited. That is to say, there needs to be a testimony that gives account of silences so full of meaning.

In practical terms, this is also a question of language in general, and languages in particular: of those languages that we learn as our mother tongue or as a foreign one; of the languages in which we are versed and versatile and through which we position ourselves on the side of whoever can speak; of those that we have not 'mastered' and which therefore do not allow an equivalent positioning; and of languages that become confounded with the language of one's own subjectivity. In short, it concerns language, languages and speech as both power and empowerment (*pouvoir-être*) both in the *polis* and for oneself, in the good Western hypermodern manner in which we live, namely through new communications tools accessible to a growing number of people in all countries, and social classes (cell phones, Internet and social networks).

The work of restoring silences around Fernanda's case allows us to recognise the need to free ourselves from the rules and canons which ignore all that is uncertain. From the outset, these compromise the exercise of articulating forgetting, amnesia and invisible subjectivities which have ceased to exist or reveal themselves to the more attentive amongst us (belying appearances). This work has of course to be accompanied by a parallel effort at self-reflexivity on the part of hegemonic knowledge that tends to indulge in monologues, imposing pre-existing categories of understanding rather than trying to know more. Despite apparent methodological insignificance, the acts of listening to silence and paying attention to the contradiction between the doctor's diagnosis and the patient's behaviour become moments and sites of substantive production. They can teach us how to tell stories from the gaps in them. As such, this procedure offers not only a methodological and technical challenge but also an epistemological one.

In fact, there is a great deal of knowledge that can be produced from Fernanda's silences, concerning not only the distant historical context of the relationship between Portugal and its ex-colonies, but also the equally colonial history of the framework in which we met her – the psychiatric consultation – (Beneduce, 2009) and the situational contexts of her encounter with Portuguese institutions, her history as a former street-seller or hawker[3] and her status in Portugal as a refugee with children living in different countries. This yields a civic conception of knowledge, which should enable us to escape the conventionalised bounds of how to conduct 'scientific' analyses or interviews in order to allow other meanings – less obvious ones – to emerge. Fernanda's silence did not seem to be a form of resistance in the conscious or political sense of someone who is able to speak but chooses not to do so. Instead, her resistance might be interpreted as the result of a violence and oppression that she experienced throughout her personal, family and generational history as a woman in a particular cultural context who migrated to another African country alone and later took refuge in a European country, the country that had once colonised her own.

Fernanda's silence is comparable to the hugs and kisses that do not fit into the psychiatrist's diagnosis: they resist classification, though did not have the power to question the knowledge of someone such as the doctor. In order for the hegemonic knowledge of medicine and mainstream social science to question itself, there is a need to develop a historical consciousness of the positions of power occupied by their everyday representatives (i.e. doctors and social scientists), as well as a (non-quotidian) capacity to tune into the instruments of knowledge that are our own bodies, beneath and beyond the imperative of macrocephalic rationality, or that which Derrida called 'the dogmatism of the paternal *logos*' (2000).

## Dialogic encounters in contexts of asymmetry: the framework of biographical research

Biographical research plays an important role in exploring the plasticity of contexts of asymmetry in its fields of inquiry. As attested by the work of authors such as Franco Ferrarotti (1981), Gaston Pineau (1996) and the Geneva school in Adult Education, biographical research creates the times and spaces to emancipate 'identity narratives', and forge possible reciprocities among researchers and the researched. Ferrarotti (1981) defended the 'autonomy of the biographic method' in sociology, and pledged for the heuristic value of life stories, life narratives and oral history. He placed emphasis on the *synthetic praxis* of human actions (simultaneously, individual and collective and singular and historical), including speech, thoughts, dreams or aspirations. Drawing from Sartre's existentialism, the Italian sociologist defended the idea that the epistemological legitimacy of biography relies in a necessary shift from a monothetic logic of understanding social life towards an ideographic one. In this sense, life experiences translate social worlds and social worlds are translated by life experiences, stories and narratives, including silent ones. For the researcher to get to know the ideographic forms and contents of (social) life, there is the need to work from the standpoint of what Ferrarotti calls 'the clinical pole of sociology'. Consequently, it is a qualitative, intimate work of relation with concrete people in the field. In this sense, it deals necessarily with asymmetries and differences – sometimes, radical ones, like the ones analysed in this paper.

More recently, Christine Delory-Momberger (2004, 2006, 2009) and Jeanne-Marie Rugira (2008) developed theoretical and practical work about the use of life narratives and the role of the researcher in this work. These two scholars are important names in both fundamental research and action-research with life stories, biographical accounts, processes of biographisation, biographical workshops and sensitive listening. Jeanne-Marie Rugira (2008) questions the place of bodily relations and sensorial expression within research and training in the social sciences dealing with such tools and objects. She argues that the relationship with the body constitutes an incontestable pillar for the collective production of meaning and knowledge. It is that relationship that restores the capacity to learn, adapt and react in a way that transcends automatic socially conditioned responses. Biographical workshops orchestrated by Rugira, as well as by Josso (1991), and Delory-Momberger (2004) develop the skills of attention and perception in order to learn, understand and act within an experimental procedure used in phenomenologically inspired biographic research. More recently, we have developed a research project with immigrants in Portugal based on these workshops, where an attuned listening exercise introduces the participants to an experience of 'shared diversity', or communality in diversity, since each one experiences the same exercise in very different ways. A paper in Portuguese examines in detail the functioning and analytical dimensions of the workshops (Lechner, 2012).

Rugira quotes Simone Weil about the transition from attention to perception: 'Extreme attention is what constitutes man's creative faculty [...] The amount of creative genius in a period is rigorously proportional to the amount of extreme attention'. For Rugira, research, training and social intervention are creative enterprises that involve tracing pathways that open up new possibilities; meanings are unveiled in the process of learning how to perceive, reflect, dialogue and understand oneself, others and the world. The way each person perceives the world both depends upon and determines the experience that he or she has of it. For this, we have to train ourselves to see properly. Merely assessing or examining is not enough. It is necessary to learn through experience, not only with thought. Rugira says that we have to become 'visionaries of our own activity', suspending mindless action and taking responsibility for enriching our own perceptions. We have to denounce crude representations of ourselves, others and worlds, and deplore our own incapacities in order to refine our approach to lived experience, learning to embody that which we know or wish to explain. This involves explaining what we know as experience through the practice of *epoche*, as both practice and attitude, within processes of research, learning and understanding.

However, Rugira also recognises that the human ability to explore its own experience is not spontaneous, that it is necessary to cultivate and train it if we want to do more than merely scratch the surface. Her theoretical and practical suggestions, which Lechner has had first-hand experience of as a trainee,[4] become all the more relevant when we understand Rugira's personal and theoretical background. It is significant that she was originally from Rwanda and witnessed genocide, followed by exile in Canada, living far away from her children and husband and having to struggle to acquire Canadian nationality. From these traumatic experiences, she developed a privileged capacity to apprehend new perceptions of herself, others and the world (she had been a militant educator in her country of origin). In exile, the new perception of herself was a question of survival – as she describes in the below-cited article. Now it is a question of necessity. She says:

> I learned to get in touch with subjective experience and understood myself as a subject. I noticed, with delight, that by experiencing an inner gesture and describing it with precision in a way that suspended ordinary cerebral activity, I was able to develop a richer sensorial response that enabled me to *take body*. (2008, p. 78, my italics)

For Rugira, the survivor of genocide, the body must be at the centre of our research projects. It is the sine qua non of our inhabited knowledge, and can give access to a form of empowerment (*pouvoir-être*), provided it is spoken, shared and divulged.

Here we turn again to Fernanda's silences. Like those of all the other migrants who we can encounter in many different terrains, they teach us more about what an interview is and how we should position ourselves in that delicate work of listening. In the wake of this sensitive listening that hears the silences and lingers on them, the theoretical and practical work of biographical research, namely through biographical workshops, is interested also in the performative, mnemonic and political dimensions of life narratives. These workshops involve exercises in listening, autobiographical writing and sharing, through which participants can experience (if they want and are able to) the difference between sensitive listening and the kind of listening that has no time to look/feel the *resonances* and *impressions* because it has no pauses.

As a dimension of training in biographical research, biographical workshops offer a form of group work in which the *situated* nature of listening is laid bare (each participant interprets the same accounts in his/her own way) and where experiences are reported in all their diversity. As in an African 'word tree' (*arbre à palabre*), where the group sits around a baobab tree, thus providing each person with a unique perspective of that tree that is different from the others', here too each participant experiences a range of possible readings of the same object of contemplation (each account is read aloud). The biographical workshops also encourage the exchange of impressions about the autobio-graphical narratives of the other participants based on the resonances that they provoke in the body. Sensitive listening foregrounds a kind of listening that is anchored in the body – of both researchers and the researched – and which attempts to develop a methodological vigilance to guard against rash judgements that are merely cognitive in nature. The act of knowing or trying to understand from this bodily awareness produces results that are substantially different from the act of knowing based on a head isolated from the trunk, limbs or gut.

But it requires courage to put this into practice in the context of ethnographic research or academic training. It requires a shift to a paradigm of knowledge that is based less on a belief in the objectivity of the objects of social studies and which is more secure about the changing, unstable and unpredictable nature of those same objects. It creates concrete challenges to the status of the parties involved in each research, bringing forth an anthropology of reciprocity (Temple, 2003). The fundamentals of such work are at the antipodes of hegemonic knowledge production and challenge ethnography in very practical terms: reciprocities, asymmetries and coauthorship.

At this point, we are reminded of Fernanda. Having survived other exiles – at the reception centre, in her family, in herself and in the country that received her as a refugee – she was finally exiled from herself, like so many other migrant women, who suffer in body and mind what words cannot express, what words only mask in the contradiction of wanting to speak silences, obliterations and the amnesias of history, which are collective and leave out the echoes of the cries of pain and affliction.

In fact, referring back to the original aim of this paper, we can say that silences and silencing in our ethnographic work reflected not only the confiscated voice of the patient but also that of the doctor and the anthropologist. Like the characters in a play on post-colonial encounters set in the context of contemporary south/north relations and migrations, all parties involved cohabited a shared historical inheritance but with fundamentally different discursive positions.

The position (material, symbolic and political) of the interlocutors is then decisive for understanding the meaning and forms of communication and dialogue in the reported case study, requiring a concomitant shift if the aim is to overcome the impossibility of dialogue. By escaping the monologue of the medical hegemonic knowledge, cross-cultural/

international psychiatry enables to create spaces of encounter and therapeutic strategies that help critically examine the patient–doctor relation, as well as their respective knowledge. In the same way, biographical research posits researchers and the researched in a kind of interaction that brings to the front the relational dimension of ethnographic work. The intrinsic relational nature of these interactions, in its turn, brings the possibility of communication and inter-knowledge. If 'all knowledge is inter-knowledge' (Sousa Santos, 2007), the advocacy of reason and truth in one sole subject position does not proceed. An ecology of knowledge is the epistemic way to go beyond abyssal thinking and colonial action over the other.

If we have to choose between a grotesque obedience to ways of thinking and doing research that fail to listen to the words not said, and the courage to write about silences that 'take body' in our fieldwork, it would seem more useful to opt for the latter. For it is there that the silences are in fact expressed. As Nourbese Philip says:

> When silence is
> Abdication of Word tongue ... and lip
> Ashes of once in what was
> ... Silence
> Song Word Speech
> Might I ... like Philomena ... sing
> Continue
> Over
> Into
> ... pure utterance.

(Marlene NourbeSe Philip, 1989)

## Funding

This research was funded by The Portuguese National Science Foundation (Fundação para a Ciência a Tecnologia). [grant number FCT/BPD/11548/2002], Instituto de Ciências Sociais da Universidade de Lisboa, [grant number FCT/BPD/26099/2005], CEAS/ISCTE, Lisbon, Portugal.

## Notes

1. The transcultural consultation (*Consulta do Migrante*) at Miguel Bombarda was open to public in 2004 after the initiative of a small group of practitioners with experience with foreign patients or clinical settings. Namely, the founder director of this service had worked for several years in the Portuguese Hospital of Macau, until the transition of the territory Portuguese sovereignty to China.
2. Post-doc project granted by the Portuguese National Science Foundation which produced, among other scientific and academic outputs, an edited volume on 'Migrations, health and cultural diversity' (Migração, Saúde e Diversidade Cultural, ICS, Lisbon: 2009).
3. Hawkers are agents of a type of trade that economics dismisses as 'informal'. However, in Cape Verde, this type of activity forms an important axis of the transnational economic and cultural movements that traverse this island country of migrants and connect it to the world. It involves networks of men and (especially) women that operate at the (often silenced) margins of the economic and cultural hegemonies that make up today's globalised world (Marzia Grassi, ICS, 2003).
4. Biographical workshop (*Atelier biographique*), Univerity of Paris, June 2004.

## Notes on contributors

Elsa Lechner, Ph.D. in social anthropology (Paris, 2003), is a principal investigator at the Center for Social Studies of the University of Coimbra where she coordinates a research project on collaborative research among immigrants in Portugal funded by the Portuguese National Science Foundation. She has conducted her doctoral research among Portuguese emigrants in France, and her Post-doc project at the Transcultural Consultations for Migrants in a Psychiatric Hospital in Lisbon (2004–2007). Currently, she is a Fulbright Scholar in the USA conducting an exploratory study about the Portuguese in Newark, New Jersey, hosted by Brown and Rutgers Universities.

Olga Solovova, Ph.D. in sociolinguistics (Coimbra, 2014), is a researcher at the Centre for Social Studies in the Humanities, Migrations and Peace Studies Group. She is a member of the project implementing collaborative research among immigrants in Portugal, and of a European project on learning languages online e-learning. Her Ph.D. thesis examines policies of language-in-education that sustain the existence of complementary schools for Eastern European immigrant children in Portugal. Her research interests include language ideologies and policies, discursive construction of cultural identity in multilingual societies as well as multilingual and biliterate literacy practices.

## References

Agier, M. (2008). *Gérer les indésirables. Des camps de réfugiés au gouvernement humanitaire* [Managing the undesirables. Refugee camps and humanitarian government]. Paris: Flammarion.

Agier, M. (2011). *Le couloir des exilés. Être étranger dans un monde commun* [Corridors of exile: A worldwide web of camps by Michel Agier]. (E. Rosencrantz, Trans.). Bellecombe-en-Bauge: éditions du Croquant.

Andersen, T. (2007). Human participating: human 'being' is the step for human 'becoming' in the next step. In H. Anderson & D. Gehart (Eds.), *Collaborative therapy: Relationships and conversations that make a difference* (pp. 81–95). New York, NY: Routledge/Taylor & Francis.

Ashcroft, B., Griffiths, G., & Tiffin, H. (1995). *The post-colonial studies reader.* London: Routledge.

Bahktin, M. (1981). *The dialogic imagination.* Austin: The University of Texas Press.

Bailey, A. (1998). Privilege: Expanding on Marilyn Fry's oppression. *Journal of Social Philosophy, 29*(3), 104–119.

Barker, P., & Stevenson, C. (Eds.). (2000). *Construction of power and authority in psychiatry.* Oxford: Butterworth-Heinemann.

Bauman, Z. (1998). *Globalization: The human consequences.* New York, NY: Columbia University Press.

Beneduce, R. (1998). *Frontiere dell'identità e della memoria. Etnopsiquiatria e migrazioni in un mondo creolo* [Frontiers of identity and memory. Ethnopsychiatry and migrations in a creole world]. Milan: Franco Angeli.

Beneduce, R. (2009). Etnopsiquiatria e migração: a produção histórica e cultural do sofrimento [Ethnopsy chiatry and migration:The historical and cultural production of suffering]. In Elsa Lechner (org.), *Migração, saúde e diversidade cultural* [Migration, health, and cultural diversity]. Lisboa: Imprensa de Ciências Sociais.

Bhabha, H. (1983). The other question … Homi K. Bhabha reconsiders the stereotype and colonial discourse. *Screen, 24*(6), 18–36. doi:10.1093/screen/24.6.18

Caruth, C. (1996). *Unclaimed experience. Trauma, narrative, and history.* Baltimore: John Hopkins University Press.

Comelles, J. M. (2013). De la locura como exceso a la locura como enfermedad [From madness as an excess to madness as illness]. In D. S. Lorda, C. G. Rodriguez, & A. C. Vasquez y Olga Villasante (Eds.), *Razón, locura y sociedad. Una mirada a la historia desde el siglo XXI* [Reason, madness and society: A glance to history in the 21st century] (pp. 143–163). Madrid: Asociación Española de Neuropsiquiatria, Estudios, 51.

De Certeau, M. (1988). *L'Écriture de l'Histoire* [The writing of history]. New York, NY: Columbia University Press.

Delory-Momberger, C. (2004). *Les Histoires de Vie : de l'invention de soi au projet de formation* [Life stories: From the invention of oneself to educational project] (2nd éd.). Paris: Anthropos.

Delory-Momberger, C. (2006). Les ateliers biographiques de projet [Formation and socalization: The project biographical workshops]. *Educação e Pesquisa, 32*(2), 359–371. São Paulo.

Delory-Momberger, C. (2009). *La Condition Biographique; Essais Sur Le Récit De Soi Dans La Modernité Avancée* [The biographical condition: Essais on self-narrative in advanced modernity]. Paris: Téraèdre.

Delory-Momberger, C. (2012). La langue coupée. Quand le récit doit faire preuve [Tongue cut. When the story must prove]. In A. Brossat & M. Déotte (Dir.), *Corps subalternes: Migrations, expériences, récits* (pp. 159–172). Paris: L'Harmattan.

Derrida, J. (1995). *Mal d'Archive : une impression freudienne* [Archive fever: A freudian impression] (E. Prenowitz, Trans.). Paris: Galilée.

Derrida, J. (2000). *Of hospitality*. Stanford: Stanford University Press.

Fanon, F. (1952). *Peau noire, masques blancs* [Black skin, white masks]. Paris: Seuil.

Fanon, F. (1961). *Les Damnés de la Terre* [The wretched of the earth]. Paris: François Maspero.

Farmer, P. (2004). An anthropology of structural violence. *Current Anthropology, 45*, 303–325. doi:10.1086/382250

Fernando, S. (2003). *Cultural diversity, mental health, and psychiatry: The struggle against racism*. Hove: Brunner-Routledge.

Ferrarotti, F. (1981). Epistemological and methodological issues – On the autonomy of the biographical method. In D. Bertaux (Ed.), *Biography and society. The life history approach in the social sciences* (pp. 19–29). London and Beverly Hills: Sage.

Giordano, C. (2008). Practices of translation and the making of migrant subjectivities in Contemporary Italy. *American Ethnologist, 35*, 588–606. doi:10.1111/j.1548-1425.2008.00100.x

Grassi, M. (2003). *Rabidantes*. Lisbon: ICS.

Harding, S. (1995). Subjectivity, experience and knowledge: An epistemology for rainbow coalition politics. In J. Roof & R. Wiegman (Eds.), *Who can speak?: Authority and critical identity*. Chicago: University of Illinois Press.

Jadhav, S. (2009). What is cultural validity and why is it ignored? The case of expressed emotions research in South Asia. In S. van der Geest & M. Tankink (Eds.), *Theory and action: Essays for an anthropologist* (pp. 92–96). Amsterdam: AMB.

Jaworski, A. (1993). *The power of silence: Social and pragmatic perspectives*. Newbury Park, CA: Sage.

Josso, M.-C. (1991). *Cheminer vers soi* [Walking towards oneself]. Paris: L'age d'homme.

Kirmayer, L. (2000). The future of cultural psychiatry: An international perspective. *Canadian Journal of Psychiatry, 45*, 438–446.

Kirmayer, L. (2001). Cultural variations in the clinical presentation of depression and anxiety: Implications for diagnosis and treatment. *Journal of Clinical Psychiatry, 62*, 22–30.

Kleinman, A. (1980). *Patients and healers in the context of culture: An exploration of the borderland between anthropology, medicine, and psychiatry*. Berkeley: University of California Press.

Kleinman, A. (1985). *Culture and depression: Studies in the anthropology and cross-cultural psychiatry of affect and disorder*. (A. Kleinman & B. Good, Eds.). Berkeley and Los Angeles: University of California Press.

Kleinman, A. (1995). *Writing at the margin: Discourse between anthropology and medicine*. Berkeley and Los Angeles: University of California Press.

Laacher, S. (2007). *Le peuple des clandestins* [The clandestine people]. Paris: Calmann-Lévy.

Laacher, S. (2009). *Mythologie du sans-papier* [Mythology of the irregular migrant]. Paris: Le Cavalieu Bleu.

Lemke, J. (2008). Identity, development and desire: Critical questions. In C. Caldas-Coulthard & R. Iedema (Eds.), *Identity trouble. Critical discourse and contested identities* (pp. 17–41). Basingstoke, NY: Palgrave Macmillan.

Lechner, E. (2012). Oficinas de trabalho biográfico: pesquisa, pedagogia e ecologia de saberes [Biographical workshops: Research, pedagogy, and ecology of knowledge]. *Revista Educação e Realidade, 37*(1), 71–87.

Littlewood, R. (1990). From categories to contexts: A decade of the 'new cross-cultural psychiatry'. *British Journal of Psychiatry, 156*, 308–327. doi:10.1192/bjp.156.3.308

Littlewood, R. (2006). *Aliens and alienists: Ethnic minorities and psychiatry*. London: Taylor & Francis.

Moro, M.-R. (2005). *Avicenne l'andalouse: Devenir thérapeute en situation transculturelle* [Avicenne the Andalusian: Becoming a therapist in a transcultural situation]. Paris: la Pensée Sauvage.

NourbeSe Philip, M. (1989). *She tries her tongue: Her silence softly breaks*. Charlotte Town: Ragweed Press.

NourbeSe Philip, M. (2008). *Zong!* Middletown, CT: Wesleyan University Press.

Pandolfo, S. (1997). *Impasse of the angels. Scenes from a Moroccan space of memory.* Chicago: Chicago University Press.

Pease, B. (2006). Encouraging critical reflections on privilege in social work and the Human Services. *Practice Reflexions,* *1*(1), 15–26.

Pineau, G. (1996). Les histoires de vie comme art formateur de l'existence [Life stories, a formative art of the being]. *Pratiques de formation,* (31), 65–80.

Portes, A. (2011). Tensions that make a difference: Institutions, interests, and the immigrant drive. *Sociological Forum,* *27,* 563–589. doi:10.1111/j.1573-7861.2012.01335.x

Rousseau, C. (2002). Incertitude et clinique transculturelle [Uncertainty and transcultural clinical practice]. *L'Évolution psychiatrique,* *67,* 764–774. doi:10.1016/S0014-3855(02)00168-8

Rousseau, C., Gauthier, M.-F., Lacroix, L., Benoît, M., Moran, A., Rojas, M. V., & Bourassa, D. (2006). Du jeu des identités à la transformation de réalités partagées: Un programme d'ateliers d'expression théâtrale pour adolescents immigrants et réfugiés. *Santé mentale au Québec, XXXI* (2), 135–152.

Rugira, J.-M. (2008). A relação com o corpo e com a sensorialidade na história de vida: por uma abordagem somatopedagógica [Body and sensoriality in the life histories approach: Towards a somatopedagogy]. In Maria da Conceição Passeggi (Ed.), *Tendências da pesquisa (auto) biográfica* [Tendencies of (auto)biographical research] (pp. 73–93). São Paulo: Paulus.

Scarry, E. (1985). *The body in pain. The making and unmaking of the world.* New York: Oxford University Press.

Scott, J. (1985). *Weapons of the weak: Everyday forms of peasant resistance.* New Haven, CT: Yale University Press.

Seikkula, J., & Olson, M. E. (2003). The open dialogue approach to acute psychosis: Its poetics and micropolitics. *Family Process,* *42*(Fall), 403–418. doi:10.1111/j.1545-5300.2003.00403.x

Seikkula, J., Alakare, B., Aaltonen, J., Holma, J., Rasinkangas, A., & Lehtinen, V. (2003). Open dialogue approach: Treatment principles and preliminary results of a two- year follow-up on first episode schizophrenia. *Ethical and Human Sciences and Services,* *5,* 163–182.

Sousa Santos, B. (2007). Beyond abyssal thinking. From Global lines to ecologies of knowledges. *Review, XXX*(1), 45–80.

Spivak, G. (1988). Can the subaltern speak? In C. Nelson and L. Grossberg (Eds.), *Marxism and the interpretation of culture* (pp. 66–111). London: Macmillan.

Temple, D. (2003). *Teoría de la reciprocidad* [Theory of reciprocity] (3 volumes). La Paz: Padep-Gtz.

Wagner, R. (2012). Silence as resistance before the subject, or could the subaltern remain silent? *Theory, Culture and Society,* *29*(6), 99–124. doi:10.1177/0263276412438593

Winter, J. (2010). Thinking about silence. In E. Ben-Ze'ev, R. Ginio, & J. Winter (Eds.), *Shadows of war. A social history of silence in the twentieth century* (1st ed., pp. 3–31). Cambridge: Cambridge University Press.

# Interpretation, translation and intercultural communication in refugee status determination procedures in the UK and France

Robert Gibb[a] and Anthony Good[b]

[a]School of Social and Political Sciences, University of Glasgow, Glasgow, UK; [b]School of Social and Political Science, University of Edinburgh, Edinburgh, UK

This article explores the interplay between language and intercultural communication within refugee status determination procedures in the UK and France, using material taken from ethnographic research that involved a combination of participant observation, semi-structured interviews and documentary analysis in both countries over a two-year period (2007–2009). It is concerned, in particular, to examine the role played by interpreters in facilitating intercultural communication between asylum applicants and the different administrative and legal actors responsible for assessing or defending their claims. The first section provides an overview of refugee status determination procedures in the UK and France, introducing the main administrative and legal contexts of the asylum process within which interpreters operate in the two countries. The second section compares the organisation of interpreting services, codes of conduct for interpreters and institutional expectations about the nature of interpreters' activity on the part of the relevant UK and French authorities. The third section then explores some of the practical dilemmas for interpreters and barriers to communication that exist in refugee status determination procedures in the two countries. The article concludes by emphasising the complex and active nature of the interpreter's role in UK and French refugee status determination procedures.

Cet article examine l'interaction entre le langage et la communication interculturelle dans les procédures de détermination du statut de réfugié au Royaume-Uni et en France. Il s'appuie sur les résultats d'une recherche ethnographique (observation participante, entretiens semi-directifs et analyse documentaire) menée entre 2007 et 2009 dans les deux pays. En particulier, il s'attache à examiner le rôle joué par les interprètes en facilitant la communication interculturelle entre les demandeurs d'asile et les différents acteurs administratifs et juridiques chargés de l'examen ou de la défense de leurs demandes. L'article est divisé en trois parties: la première donne un aperçu des procédures de détermination du statut de réfugié au Royaume-Uni et en France; la deuxième compare l'organisation des services d'interprétariat, les codes de déontologie pour interprètes, et les attentes institutionnelles concernant l'activité de l'interprète dans les deux pays; et la troisième examine les dilemmes pratiques auxquels les interprètes sont souvent confrontés et les obstacles à la communication qui existent dans les procédures d'asile au Royaume-Uni et en France. L'article conclut en insistant sur le rôle complexe et actif joué par l'interprète dans les procédures de détermination du statut de réfugié dans les deux pays.

## Introduction

Article 1A(2) of the 1951 United Nations Convention Relating to the Status of Refugees defines a 'refugee' as someone who has a 'well-founded fear of being persecuted for reasons of race, religion, nationality, membership of a particular social group or political opinion'. The administrative and legal procedures adopted by signatories to the convention for determining whether an individual satisfies this definition characteristically involve complex processes of cultural and linguistic translation and interpretation. In the following article, we explore the interplay between language and intercultural communication within refugee status determination procedures in the UK and France, comparing the ways in which linguistic and intercultural issues are addressed, in theory and in practice, in the two countries. We will be concerned, in particular, to examine the role played by interpreters in facilitating intercultural communication between, on the one hand, asylum applicants and, on the other, the different administrative and legal actors (e.g. civil servants, *rapporteurs*, lawyers and judges) responsible for assessing or defending their claims.

The United Nations High Commissioner for Refugees (UNHCR) *Handbook* recommends that '[t]he applicant should be given the necessary facilities, including the services of a competent interpreter, for submitting his [*sic*] case to the authorities concerned' (UNHCR 1992) [para. 192 (iv)]. Similarly, para. 13 of the Introduction to the European Council Directive 2005/85/EC of 1 December 2005 (the 'Procedures Directive') states that:

> the procedure in which an application for asylum is examined should normally provide an applicant at least with (…) access to the services of an interpreter for submitting his/her case if interviewed by the authorities, (…) and the right to be informed of his/her legal position at decisive moments in the course of the procedure, in a language he/she can reasonably be supposed to understand.

More specifically, Article 13.3(b) of the Procedures Directive asserts, with regard to the personal interview conducted with an asylum applicant, that it is incumbent on Member States to:

> select an interpreter who is able to ensure appropriate communication between the applicant and the person who conducts the interview. The communication need not necessarily take place in the language preferred by the applicant for asylum if there is another language which he/she may reasonably be supposed to understand and in which he/she is able to communicate.[1]

Among the issues raised by the wording of the UNHCR recommendation, and by the Procedures Directive in both its original and recast forms, are what constitutes 'appropriate communication', how is the competence of an interpreter to be defined and assessed and how is the applicant's understanding of and ability to communicate in a language other than their preferred one to be defined and established.[2] This article investigates how such questions have been approached within refugee status determination procedures in the UK and France, using material taken from ethnographic research that involved a combination of participant observation, semi-structured interviews and documentary analysis in both countries over a two-year period (2007–2009).

The first section of the article provides an overview of refugee status determination procedures in the UK and France, introducing the main administrative and legal contexts of the asylum process within which interpreters operate in the two countries. The second section compares the organisation of interpreting services, codes of conduct for interpreters and institutional expectations about the nature of interpreters' activity (particularly with regard to the extent to which this is defined as 'translation' or 'interpretation') on the part of the relevant UK and French authorities. The third section then explores some of the practical dilemmas for interpreters and barriers to communication that exist in refugee status determination procedures in the two countries. The article concludes by emphasising the interplay of language issues and intercultural communication and the complex nature of the interpreter's role in UK and French refugee status determination procedures.

## Refugee status determination processes in the UK and France

In the UK, asylum claims are administered by a branch of the Home Office: the UK Border Agency (UKBA). As soon as UKBA receives a claim, it conducts a screening interview with the applicant in order to establish their identity and collect basic personal information. A far more detailed interview with a UKBA case-owner takes place a few weeks later. This second interview usually lasts for several hours and follows a rigid question and answer format. The case-owner focuses here on establishing the basic chronology of the applicant's narrative and on testing its internal credibility. At both interviews interpreters hired by UKBA are present.[3]

After the interview, the case-owner must decide whether the asylum claim should be granted or refused. In the former case, the applicant is granted refugee status or another form of international protection, and notified of this decision without any specific reasons being given. More frequently, however, the claim is refused and the case-owner writes a Reasons for Refusal Letter (RFRL) explaining and justifying this decision. Most RFRLs claim that the applicant's story lacks credibility as a result of alleged inconsistencies in their answers or on the grounds that aspects of their narrative are inconsistent with the cited Country of Origin Information (COI) or because their story is deemed inherently unlikely.

An appeal to an Immigration Judge (IJ) in the First-tier Tribunal (Immigration and Asylum Chamber) is possible following most refusals of asylum by UKBA.[4] A solicitor assembles the documents for the appeal, including the appellant's own witness statement as taken down by the solicitor with the aid of their own interpreter, and any relevant COI, but (in England though generally not in Scotland) the advocate who actually represents the appellant in court is normally a barrister (counsel). UKBA is generally represented in court by a Home Office Presenting Officer (HOPO), who is a civil servant rather than a professional lawyer.

An appeal hearing begins with the appellant's 'examination-in-chief'.[5] Usually very short, this involves an appellant being asked by their counsel simply to confirm that the contents of their asylum interview transcript and witness statement are true (clarifying any points that are claimed to be inaccurate) and that they wish to submit these documents as evidence. The HOPO then cross-examines the appellant. Typically lasting one or two hours, this is the longest part of the hearing. If the barrister wishes, they may then re-examine their client, and very occasionally other witnesses may be called to corroborate the appellant's story or give expert evidence.

The final part of the hearing begins with closing submissions to the IJ by the HOPO, who argues that the refusal of asylum should be upheld. The HOPO's submissions generally involve attacks on the credibility of the appellant's narrative, but 'objective evidence' in the form of COI about the situation in the appellant's country of origin is also cited, with the claim that it supports the UKBA's original decision. The appellant's barrister then attempts to rebut the credibility points and offers rival interpretations of the COI. After the hearing, the IJ produces a written determination announcing the decision and indicating how much weight has been given to each piece of evidence, including COI.[6]

In France, asylum applications are examined in the first instance by the French Office for the Protection of Refugees and Stateless Persons [*Office français de protection des réfugiés et apatrides* (OFPRA)].[7] Established in 1952, the OFPRA is a public institution endowed with legal personality as well as financial and administrative autonomy. It currently works under the authority (*tutelle*) of the French Ministry of the Interior (*Ministère de l'intérieur*).

After being received by the OFPRA, an asylum application is assigned to a caseworker (*officier de protection*) who, in most cases, subsequently interviews the applicant. Asylum interviews can vary considerably in length, but usually last between an hour and an hour and a half. They tend to be divided into two parts: in the first, the caseworker seeks to establish the applicant's identity and to collect other basic personal information; in the second, the focus is on the applicant's narrative and reasons for applying for asylum. With non-francophone applicants, either an interpreter is provided by the OFPRA or the caseworker conducts the interview directly in a language other than French. After the interview, the caseworker forwards a proposal to accept or reject the application to the head of their section (or division), the person responsible for signing the final decision. The applicant is then sent a letter informing them of the outcome of their application.

Appeals against the OFPRA's decisions can be made to an administrative court: the National Asylum Court [*Cour nationale du droit d'asile* (CNDA), known until 1 January 2008 as the *Commission des recours des réfugiés* (CRR)/Refugee Appeals Board]. Appellants are entitled to be assisted by a barrister (*conseil*) and an interpreter when their case comes before the CNDA. In advance of the actual hearing, a CNDA official (known as a *rapporteur*) writes a report that concludes with an opinion (*avis*) as to whether the appeal should be accepted or rejected, based on the current state of the case file.

At the CNDA, most appeals are heard by panels of three judges. In any one morning or afternoon session, a panel of judges may hear up to 13 different appeals. How long the examination of an individual case lasts varies, depending on its complexity and a number of other factors. However, the Cimade (*Comité inter-mouvements auprès des evacuées*), a French association that provides legal advice and other support to asylum seekers and refugees, observed 203 cases at the CNDA over a three-month period in 2009 and found that the average time taken to hear an individual appeal – including the report, which the *rapporteur* reads out at the start, and the barrister's statement – was 33 minutes (Cimade, 2010, p. 47). After the hearing, the three judges discuss all the appeals that have just come before them, deciding in each case whether to annul OFPRA's original decision (and therefore grant refugee status or subsidiary protection) or to reject the appellant's appeal against this decision. A letter is subsequently sent to the appellant, informing them of the outcome of their appeal.

## Interpreting services, codes of conduct and institutional expectations

A distinction is usually drawn between 'interpretation', i.e. 'the oral transfer of meaning between languages', and 'translation', the 'process of transferring meaning from a written text in one language to a written text in another' (Colin & Morris, 1996, p. 16). As indicated in the previous section, refugee status determination procedures in the UK and France usually require both the translation of written documents and the interpretation of oral exchanges in asylum interviews and appeals hearings. However, only the second of these forms of intercultural communication will be examined in the rest of this article. It is important to note before doing so that legal professionals in both countries also refer to 'interpretation', in the context of their own activities, as the process of determining the 'true meaning' of a legal text or document (Colin & Morris, 1996, p. 16; Cornu, 2007, p. 510). As Colin and Morris (1996, p. 17) explain, in their study of interpreters in the legal process in England and Wales, this frequently leads lawyers to insist in court that interpreters 'translate' rather than 'interpret' a speaker's utterances, by which they mean provide a literal or *verbatim* 'translation' (as opposed to an 'interpretation', in the legal sense). Colin and Morris (1996, p. 17) point out, however, that 'word-for-word or literal translation often produces distorted communication', due partly to the fact that words depend for their meaning on how they are combined with other words within a given utterance; an understanding of this context is required for accurate translation and interpretation to be possible. Against this background, the remainder of the present section will describe and compare the provision of interpreting services and the expectations surrounding the interpreter's work (as reflected in codes of conduct) in the different administrative and legal settings associated with the UK and French asylum processes.

In England and Wales, following a 1993 recommendation by the Runciman Royal Commission on Criminal Justice, the National Register for Public Service Interpreters (NRPSI) was set up, together with a qualifying diploma examination in Public Service Interpreting. From 1997 onwards, a National Agreement required every interpreter working in courts to be registered with one of four professional bodies, all of which had codes of professional conduct[8]: similar arrangements governed UKBA procedures. However, a January 2010 audit found that booking and payment arrangements were inefficient, quality assurance systems were inadequate, and some courts used outdated NRPSI lists or unregistered interpreters. The costs of the system were not clear. In August 2011 the Ministry of Justice (MoJ) therefore signed a four-year contract with a private company, Applied Language Solutions (ALS), following a competitive tendering process, and ALS began supplying interpreters to courts and tribunals from 30 January 2012. The initial months of this contract were dogged by complaints and controversy, however. Many experienced interpreters refused to work under the greatly reduced pay scales offered by ALS, and the MoJ itself admitted to an 'unacceptable' number of problems, such as failures to provide interpreters or provision of incompetent interpreters, leading to repeated adjournments (House of Commons Justice Committee [HCJC], 2013, pp. 5–11, 41n). By the end of February 2012, the MoJ was forced to allow courts to revert to the old system as an interim measure to avoid further interpreter-related delays. In October 2012, ALS was taken over and rebranded as Capita Translation and Interpreting, but complaints about pay rates and about the reduction or removal of travelling expenses have continued.

While the use of interpreters in French refugee status determination procedures is not a new phenomenon, a specific 'interpreting service' (*service d'interprétariat*) was only created at the CRR/CNDA in 1994 and at the OFPRA in 2001. In both cases, this was largely a response to an increase in the number of asylum applications and appeals received and of the languages spoken by asylum applicants. Since 2003, the provision of interpreters has been organised through a system of 'competitive tendering' (*marchés publics*), covering both the OFPRA and the CRR/CNDA. While 46% of asylum interviews at the OFPRA were conducted in the presence of an interpreter in 2003, this had risen to 82% in 2011 (OFPRA, 2011, p. 106, 2012, p. 63). Not surprisingly, the cost of providing interpreting services at the OFPRA has also increased, from 1.1M€ in 2005 to 2.4M€ in 2011 (OFPRA, 2007, p. 38, 2012, p. 59). At the CNDA, 95% of appellants are not French speakers (CRR, 2007, p. 19), and the cost of interpreting services was 1.1M€ in 2008 although this is likely to have risen since then, as has been the case at the OFPRA (2009, pp. 44, 50). In 2011, the OFPRA received 40,464 first applications, an increase of 9.6% compared to the previous year, while 31,983 appeals were lodged at the CNDA, a rise of 16.5% in one year (Conseil d'État, 2012, p. 33; OFPRA, 2012, p. 74).

Both UKBA's Central Interpreters Unit and the Tribunals Service have codes of conduct for the interpreters they use. While mostly concerned with general professional behaviour, the UKBA code does include a section on 'Accurate and Precise Interpretation'. Typically, this begins by stressing that interpreters must 'retain every single element of information that was contained in the original message, and interpret in as close *verbatim* form as English style, syntax and grammar will allow' (italics added).[9] Similarly, the Tribunals Service's *Handbook for Freelance Interpreters* (2011) instructs interpreters to 'use the witness's exact words. If you cannot make a direct or exact interpretation, interpret it as accurately as possible in the witness's own words and then inform the Judiciary what the phrase means'; later, it re-emphasises 'Please do not ... use an English expression or phrase which is not an exact translation of the witness's own words' (Henderson & Pickup, 2012, para. 34.24). What constitutes an 'exact translation' is left unclear.

In France, there is a code of conduct for interpreters at the CNDA but not at the OFPRA. The CNDA code (a copy of which is displayed on the wall of the interpreters' room at the Court) sets out the five 'duties' (*devoirs*) of interpreters working there: punctuality and diligence, impartiality and independence, neutrality, accuracy (*la justesse de l'interprétation*) and confidentiality (*le secret professionnel*). Although an equivalent document does not exist at the OFPRA, a number of 'basic rules' (*règles élémentaires*) for interpreters, such as neutrality, are written into the specification or tender documents (*cahier des charges*) used in the competitive tendering procedure through which the provision of interpreting services there (and at the CNDA) is organised (interview with Head of the Interpreting Service, OFPRA). Although a single system of competitive tendering covers interpreting services at the OFPRA *and* the CNDA, and the same interpreter may therefore be contracted to work at both institutions, what is expected of the interpreter in practice is not the same in the two settings. Semi-structured interviews conducted in 2008 and 2009 with the Head of the Interpreting Service at the OFPRA, her counterpart at the CNDA, interpreters working at the OFPRA and/or CNDA, OFPRA caseworkers and CNDA *rapporteurs*, as well as observation of asylum interviews and appeal hearings, highlighted a number of important differences.[10] One of these relates back to the distinction between 'translation' and 'interpretation' introduced at the beginning of this section. Thus, the Head of the Interpreting Service at the OFPRA commented in the following way on the interpreter's role at the administrative institution:

> The interpreter – what I always say to interpreters – for me, interpreters here [i.e., at the OFPRA] – and it is not pejorative, on the contrary – are instruments of communication. And that is no small matter. (...) I explain to interpreters that their role is to **translate**[11] (*traduire*), and I'm using this term **translate** (*traduire*) deliberately. Because you know that in French interpret (*interpréter*) can be something else. (...) So, the interpreters should translate. It's an essential role and it's not as simple as it might appear.

Thus, the expectation at the OFPRA – and this was confirmed by interpreters interviewed for the research, as will be shown below – is that interpreters will 'translate' rather than 'interpret' the speaker's words, in the sense of providing a word-for-word or *verbatim* translation. Although the OFPRA is an administrative institution and not a court, the perspective on the interpreter's role here appears similar to the one held by many lawyers in English and Welsh courts, as discussed above.

In contrast, what is expected of the interpreter at the CNDA, an administrative court, is not a literal or *verbatim* translation but instead the transmission of an equivalent message or meaning from one language to another. The following comment from the Head of the Interpreting Service at the CNDA makes this clear:

> I am not sure that I ask them [i.e. interpreters] to do the same job (*le même métier*). At the Office [OFPRA], they want word-for-word, a word-for-word translation. What I ask them to do is to transcribe the **meaning** (*sens*) of what is said. (...) That is a fundamental difference.

A 25-page document entitled 'Interpreting at the Refugee Appeals Board: Code of Conduct and Organisation' (CRR, 2007), written by the Head of the Interpreting Service at the CNDA and distributed to all interpreters working at the Court, appears to make a similar distinction when it states that: 'The role of the translator[12] is not to transcode (*n'est pas de faire du transcodage*) but rather to render the meaning (*sens*) contained in the appellant's discourse and in the questions asked by the panel of judges' (p. 14). This sentence is immediately followed by a paragraph in which it is emphasised that interpreters should not 'limit themselves to a mechanical translation (*une traduction machinale*) of the questions and answers' uttered by the various participants in the hearing, but must also attempt to reflect the 'nuances' contained in the questions asked by the judges when interpreting these for the appellant (p. 14).

Interpreters with experience of working at both the OFPRA and the CNDA confirmed that expectations with regard to their role were not the same at the two institutions. As one interpreter stated:

> In fact, there is a huge difference. At the OFPRA, what we are asked for is more a translation, in the literal sense of the term, that is to say an almost literal translation of the asylum seekers' words. What we are asked for here [at the OFPRA] is really a translation of the words, practically an oral translation. They call it here – I like the expression very much – *brut de décoffrage*. *Décoffrage* is when you make cement, and as soon as you remove [the framework or *coffrage*], you see exactly what is there. That is to say, they want to have the unprocessed material (*la matière brute*). That's the first big difference. At the CNDA, it is more the case that we do oral interpretation.[13]

In other words, the interpreter at the OFPRA is generally called upon to provide a word-for-word or *verbatim* translation of the asylum applicant's words that leaves them in a 'raw' or 'untreated' state, available for subsequent 'interpretation' by the caseworker. The situation is different at the CNDA, where accurate and precise interpretation is not equated with a literal translation of words from one language to another. There is thus a striking contrast between the two French institutions in this respect, whereas the expectations of their British counterparts appear broadly similar to each other.

From the users' perspective, it is worth noting, finally, that the MoJ in the UK has general guidance for criminal court staff on working with interpreters, but the Civil Procedure Rules say nothing whatever about this.[14] Similarly, the Tribunal's *Practice Directions* and *Practice Notes* (www.justice.gov.uk/tribunals/practice; accessed 6 March 2013) do not discuss interpreters or how to work with them, even though judges are expected to assess their performance after every hearing.[15] However, its *Guidance Notes* do provide a script for IJs to follow when explaining the interpreter's role to the appellant and establishing that the appellant and the interpreter understand one another. Rather oddly, the (very basic) checking of mutual comprehension is left right to the end of this script, *after* the judge has explained the structure of the hearing and the role of the interpreter, all of which have to be translated even though it has yet to be confirmed that the appellant understands it.[16] Another guideline states that if applicants are unrepresented in court, which is increasingly common following cuts to legal aid, requirements of fairness may entail the interpreter reading out the asylum interview transcript, RFRL, and other case documentation to them, possibly in full, while 'Summaries of the objective evidence may be prepared in advance to be translated to the appellant in Court'.[17] The guidance does not say whose responsibility it is to prepare such summaries. Guidance for lawyers on working with court interpreters in asylum hearings is given in the Immigration Law Practitioners Association's *Best Practice Guide* (Henderson & Pickup, 2012, chap. 34). Unlike the other UK documents mentioned, this discussion does reveal an awareness of the limitations of even the most competent interpretation, especially when, as is invariably the case, different interpreters have been used at each stage of the refugee status determination process (Henderson & Pickup, 2012, paras. 34.4–34.8).

## Fragmented narratives, interpreting dilemmas and barriers to communication

At all the different stages described in the previous sections the interposition of interpreters creates barriers to communication, irrespective of their competence. For example, in the UK each of the various codes and guidance stresses the need for asylum applicants to answer questions in short phrases or sentences, so that these can be fully translated. While it is of course important that everything an applicant says *is* communicated to their interlocutor, this fragmentation of the narrative introduces limitations of its own, as interpreters themselves are fully aware; they also know that questioners turn these limitations to their own advantage. As one interpreter commented:

> People are discouraged from talking, and the interpreter is always made the excuse for that; you know, that you need to give short answers so that the interpreter can translate? That is another constraint brought on by the interpretation process itself … and it works in the favour of the Home Office because people do not speak like that naturally, and they will lose track; they will say less than they mean to say simply because they have to break it down. I've seen it on their faces; they just give up, you know? They try to do it for a bit and then they give up. And let's not forget, the interpreter has practice at doing this, so do the Presenting Officers, so do the judges, so do the lawyers, but the asylum applicant doesn't. He's the only one who comes to this all fresh and raw and natural, and the flow of speech, when it's constrained like that, very often dries up.

While this applies to the entire asylum process, its different stages do vary in practice in terms of the restrictions that interpreters themselves are under. When comparing screening and substantive interviews, one interpreter with more than a decade of experience in Home Office work stated:

> With the substantive interview … the interpreter isn't supposed to intervene all that much, whereas in a screening interview it's okay to intervene because it's just collecting the data. It's less formal. I think the interviewing officers are taking the substantive interview more seriously in the sense that there's more important stuff to talk about. They know the screening interview is just provisional, and they often stop people from talking, 'No, not now, not now, you're going to tell me later, you're going to tell me later'. So that is done in quite a hurry.

Whereas those assignments both involve almost entirely the consecutive interpretation of questions and answers, at hearings themselves the interpreter is also supposed to provide the appellant with whispered simultaneous interpretation of dialogue involving other participants. Often this does not happen, however, not least because it is extremely demanding for interpreters to have to work continuously for such long periods, especially when required to switch to and fro between consecutive and simultaneous modes. Even when they do attempt this judges sometimes ask them to stop, as they find it distracting.

The various UK codes and guidelines also specify that interpreters should, as the Tribunal's *Handbook* puts it, 'endeavour to reflect the type of language that is being used, whether it is simple, formal, colloquial etc.' (Henderson & Pickup, 2012, para. 34.24). This may place the interpreter in a quandary when appellants speak ungrammatically, rudely or colloquially[18]:

> That's a dilemma. I find myself actually (laughs) brushing up [their] speech because I certainly don't want to come across as a bad interpreter and it can be believed that it is me who is making the grammatical errors.[19] And also, for me, it is difficult to interpret in a different register to the one I usually speak in. I realised that for a long time I did that, when interpreting for [one particular minority group] at the Home Office. I would use polysyllabic words ... and then I thought, hang on, these people are going to go to appeal and the way they speak is going to come across so, so disjointed from how they came across in the asylum interview. What's that going to do to their credibility?

In addition to having possible implications for perceptions of the credibility of an appellant's narrative, differences in the register of speech employed by participants in the hearings constitute potential barriers to communication and pose further challenges for interpreters. The need for interpreters sometimes to adapt the wording of questions in order to ensure effective communication is explicitly acknowledged in the code of conduct for interpreters at the CNDA in France. Under the heading 'The Accuracy of Interpretation', it is stated that:

> [The Interpreter] must behave in a useful and positive manner: to the extent that is strictly necessary for the expression of justice, the interpreter is authorized to adapt their language and to reformulate the questions when the appellant has a level of language that is less sophisticated (*moins élaboré*) or in the case of incomprehension.

The following extract from an interview with an interpreter who had experience of working at both the OFPRA and the CNDA provides some examples of this kind of adaptation:

> Interpretation at the Court is more difficult, technically speaking. Why? Because you must remain faithful to the translation, to the appellant's words, but at the same time you must make a dialogue possible. Now, on the one hand I have judges who have a string of qualifications (*qui ont fait bac plus 36*) and on the other peasants, fishermen, farmers, people who don't know *anything* about the system in their country and even less about the system in France. So, for example, if I'm asked to translate 'Were you arrested and kept in police custody (*arrêté en garde à vue*)? Were you brought before an examining magistrate (*déféré devant un juge d'instruction*)?' I can translate that to the person, absolutely, but they won't understand a thing. Do you see? Therefore, while remaining faithful to what was meant and to the words, I have to adapt my language in such a way that it is understood, because if the legal dialogue (*le dialogue judiciaire*) is not possible, I'm not being of use. (...) [At the OFPRA] they don't want this adaptation; they want the raw material (*ils veulent du brut*).

This highlights the fact that while there is often an institutional requirement or expectation that the interpreters will be 'invisible',[20] the latter's role in practice is often that of 'an active verbal participant' (Berk-Seligson, 2002, p. 64) in the interactions that take place in UK and French asylum interviews and appeal hearings.

The issue of the interpreter's role can be explored further by returning to the UK guidelines and codes of conduct discussed earlier. These stress that the interpreter's task is to provide *verbatim* or 'exact' translation and that they must not, as the UKBA code of conduct puts it:

> ask the interviewee what they mean by a particular answer ... try to anticipate what the interviewer or interviewee is trying to say or give an answer other than what is being said (or) let your own experience or views get in the way of how you interpret the evidence.

The assumption here, very clearly, is that the interpreter's own understanding of what the interviewee means to say is to be suppressed because it will 'get in the way' of the desired *verbatim* translation.

Such naivety about the translation process is of course not confined to legal contexts. However, its stress here seems partly also to reflect the centrality of language to the entire legal process. As Wadensjö argues, building upon Morris's work cited earlier (and also Morris, 1995):

> established legal systems show little or no readiness to acknowledge the interpreter-mediated situation as essentially different from the ordinary, monolingual one, and the court interpreter's task as truly interpretive. Instead, the court interpreter is defined as a disembodied mechanical device. (Wadensjö, 1998, p. 74)

This, she argues, is partly because law itself, as performed in court, depends so heavily on the skilful manipulation of language by lawyers and its incompetent or untrained use by those under cross-examination (which will almost certainly be portrayed in asylum contexts as damaging their credibility). As Atkinson and Drew (1979) pointed out in their seminal study of courtroom dialogue, cross-examination seeks to 'to challenge or blame the witness' by getting them to agree to the 'facts' progressively brought out during the questioning (pp. 105, 106). Both questions and answers are moulded by expectations over what the interlocutor will say next. For example, barristers expect that their accusations will produce denials, and try to turn that expectation to advantage by choosing forms of words such that witnesses damage their standing or credibility whatever answers they give ('when did you last beat your wife?'). Witnesses themselves may respond by 'hedging' to mitigate any potential admission; instead of a simple 'yes', they reply 'I suppose so'. These processes become far more difficult for lawyers when they are forced to work through interpreters, and legal efforts to limit and 'mechanise' the interpreter's role can be seen as attempts to maintain as far as possible the hegemony of the examining lawyer. Thus, as Wadensjö (1998) notes:

> it would obviously be a challenge to the court if interpreters were ... allowed to clarify an attorney's deliberately ambiguous question. It would be a threat to the system if interpreters were allowed to improve the image of witnesses ... by rendering eloquently and precisely statements which were originally voiced carelessly and imprecisely. (p. 75)

On the other hand, the UK Tribunal's *Handbook for Freelance Interpreters* also provides potentially contradictory guidance:

You may intervene at the hearing for the following reasons: to seek clarification if you have not fully understood what [has] been asked to interpret; to alert the Judiciary that although the interpretation was correct, the question or statement may not have been understood; to alert the court to a possible missed cultural inference – such as when an item of information has not been stated but knowledge of which has been assumed. (in Henderson & Pickup, 2012, para. 34.24; their gloss)

Clearly then, interpreters constantly have to use their judgement over whether to 'intervene' and explain that a misunderstanding or missed inference may have occurred. Not surprisingly, they differ greatly in the extent to which they do this in practice. Their behaviour is likely to reflect not only their own personal shyness or ebullience but also the professional stress upon self-effacement. They also know very well that if they intervene in this way too often, this is likely to be attributed to their incompetence rather than their alertness and sensitivity.

Missed social and cultural inferences are rendered more likely by what Rycroft labels the 'silent actors' in asylum hearings, namely, the legal elements of refugee law that motivate particular questions but of which the appellant is usually unaware. For example, a person is only recognised as a genuine refugee if they have first exhausted all avenues of domestic protection, so they are almost always asked about relocating within their own country:

Thus the ubiquitous question is: 'Have you tried to move to a different part of Romania?' Many applicants say, 'No, because the police are hand in hand.' The fact that they did not attempt to relocate will count against them, although, had the applicants known where the question was aiming, they may have explained that in Romania the police keep centralised records, and that in order to move away one has to request a residence visa from the police. (Rycroft, 2005, p. 241)

As an experienced legal interpreter who is herself Romanian, Rycroft is fully aware of this unspoken contextual background, both the legal reasons for the question and the relevant information missing from the appellant's answer. The dilemma for her is whether to interpose her own explanation. Some judges will accept such behaviour by an interpreter, at least occasionally, but they are more likely to rebuke her for exceeding her duties by giving evidence as though she were herself a witness.

Elsewhere, one of us gave a lengthy example involving an exceptionally proactive Farsi interpreter, showing how his own interpolations frequently helped the court by clarifying the appellant's answers, but also sometimes disrupted it, to the extent even of 'correcting' lawyers questions and – on one occasion – actually subverting the normal order of proceedings (Good, 2007, pp. 167–169, 177–178). The excerpts cited there also illustrated that there are certain matters, such as dates in non-Western calendars, or kin terms where kinship itself is structured very differently, that are inherently impossible to translate exactly or *verbatim* (see also Kalin, 1986). Different interpreters, or the same interpreter on different occasions, may offer differing but equally valid English (or French) equivalents, creating, purely as an artefact of interpretation, the impression that the appellant is confused and possibly untruthful.

## Conclusion

Interpreters play a crucial role in facilitating intercultural communication in the context of asylum interviews and appeal hearings in countries such as the UK and France that are signatories to the 1951 Refugee Convention. As this article has highlighted, however, their task is a complex one. First, the institutions in which they work sometimes have differing expectations as to the nature of their activity (e.g. providing a literal/*verbatim* translation or transmitting the 'meaning' of messages from one language to another), and these shape the definition of 'appropriate communication' in the particular contexts concerned. Second, institutional codes of conduct or guidance for interpreters can provide potentially contradictory advice, confronting them with dilemmas and requiring them to exercise their judgement on a range of matters. The latter include whether or not to intervene to explain a cultural misunderstanding, how to negotiate different registers of speech without potentially damaging the perceived credibility of an applicant's or appellant's narrative and how to 'adapt' or reformulate questions (and answers) in order to ensure effective communication between the parties involved. Third, the fragmentation of applicants' or appellants' narratives that results from their having to answer questions in short phrases or sentences introduces barriers to communication and imposes restrictions on even the most competent of interpreters (as well as on the other parties involved in the process). Despite these constraints, interpreters are active participants in the often multilingual and intercultural exchanges that take place in asylum interviews and appeal hearings, although the mechanistic views of interpretation and ideas about the 'invisibility' of the interpreter that are sometimes (but not always, as has been emphasised) found in these legal and administrative contexts can obscure this fact.

## Acknowledgements

Robert Gibb is grateful to François Bernard (former president, National Asylum Court, France) and Jean-François Cordet (former director general, French Office for the Protection of Refugees and Stateless Persons) for granting him permission to conduct interviews with staff at the two institutions; to Vera Zederman (director, Legal Information Centre, National Asylum Court, France), Pascal Baudouin and Myriam Djegham (Research and Communication Service, French Office for the Protection of Refugees and Stateless Persons) for arranging interviews with staff; and to the individual members of staff who agreed to be interviewed. All errors and omissions are the sole responsibility of the authors.

## Funding

The research was supported by AHRC [grant number AH/E50874X/1] under its Diasporas, Migration and Identities Programme.

## Notes

1. In the 'Amended proposal for a Directive of the European Parliament and of The Council on common procedures for granting and withdrawing international protection status (Recast) (1.6.2011)', Article 13.3(c) has been recast as follows:

   [Member States shall] select a competent interpreter who is able to ensure appropriate communication between the applicant and the person who conducts the interview. The communication shall take place in the language preferred by the applicant unless there is another language which he/she understands and in which he/she is able to communicate clearly. Wherever possible, Member States shall provide an interpreter of the same sex if the applicant so requests. (Article 15.3(c) of the 'Amended Proposal')

2. On this final issue, by contrast, case law in the UK has emphasised that appellants should *not* be required to give evidence in a language other than the first or preferred language (*Kaygun v. Secretary of State for the Home Department*).
3. For more details on the UK process and the importance of credibility, see Good (2011a, 2011b). The two kinds of interviews have been nicely described, from an interpreter's perspective, by

Rycroft (2005, pp. 227–232). There is also a 'fast track' process (not described here) involving less scrutiny and procedural short cuts.

4. The organisational structure of the immigration courts and the titles given to IJs have changed several times in recent years, but the format of the actual appeal hearings has not changed.

5. Interpreters at appeal hearings are hired by the Ministry of Justice, as discussed in the following section.

6. Subsequent appeals to higher tribunals or courts are limited to matters of law, and although the boundary between law and fact is often hazy in asylum claims, there is mostly no fresh evidence at these later hearings. Consequently the applicants themselves rarely attend and no provision is normally made for interpretation.

7. For more detailed accounts of refugee status determination procedures in France, see Cimade (2010) and Gibb and Good (2013, pp. 295–297).

8. These were NRPSI, the Chartered Institute of Linguists, the Institute of Translation and Interpreting and the Association of Police and Court Interpreters.

9. The UKBA code appears to date from 2008. See www.ukba.homeoffice.gov.uk/sitecontent/documents/policyandlaw/asylumprocessguidance/relateddocuments/Theasyluminterview/conductingtheasylumintervie2.pdf?view=Binary (accessed 6 March 2013).

10. Although it will not be discussed here, one difference is that a 'swearing in' ceremony for new interpreters (*assermentation*), at which an oath is administered (valid only for the CNDA), is held annually at the CNDA (an administrative court), whereas no equivalent procedure occurs at the OFPRA (an administrative institution).

11. Bold is used here, and in subsequent extracts from interviews, to indicate words emphasised by the speaker. All extracts from interviews conducted in French that are reproduced in this article have been translated by the first author.

12. The words 'translator' and 'translation' are sometimes used in this document when it is a question of the interpretation of oral exchanges rather than the translation of texts.

13. Another interpreter who had worked at both institutions expressed the difference in expectations as follows: 'The [OFPRA] case-workers insist on a much more literal translation, whereas at the Commission [CNDA] we are allowed to reformulate the words in order to make them, you could almost say, clearer in fact'.

14. For criminal court guidance, see http://rpsi.name/docs/interpreters_good_practice_guide%20sept 10.pdf; for the Civil Procedure Rules, see www.justice.gov.uk/courts/procedure-rules/civil/rules (both accessed 7 March 2013).

15. They are asked to assess 'Overall standard of English; Comprehension; Fluidity; Overall standard of interpretation; Appropriate body language/tone of voice; Adherence to Tribunal Service protocol; Professionalism', but clearly an IJ 'will have no way of judging the real standard of interpretation unless he is familiar with the language in which the witness is giving evidence' (Henderson & Pickup, 2012, para. 34.21). In France, judges at the CNDA were asked to provide a similar assessment of interpreters over the course of a month in 2008.

16. See www.justice.gov.uk/downloads/tribunals/immigration-and-asylum/lower/GuideNoteNo3.pdf (accessed 6 March 2013).

17. See www.justice.gov.uk/downloads/tribunals/immigration-and-asylum/lower/GuideNoteNo3.pdf and www.justice.gov.uk/downloads/tribunals/immigration-and-asylum/lower/GuidanceNote.pdf (accessed 6 March 2013).

18. This of course applies to all participants in the hearing, not just the appellant. This is extremely demanding; as Rycroft (2005) notes, 'the interpreter will interpret what is said by four different parties and must maintain consistency with the tone and demeanour of each one … like an actor playing several roles' (pp. 233–234).

19. See Pöllabauer (2004, pp. 163–168) for a discussion of 'face-saving strategies' in asylum interviews.

20. For example, while the document 'Interpreting at the Refugee Appeals Board: Code of Conduct and Organisation' distances itself from a mechanistic view of interpretation, as noted above, it nevertheless states that: 'A good interpreter should pass unnoticed (*Un bon interprète doit passer inaperçu*)' (CRR, 2007, p. 14). The problematic nature of ideas about the 'invisibility' of the translator has been extensively discussed in the literature (see, for example, Venuti, 2008).

## Notes on contributors

Robert Gibb is a Lecturer in the School of Social and Political Sciences at the University of Glasgow. He has conducted research on the antiracist movement in France and, more recently, a comparative study of asylum processes in the UK and France (with Anthony Good). Recent publications include: 'Do the facts speak for themselves? Country of origin information in French and British refugee status determination procedures'. *International Journal of Refugee Law*, 25, 291–322 (2013, co-authored with Anthony Good).

Anthony Good is Emeritus Professor of Social Anthropology at the University of Edinburgh, and was formerly head of its School of Social and Political Science. His research interests cover South India and Sri Lanka, focusing on kinship and religion. He frequently acts as an expert witness in asylum appeals involving Sri Lankan Tamils. His recent research concerns uses of expert evidence in British asylum courts and (with Robert Gibb) a comparative study of asylum processes in the UK and France. Recent publications include *Worship and the Ceremonial Economy of a Royal South Indian Temple* (2004) and *Anthropology and Expertise in the Asylum Courts* (2007).

## References

Atkinson, J. M., & Drew, P. (1979). *Order in court: The organisation of verbal interaction in court settings*. London: Macmillan.
Berk-Seligson, S. (2002). *The bilingual courtroom: Court interpreters in the judicial process*. Chicago, IL: University Press.
Cimade. (2010). *Voyage au centre de l'asile: Enquête sur la procédure de détermination d'asile* [Voyage to the centre of asylum: An investigation into the asylum determination procedure]. Paris. Retrieved from http://www.cimade.org/publications/39
Colin, J., & Morris, R. (1996). *Interpreters and the legal process*. Winchester: Waterside Press.
Commission des recours des réfugiés. (2007). *L'interprétariat à la Commission des recours des réfugiés: Les règles de déontologie et l'organisation* [Interpreting at the Refugee Appeal Board: Code of conduct and the organisation]. Paris: CRR.
Conseil d'État. (2012). *Le Conseil d'État et la justice administrative en 2011* [The Council of State and Administrative Justice in 2011]. Retrieved from http://www.conseil-etat.fr/bilan-activite2011/
Cornu, G. (2007). *Vocabulaire juridique* [Legal vocabulary] (8th ed.). Paris: Quadrige/PUF.
Gibb, R., & Good, A. (2013). Do the facts speak for themselves? Country of origin information in French and British refugee status determination procedures. *International Journal of Refugee Law*, 25, 291–322. doi:10.1093/ijrl/eet015
Good, A. (2007). *Anthropology and expertise in the asylum courts*. London: Routledge/Clarendon.
Good, A. (2011a). Tales of suffering: Asylum narratives in the refugee status determination process. *West Coast Line*, 68, 80–89.
Good, A. (2011b). Witness statements and credibility assessments in the British asylum courts. In L. Holden (Ed.), *Cultural expertise and litigation: Patterns, conflicts, narratives* (pp. 94–122). London: Routledge.
Henderson, M., & Pickup, A. (2012). *Best practice guide to asylum and human rights appeals*. Retrieved from http://www.ein.org.uk/bpg/contents.
House of Commons Justice Committee. (2013). *Interpreting and translation services and the Applied Language Solutions contract* (HC 645). London: Stationery Office.
Kalin, W. (1986). Troubled communication: Cross-cultural misunderstandings in the asylum-hearing. *International Migration Review*, 20, 230–241. doi:10.2307/2546033
*Kaygun v. Secretary of State for the Home Department*, 17213, 29 March 1998.
Morris, R. (1995). The moral dilemmas of court interpreting. *The Translator*, 1(1), 25–46. doi:10.1080/13556509.1995.10798948
Office français de protection des réfugiés et apatrides. (2007). *Rapport d'activité 2006* [Annual Report 2006]. Retrieved from http://www.ofpra.gouv.fr/documents/rapport_Ofpra_2006.pdf
Office français de protection des réfugiés et apatrides. (2009). *Rapport d'activité 2008* [Annual Report 2008]. Retrieved from http://www.ofpra.gouv.fr/documents/Rapport_Ofpra_2008_com-plet_BD.pdf

Office français de protection des réfugiés et apatrides. (2011). *Au coeur de l'Ofpra: Demandeurs d'asile et réfugiés en France* [At the heart of the OFPRA: Asylum seekers and refugees in France]. Paris: La documentation française.

Office français de protection des réfugiés et apatrides. (2012). *Rapport d'activité 2011* [Annual Report 2011]. Retrieved from http://www.ofpra.gouv.fr/documents/OfpraRA2011.pdf

Pöllabauer, S. (2004). Interpreting in asylum hearings: Issues of role, responsibility and power. *Interpreting, 6,* 143–180. doi:10.1075/intp.6.2.03pol

Rycroft, R. (2005). Communicative barriers in the asylum account. In P. Shah (Ed.), *The challenge of asylum to legal systems* (pp. 223–244). London: Cavendish.

United Nations High Commissioner for Refugees. (1992). *Handbook on procedures and criteria for determining refugee status under the 1951 Convention and the 1967 Protocol relating to the status of refugees. HCR/IP/4/Eng/REV.1 Reedited.* Geneva: UNHCR.

Venuti, L. (2008). *The translator's invisibility: A history of translation* (2nd ed.). London & New York, NY: Routledge.

Wadensjö, C. (1998). *Interpreting as interaction.* London & New York, NY: Longman.

# Index

Entries in *italics* refer to figures.

For Product Safety Concerns and Information please contact our EU
representative GPSR@taylorandfrancis.com Taylor & Francis Verlag GmbH,
Kaufingerstraße 24, 80331 München, Germany

Batch number: 08153807

Printed by Printforce, the Netherlands